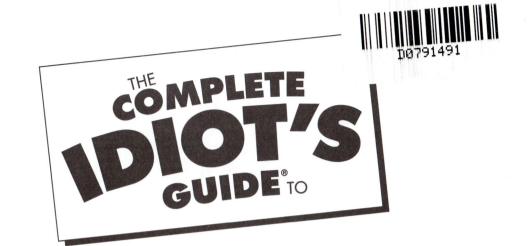

THE COMPLETE IDIOT'S GUIDE® TO

Understanding Saudi Arabia

by Colin Wells

ALPHA

A member of Penguin Group (USA) Inc.

This book is dedicated with love and gratitude to my parents.

Copyright © 2003 by Colin Wells

All rights reserved. No part of this book shall be reproduced, stored in a retrieval system, or transmitted by any means, electronic, mechanical, photocopying, recording, or otherwise, without written permission from the publisher. No patent liability is assumed with respect to the use of the information contained herein. Although every precaution has been taken in the preparation of this book, the publisher and author assume no responsibility for errors or omissions. Neither is any liability assumed for damages resulting from the use of information contained herein. For information, address Alpha Books, 800 East 96th Street, Indianapolis, IN 46240.

THE COMPLETE IDIOT'S GUIDE TO and Design are registered trademarks of Penguin Group (USA) Inc.

International Standard Book Number: 1-59257-113-1
Library of Congress Catalog Card Number: 2003111791

05   04   03   8   7   6   5   4   3   2   1

Interpretation of the printing code: The rightmost number of the first series of numbers is the year of the book's printing; the rightmost number of the second series of numbers is the number of the book's printing. For example, a printing code of 03-1 shows that the first printing occurred in 2003.

Printed in the United States of America

Note: This publication contains the opinions and ideas of its author. It is intended to provide helpful and informative material on the subject matter covered. It is sold with the understanding that the author and publisher are not engaged in rendering professional services in the book. If the reader requires personal assistance or advice, a competent professional should be consulted.

The author and publisher specifically disclaim any responsibility for any liability, loss, or risk, personal or otherwise, which is incurred as a consequence, directly or indirectly, of the use and application of any of the contents of this book.

Most Alpha books are available at special quantity discounts for bulk purchases for sales promotions, premiums, fund-raising, or educational use. Special books, or book excerpts, can also be created to fit specific needs.

For details, write: Special Markets, Alpha Books, 375 Hudson Street, New York, NY 10014.

Publisher: *Marie Butler-Knight*
Product Manager: *Phil Kitchel*
Senior Managing Editor: *Jennifer Chisholm*
Acquisitions Editor: *Gary Goldstein*
Development Editor: *Jennifer Moore*
Production Editor: *Billy Fields*
Copy Editor: *Sara Fink*
Illustrator: *Chris Eliopoulos*
Cover/Book Designer: *Trina Wurst*
Indexer: *Angie Bess*
Layout/Proofreading: *Rebecca Harmon, Ayanna Lacey, Donna Martin*

Contents at a Glance

Contents

Foreword

When it was learned within days of September 11, 2001 that 15 of the 19 hijackers were citizens of Saudi Arabia, along with attack mastermind Osama bin Laden, it was no longer possible for many Americans to view the Desert Kingdom, its rulers, and people in the same way. The image of the country once seen as not much more than a very large gas station for America and the modern world underwent a drastic change.

Almost literally overnight a benign if not cartoonish take on a complicated nation—that is in fact a strategic ally—morphed into a not-so-benign if equally cartoon-like image. Initial denials from Saudi government officials about the role of Saudi citizens only fueled the American view that this was a nation that not only encouraged terrorists but educated them, turning a blind eye to Islamic clerics spewing hatred for America and the West in their teachings. Was this an ally who could be a partner in the modern world—or a country insistent on sanctions repressing women as the main order of the day? Underlying this swift change was a sense of betrayal by a longtime friend and ally. How could citizens from a nation befriended by over 60 years of American presidents from Franklin Roosevelt to George W. Bush, a country America had saved from the clutches of Saddam Hussein in the 1991 Gulf War, brutally murder thousands of innocent Americans? Was Saudi Arabia really an ally at all?

The reality of the Royal Kingdom of Saudi Arabia is at once black and white with a considerable amount of gray. This is a nation with a vast amount of dramatic religious, cultural, and political history. It is a history that expresses itself in a kaleidoscope of swirling currents, mixing the staggeringly ancient with twenty-first century modern. Colin Wells has written extensively on Saudi Arabia, and is well-positioned to explain this reality with all of its shadings. From the arrival of Prophet Muhammad 14 centuries ago to the current oil-rich Saudi royal family and its nemesis, the expelled Osama bin Laden, from camel-riding Bedouin to the interaction between Wahhabi Islamic traditionalists and the onslaught of the outside world via the Internet and satellite TV, Wells weaves it all together in a story that Americans can no longer afford to ignore. He makes a persuasive case for looking at Saudi society and its contradictions, tensions, prejudices—even outright paranoia—with a fresh eye to understanding.

The indelible memory of the smoking rubble that was the World Trade Center makes it more imperative than ever for Americans to take a hard look at what is going on inside this all-important country. What does it mean to have the two most important religious sites in the Islamic religion within its borders? What is Wahhabism, who created it, and why does it hold such incredible sway with Saudi Muslims, including the ruling Al Saud family? How should Americans deal with an allied nation where many of its people deeply believe there is a Jewish plot to control the world—and that America is controlled by those same Jews? Can democracy take root in such a society where everything from the educational system to its wealthy charities are now suspect in the wider world? Can America ever deal honestly with a country that has beneath its soil such massive reserves of oil? Will the global communications revolution finally prove to be too powerful for even this closed society?

The *Complete Idiot's Guide to Saudi Arabia* explores and answers these questions and many more. Colin Wells has used his experience and writings of the Middle East to not only inform but to genuinely discuss the problems—and opportunities—that face America as it comes to grip with the tidal wave of consequences that overtook it that bright, sunny day in September of 2001. It is a discussion Americans have learned to ignore at their peril.

—Jeffrey Lord

Jeffrey Lord, a White House aide in the Reagan Administration, is now a novelist and political and screen writer whose articles have appeared in *The Weekly Standard, The Wall Street Journal, The Los Angeles Times,* and *The Philadelphia Inquirer.*

Introduction

The kingdom of Saudi Arabia first leaped into the Western consciousness in 1973, when it led the Arab oil embargo that resulted in panic-stricken gas lines around the United States. Nearly three decades later, Americans experienced another rude awakening, when 15 Saudis helped pilot two planes into the World Trade Center and one into the Pentagon.

In between times, though, Saudis were mostly known in the West for being America's friends and allies. They bought U.S. and British arms, and above all they kept the cheap oil flowing. The embargo aside, the Saudis were a responsible "swing producer," keeping prices low by using their massive excess oil production capacity to offset shortages elsewhere. And they offered their bases when it was time to oust the forces of Saddam Hussein from a brutalized Kuwait in 1991.

What lies behind these two conflicting images we have of the Saudis—of friend on the one hand, foe on the other? How can we reconcile them? And which one is the real Saudi Arabia? This book will give you the knowledge you need to answer those and other questions about the kingdom for yourself.

What You'll Learn in This Book

This book is divided into four parts that break Saudi history and culture down into manageable chunks. They're preceded by an Introduction, which briefly sketches the outline of the Saudi role in 9/11 and its aftermath, on the assumption that that's one of the main reasons you bought this book.

Part 1, "Historical Background," takes you on a tour through the history of Arabia and of the Middle East, starting with the birth of Islam in Arabia and going up to about 1990.

Part 2, "Recent History: The Gulf War and Its Aftermath," continues the story, but tightens the focus, so that most of it covers the crucial events of the 1990s: the Persian Gulf War and its aftermath. It starts, though, with an overview of the hugely important role that oil has played in the modern world. After all, that's why Kuwait mattered so much to the West.

Part 3, "Who Are the Saudis? A Closer Look at Saudi Culture Today," temporarily leaves the historical approach to give you a contemporary "snapshot" of the Saudis—their culture, religion, and family values.

Part 4, "Saudi Arabia in the Age of Global Terror," basically combines the two approaches, sticking to current events but viewing them through the lens of history, as a historian of the future might.

Finally, several useful appendixes offer quick and easy information on specific topics.

Extras

Scattered through the book you'll also find small boxes of text that will help you deepen your knowledge or understanding of specific issues. They're flagged with convenient labels:

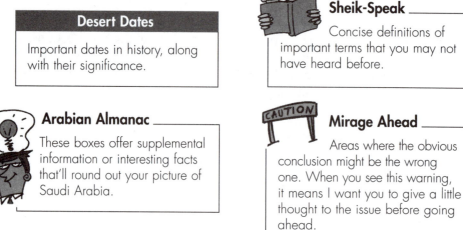

Desert Dates

Important dates in history, along with their significance.

Sheik-Speak

Concise definitions of important terms that you may not have heard before.

Arabian Almanac

These boxes offer supplemental information or interesting facts that'll round out your picture of Saudi Arabia.

Mirage Ahead

Areas where the obvious conclusion might be the wrong one. When you see this warning, it means I want you to give a little thought to the issue before going ahead.

Acknowledgments

I want to thank my parents for their steadfast support while I was writing this book. I'm more grateful than I can say to my agents, Elizabeth Frost-Knappman and Edward Knappman at New England Publishing Associates, who've both been a dream come true. Many thanks also to Anne de la Chapelle and Michelle Maron of the Westport Library Association for their help in research, and to the gang at the Depot Theatre for xeroxing privileges and moral support. Marissa Burgoyne and Chris Franciosa shared their experiences of Saudi Arabia with me; their generous, friendly, and insightful help is much appreciated, though they won't necessarily agree with some of my judgments. I'd also like to recognize the skills and professionalism of the editors who worked hard on this book, including Gary Goldstein, Jennifer Moore, Billy Fields, and

Sara Fink. Finally, I wish to acknowledge my great debt to the work of Albert Hourani, Robert Lacey, Sandra Mackey, David E. Long, Fred Halliday, Bernard Lewis, and Thomas Friedman, whose books you'll find listed in Appendix C. Many writers have helped shape the information and ideas presented in this book, but they are among the ones I've found most helpful.

Special Thanks to the Technical Reviewer

The Complete Idiot's Guide to Understanding Saudi Arabia was reviewed by an expert who double-checked the accuracy of what you'll learn here, to help us ensure that this book gives you everything you need to know about Saudi history, politics, and culture. Special thanks are extended to Donald J. Davidson.

Trademarks

All terms mentioned in this book that are known to be or are suspected of being trademarks or service marks have been appropriately capitalized. Alpha Books and Penguin Group (USA) Inc. cannot attest to the accuracy of this information. Use of a term in this book should not be regarded as affecting the validity of any trademark or service mark.

Part 1

Historical Background

Attention history buffs—this is where you'll get the lowdown on the history of Arabia from ancient times up to 1990. You'll see the Arabs transform themselves from a bunch of feuding desert tribes into a formidable fighting force, unified around a brand new faith, and then back into a bunch of feuding tribes again. In between, however, the Arabs founded one of the world's great empires.

Then, of course, there's the discovery of oil in the twentieth century, which occurred just as the modern kingdom of Saudi Arabia was being founded. Once again the Arab world was transformed, as oil revenues propelled the Saudis to a leadership role in the international Muslim community. Along with new international prestige, oil wealth also brought modernization and development—which in turn brought their own challenges to the Saudis' highly conservative and traditional society.

A Delicate Alliance

In This Chapter

- Osama bin Laden develops a grudge against the West
- Islamic fundamentalism in Saudi Arabia
- America's dependence on a shaky ruling family
- Saudi Arabia's strategic importance

Like most of us, you have the slow-motion images forever burned into your memory. The jetliner plowing into the sheer side of the monolithic World Trade Center Tower, the suspended moment when all seems impossibly and eerily normal—and then the orange fireball exploding from the shattered building. Huge, billowing dust clouds moving like dark tidal waves through New York City's financial district, as first one, and then the second, world famous landmarks collapse. The dazed and bloody figures running headlong in terror or standing listlessly, shocked beyond movement.

The massive, humped pile of still-smoking rubble. The firemen. The cops.

Then the media began to put the pieces together, and new names percolated into your awareness. *Taliban*. *Al Qaeda*. Above all, *Osama bin Laden*. But some of the pieces didn't quite seem to fit. For example, the Taliban were the rulers of Afghanistan, right? So why did so many of the al Qaeda fighters there—like their suddenly infamous leader, Osama bin Laden—originally come from Saudi Arabia? What were they doing in Afghanistan? And why were so many of the hijackers Saudis in the first place? Wasn't Saudi Arabia supposed to be friendly to the United States, a staunch U.S. ally in the Gulf War and after? What's the deal with that, anyway?

Since those questions are most likely the ones that made you pick up this book in the first place, I'll answer them first. This chapter will sketch out the basics on how Saudi Arabia fits in with the terrorist attacks of September 11, 2001—and how it will probably fit in with America's ongoing campaign against terrorism in the future. In addition, you'll get the big picture on how those issues affect Saudi Arabia's overall relationship with the United States.

Hallowed Ground

The single most important thing to know about Saudi Arabia is that it is sacred territory. As the birthplace of one of the world's great faiths, Islam, the land itself is revered by Muslims around the world. Westerners may tend to view Saudi Arabia as simply a big empty desert with lots of oil under it. Okay, so it is a big empty desert. And true, it does have lots of oil under it (discover what you need to know about Saudi oil in Chapter 5). But the point is that there's much more to it than that. If you think of the whole country as one big shrine, you'll be closer to the way a large part of humanity views it.

Mirage Ahead

Without a clear appreciation of Saudi Arabia's religious importance, you won't be able to understand Muslims' negative reactions to the Western presence there—and especially to the presence of U.S. and other armed forces. Underestimating the religious feelings that Muslims have for Saudi Arabia is the biggest mistake you can make about it.

For the world's one billion Muslims, Saudi Arabia embodies the purest and most authentic ideals of their faith. For one thing, it contains Islam's holiest sites, and millions of devout Muslim pilgrims from around the world travel there every year. But the whole country basks in a sort of religious glow, at least in the eyes of the world's Muslim community. You'll learn more about Saudi Arabia and the world's Muslims in Chapter 15. For now, just get used to thinking of Saudi Arabia as the spiritual home of one fifth of the world's population.

Sheik-Speak

The **Taliban** are the Afghan Islamic fundamentalists who took over Afghanistan in 1997. They have nothing to do with Saudi Arabia per se. Culturally and ethnically, they're not Arabs but Afghans. The name means "the students" in Pashtu.

Al Qaeda is the fundamentalist Muslim network originally founded by Osama bin Laden to assist Afghan fighters against the Soviet Union (which invaded Afghanistan in 1979). The name means "the Base" in Arabic, and the hard-core al Qaeda leadership is made up of Arabs, many of them Saudis.

Osama bin Laden—and How He Got That Way

Osama bin Laden is a good person to start with if you want to understand Saudi Arabia, and not just because he's so notorious in the West. His story also offers some revealing insights into the country and the society that produced him.

Like many ruthless revolutionaries from the pages of history, Osama bin Laden is a far cry from being a product of the downtrodden masses. In fact, his family hails from Saudi Arabia's wealthiest elite class, and as a young man he himself was given the best that money could buy.

It wasn't always that way in his family, however, for the life story of Osama's father, Muhammad bin Laden, is a classic rags-to-riches tale that parallels the history of Saudi Arabia itself. Uneducated and poor, Muhammad bin Laden immigrated to Saudi Arabia from Yemen sometime before World War II. Starting his own construction company, he won a reputation for high quality work that attracted the attention of the king. Muhammad was soon building a series of palaces for the royal family.

In the 1950s, during the construction boom that followed the discovery of Saudi Arabia's vast oil reserves, Muhammad bin Laden parlayed his contacts with the Saudi royal family into one of Saudi Arabia's largest business empires. That empire, the Saudi Binladen Group, is still owned by the bin Laden family. (Binladen is a different way of spelling the name in English. In Arabic "bin" means "son of," and in English it's also spelled "ibn." More on Arab names in Chapter 13.) Today, the Saudi Binladen Group is worth some $5 billion dollars.

It turned out that Muhammad bin Laden was busy with more than just construction. Osama is the seventeenth of Muhammad's more than fifty children by an unknown number of wives. (Islamic practice allows a man to have more than one wife, as long as he can support them all. Presumably, $5 billion can support a lot of wives.) Many of his half-brothers went into the family business, but as an adult Osama turned his back on it.

Arabian Almanac

Osama bin Laden's father, Muhammad bin Laden, gave the famous Saudi billionaire Adnan Khashoggi his start in business in the 1950s. Bin Laden let the younger man broker an important deal and gave him $50,000 as commission and bonus. As a successful agent or deal-making middleman, Khashoggi represents a common phenomenon in the Saudi business world, where contacts count for all. Khashoggi went on to build a financial empire ranging from billion-dollar arms deals to multimillion-dollar Hollywood movies, becoming a high flyer on the international party circuit.

Instead, he used his share of the family riches to go to Afghanistan and join that country's guerrilla campaign against the Soviet Union and its Communist puppet government there. The bloody civil war in Afghanistan had religious overtones, since communism is sharply atheistic. Indeed, for many Muslims—as for bin Laden—the war in Afghanistan became a *jihad* or holy war. Building up a network of Islamic fundamentalist guerrillas that called itself al Qaeda, bin Laden became something of a folk hero among the other Afghan resistance groups. At this point he was in fact loosely allied with the United States, which offered many of these groups covert assistance through the CIA. The Americans, waging the closing stages of the Cold War against the Communist Soviet Union, were happy to support anyone who opposed communism.

Sheik-Speak

No Arabic word causes more consternation in the West than **jihad,** which simply means "holy war." The problem is, what does "holy war" mean, exactly? Muslims themselves are divided. For moderates, jihad stands for a spiritual quest and has nothing to do with actual war. For some fundamentalists, however, it reflects an Islamic religious commandment to wage literal war against all infidels or unbelievers—against all non-Muslims, that is.

Soon after its troops were driven out of Afghanistan in 1989, the Soviet Union collapsed, as Russia and the other former Soviet republics went their separate ways. With that enemy gone, Islamic extremists like Osama bin Laden didn't take long to find another target for their militant zeal.

The ascetic bin Laden was already deeply hostile to the materialism and permissiveness that he saw in Western culture. In 1991, the United States and its coalition allies were welcomed by the Saudi government. They used Saudi Arabia as a major staging area for Gulf War operations against Saddam Hussein's occupation of neighboring Kuwait. The presence of all these infidel soldiers—marshaled on Saudi soil to fight against fellow Muslims—nourished Osama's growing rage against the West, and especially against the United States.

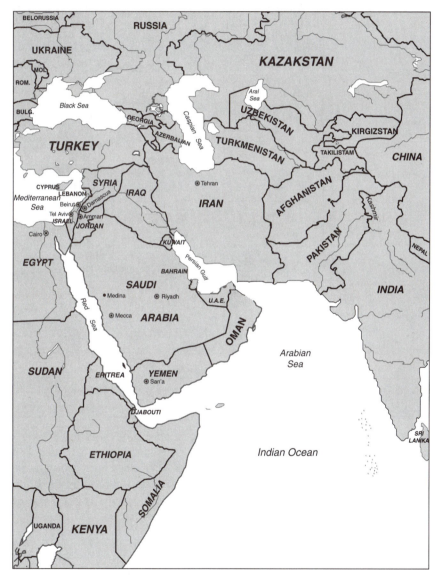

Here's a map showing some of the places I've talked about so far in this chapter.

Saudi Arabia made a perfect staging area for U.S. operations to liberate Kuwait from Iraqi occupation during the Gulf War.

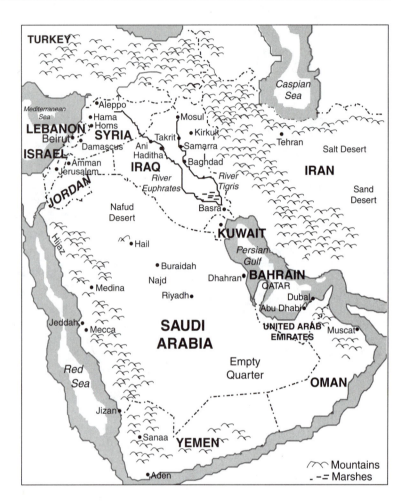

Arabian Almanac

Starting in the early 1990s, the family-owned Saudi Binladen Group made it clear to their many American employees and business partners that they wanted nothing further to do with the family's black sheep, Osama. The family has had an extensive presence in the United States, and many bin Ladens have been educated at expensive private American schools. Their American headquarters was in Boston, which a number of family members called home—until forced by circumstances to return to Saudi Arabia after 9/11.

Added to a long list of other grievances, the presence of infidel soldiers on Saudi soil also gave bin Laden the leverage he needed to stir up similar hatred among fundamentalist Muslims around the world. Osama bin Laden had found his new target. During the 1990s al Qaeda mounted a series of terrorist attacks against American targets—a long campaign that reached its horrific climax on September 11, 2001. (You'll find all this laid out step-by-step in Parts 2 and 4.)

Why Were So Many of the Hijackers Saudis?

As is now well known, 15 out of the 19 hijackers were Saudi citizens, and many of them are thought to have been recruited in Saudi Arabia itself. Yet Saudi Arabia has been (and remains) one of America's strongest allies in the Middle East, as evidenced by its support of the U.S.–led coalition in the Gulf War. So once again, what's going on here?

A Streak of Puritanism: The Wahhabis

Osama bin Laden's asceticism didn't spring out of a vacuum. It's directly related to a long tradition of Islamic puritanism that has deep roots in Saudi Arabian culture. The Saudis' puritanical version of Islam is going to play an important role in the rest of this book, and this is a good place to introduce you to it. It goes under the name *Wahhabism*, and its adherents are called *Wahhabis*.

Wahhabism is immensely influential in Saudi Arabia. It also adds luster to the Saudis' reputation for strict piety among other Muslims around the world. Three aspects of Wahhabism combine to give it special appeal:

- **Political influence.** Historically, Wahhabism has been closely allied with the Saudi royal family (you can learn more about its history in Chapter 4).

- **Religious legitimacy.** Sometimes described as a revival movement, Wahhabism is also occasionally considered to be a separate sect of Islam, though Wahhabis would argue that it's really just a distillation of true Islamic principles. That's how most Saudis see it. For the role of Wahhabism in Saudi culture today, see Chapter 14.

- **Moral authority.** The Wahhabi message is bolstered by the moral example of Saudi Arabia's widely respected Wahhabi clerics, who live according to simple, Spartan values.

> **Desert Dates**
>
> **1744:** Muhammad ibn Abdel Wahhab, the founder of Wahhabism, marries the daughter of Muhammad ibn Saud, the founder of the Al Saud or House of Saud. It's the beginning of a beautiful friendship. For generations, Saud family dynasts have rallied the faithful behind the Wahhabi banner, while the Wahhabis have enjoyed the political protection of the royal family. This long-lived relationship remains the central fact of Saudi civic life.

This potent combination helps explain why devout Saudis might be sympathetic to bin Laden's cause. Wahhabism and its puritan ideals line up very well with Osama bin Laden's anti-Western, anti-materialism message.

Royal Extravagance

While earlier Saud family leaders may have stuck to the Wahhabis' ascetic, puritan ideals, more recent scions of the royal family have been better known for Ferraris than hairshirts. In short, the corruption and extravagance of the Al Saud and their hangers-on have become legendary. They are the West's political allies, but their worldly excesses discredit them in the eyes of the Saudi public, and stand in sharp contrast to their pious Wahhabi critics. Plus, as a rule, material extravagances like Ferraris are Western imports. This, too, no doubt contributed to the anti-Western feelings that could have driven young Saudis to follow Osama bin Laden.

Lots of Money—Along with Some Guilt

Surprisingly, given Osama bin Laden's reputation among Muslims as a defender of the poor and disenfranchised, a number of the hijackers appear to have come from relatively rich, Westernized origins. As we've seen, bin Laden himself comes from one of Saudi Arabia's wealthiest families, and one with extensive ties to the United States. Most of the time, it's a case of the more money, the more luxury, and the more luxury, the more Western the outlook. Wealthy Saudis love to travel, and they are sometimes known as "airport Muslims"—for example, ordering drinks as soon as the plane leaves the runway on its outbound flight. (Muslims are forbidden to drink alcohol.) Conversely, on a flight into Saudi Arabia from a Western country you'll see well-dressed Saudi women donning their veils as the plane readies for touchdown.

However, even the most Westernized Saudi is likely to feel some Wahhabi-inspired guilt over his (or her) cultural orientation. Though mild, such feelings are actually quite a widespread phenomenon in Saudi society, and have led to something of a cultural split-personality syndrome. This residual guilt helps explain the financial support many wealthy Westernized Saudis have given to Islamic "charity" organizations that funneled cash to organizations like al Qaeda. It also helps account for the "renegade" factor: the fact that a number of the hijackers came from such wealthy, Westernized families. But there were deeper things at work there as well, and we'll save the subject of the hijackers for Chapter 17.

The Amazing Tightrope Act of the Saudi Royal Family

Given this background, it's hardly surprising that the House of Saud has started to show some cracks in its foundation. Don't write it off yet, however. The Al Saud have proven to be a remarkably resilient dynasty, and long practice has made them very good at keeping their balance amid the various forces that threaten to topple them.

Arabian Almanac _____

Since the 1950s all Saudi kings have been brothers, the sons of the dynasty's greatest monarch, King Abdel Aziz ibn Abdel Rahman Al Saud (c. 1880–1953). Often known in the West simply as Ibn Saud, King Abdel Aziz emerged from family exile in Kuwait to found the modern Kingdom of Saudi Arabia in the early twentieth century. His more than 50 sons include (with their reign years) King Saud (1953–1964), King Faisal (1964–1975), King Khalid (1975–1982), and King Fahd (1982–present).

I'll go into specifics later on in this book. For now I'll just divide these pressures into two basic categories: those from inside Saudi and Islamic culture, and those from outside it. Wahhabism is a good example of a pressure acting on the Al Saud from inside their culture, while oil money and Westernization are good examples of pressures acting from outside. Of course, lots of internal and external pressures push and pull on political leaders everywhere. While the specifics may change, all national governments have to weigh such forces against each other in order to survive. But for the Saudi royal family, a number of special factors have come together to raise the stakes. Without pushing the metaphor to include too many cliché images (like "safety nets" or "gusty winds"), let's just say that the Al Saud walk a higher tightrope than most other governments or ruling families.

Since the 1940s, the Al Saud have walked that tightrope with the watchful assistance of the United States, which has supported the Saudi royal family in exchange (essentially) for continued access to cheap oil. Yet a fundamental contradiction exists between the Saudi royal family's two alliances, that with the United States on the one hand and that with the increasingly anti-Western Wahhabis on the other. This growing conflict between external and internal forces has come to pose a serious threat to Saudi Arabia's stability.

Saudi Arabia: The "Perfect" Strategic Dilemma

Remember that movie (and the gripping book it was based on) about "the perfect storm" of 1991? That fluke monster of a nor'easter was formed by the chance coming together of smaller weather systems in just the right way to form a rare powerhouse of wind and rain and towering waves over the North Atlantic.

When it comes to Saudi Arabia's problematic place in the world of international geopolitics, the image of a "perfect storm" is a much better metaphor than the old time-tested "tightrope act." Of course, the title of the book and movie was so apt that all sorts of "perfect" whatevers began popping up after the movie came out. But at the risk of jumping on the bandwagon, I think I can make a good case for using this image to describe the strategic dilemma that Saudi Arabia presents to the West.

Two "Weather Systems" Combine ...

And I'm sure that by now you'll be able to take a pretty good guess at the two main types of "weather systems" that are going to combine to form our "perfect" strategic problem. They are, of course, economics (that is, oil) and religion (that is, Islam).

Saudi Arabia has the world's largest proven reserves of oil—that slimy, gooey stuff Western industrial nations have grown so totally addicted to. This geological accident makes it a primary focal point of Western—and especially American—attention.

Yet Saudi Arabia also happens to be the sacred home of Islam, the faith of one billion of the world's people, the vast majority of whom do not live in the wealthy industrial societies that want the oil. On top of that, Wahhabism—the Saudi version of Islam— is the most austere and unfriendly version of this otherwise generally tolerant faith.

... To Form a Superstorm Powered by Money ...

That's the satellite picture of the two weather systems before they combine. As they have combined (the process is still going on), all sorts of new turbulence patterns have emerged to begin whipping up the waves. These squalls and gales are driven by oil money, which is like the moist warm air that powers a nor'easter. A steady torrent of money pours into Saudi Arabia from Western oil-consumers like the United States. And from Saudi Arabia much of it pours right back out again, to *mosques*, schools, and individuals around the world, spreading the Saudis' extremist, anti-Western Wahhabi message as it goes. Obviously, not all the money goes into exporting extremism. Huge amounts are spent on development inside the kingdom, and lots of it is also invested in the West. But billions of dollars of oil money go to

Sheik-Speak

A **mosque** (pronounced *mahsk*) is a Muslim's place of worship, as a church is for a Christian and a synagogue is for a Jew. Also like churches and synagogues, mosques often play an important role in community life.

financing extremist mosques and schools, and hundreds of millions have flowed into the coffers of al Qaeda.

... and Precipitating Terror

It is in these Saudi-backed mosques and schools that the extremist zeal of your off-the-rack potential al Qaeda terrorist is born. The money comes into Saudi Arabia from the West and then flows out to stir up anti-Western feelings, and the more money comes in, the more goes out. We'll be examining all this more closely later, but that's the basic pattern of this perfect storm.

The big strategic problem for Western leaders (like President George W. Bush and whoever succeeds him) is how to break this destructive and violent cycle. Doing so will be absolutely essential to winning the war against terrorism. This makes it especially important for Westerners—who are responsible for choosing those national leaders, after all—to understand what makes the Saudis tick.

Look at Saudi Arabia with Fresh Eyes

Yet to the average North American or European, Saudi culture is almost completely alien. That means you'll have to abandon many of your most basic assumptions in order to understand it. Its values were forged in a harsh and unforgiving desert environment, and in many ways they may appear to reflect that harshness. But Arabia is also a land of great beauty, and Saudi culture can reflect that as well. So get rid of your assumptions, even if only temporarily. We're going to look at this fascinating people—their history and their contemporary culture—with fresh eyes.

However, all this doesn't mean you have to give up political ideals like free speech and women's rights, both of which are essentially nonexistent in Saudi Arabia. There's no reason why you should (and many why you shouldn't). Indeed, I share such convictions. All I'm asking is that you try to suspend making judgments until you have a fuller picture. Giving you that fuller picture will be my job, and I hope you enjoy discovering it as much as I'm going to enjoy painting it for you.

The Least You Need to Know

- Islam's two holiest sites are on Saudi soil.
- The Saudi version of Islam is puritanical, extremist, and anti-Western.
- Virtually all of Saudi Arabia's national income comes from oil.

◆ Saudis use oil money to support Islamic extremism around the world.

◆ This cycle will not end until either the West breaks its oil addiction or the Saudis stop exporting extremism.

The Birth of Islam

In This Chapter

- ◆ Desert caravans and ancient trading routes
- ◆ Tribal raiding for fun and profit
- ◆ Two mighty empires beat each other to a pulp
- ◆ A new faith is born

Okay, you know that Islam is a major world religion and that it was founded in Arabia by a man named Muhammad. You also know that Islam's adherents, called Muslims, make up about a fifth of the world's population today. But how did it all get started? Who was Muhammad, and what did he have to say? And why did anyone listen? What did Muhammad have to offer those who first answered his call?

This chapter will take you back more than 14 centuries, to focus on the early seventh century. Arabia is a backwater. Though trade has been growing between the Arabs and the outside world, that outside world has its attention firmly focused elsewhere. A fight to the death is going on north of Arabia, between the two superpowers of the day, Byzantium and Persia. The desert Arabs have been a relatively insignificant part of this contest, though each side has Arab allies. When other Arab tribes conduct sporadic raids into Byzantine or Persian lands, they are easily turned back by these two powerful empires.

Yet within a few years the Arabs would explode out of the desert, swallowing Persia whole and reducing Byzantium to a fraction of its former territory. The engine behind this unprecedented campaign of conquest was the new faith of Islam, and it would soon bring much of the known world under its sway. In its earliest days, however, no observer would have put much money on its future greatness—or even on the continued survival of Muhammad, the social outcast who founded it.

Frankincense and Grr

In the beginning there was … the desert. Saudi Arabia takes up four fifths of the Arabian Peninsula, and nearly all of that land is dry, barren, and sparsely inhabited. Most of it has always been empty of permanent settlements, though little is known for sure about life in ancient Arabia. It's thought that, as later, the *Arabs* were organized in tribes with some (later called *Bedouin*) living as *nomads* and some living in settled farming communities.

Sheik-Speak

Who are the **Arabs?** That's a not a simple question. In ancient times, the Arabs were an ethnic group found throughout much of the Middle East but whose ancestral homeland is commonly believed to be the Arabian Peninsula. Eventually, however, anyone who spoke Arabic as a native language was considered to be an Arab. (That now includes a lot of people whose ancestors belonged to other groups.)

The **Bedouin** were Arabs who lived as **nomads**—that is, on the move, often through the harshest desert terrain. In the case of the Bedouin, they packed their homes on the backs of camels. But other societies have nomads, too, since nomadic living is found throughout the world in areas where farming can be difficult. For more on traditional Arab life, see Chapter 11.

The peninsula's lushest areas lie along the mountainous southwestern coast, in today's Yemen, which the Greeks and Romans called Arabia Felix or "Happy Arabia." Ancient Arabia Felix was home to four successive kingdoms, whose people are called Sabaeans, Qatabanians, Minaeans, and Hadramites. The earliest of these, the Kingdom of Saba, is better known as the biblical Sheba. (As in "the Queen of Sheba," a Sabaean monarch was recorded in the Old Testament as visiting the Jerusalem of King Solomon in about the tenth century B.C.E.) Around the time Sheba was flourishing, trade routes arose linking Arabia Felix with Mediterranean civilizations to the north such as Greece and Rome. The routes ran north-south along the Red Sea, through the mountainous coastal region called the Hijaz, in what is now western Saudi Arabia. Check this chapter's map to get a fix on Arabia Felix, the Hijaz, and other places mentioned in the chapter.

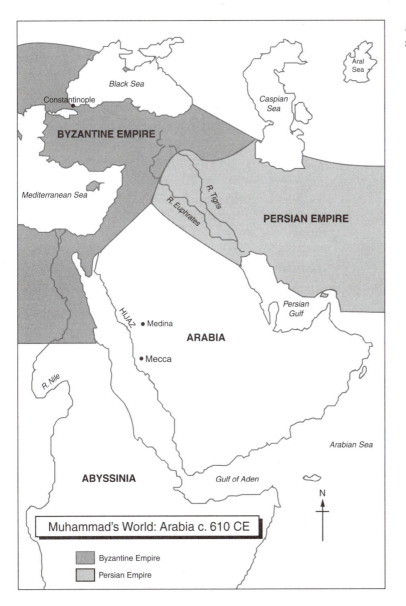

Here's a map of the places mentioned in this chapter.

Arabian Almanac

From the tenth century B.C.E. through the Middle Ages, the most valuable exports from Arabia Felix were frankincense and (you guessed it) myrrh. Aromatic resins, they are derived from the saps of two kinds of thorny tree and were used for incense, perfume, cosmetics, and medicines.

Desert Dates

Approximately 1000 B.C.E.: Arabs figure out how to saddle the camel so that it can carry heavy loads. This allows the rise of the camel caravan, vastly increasing trade between Arabia Felix and the Mediterranean world and bringing greater prosperity to southern Arabia.

Sheik-Speak

The word **pagan** is most often used to describe religious beliefs that fall outside of the Judaic, Christian, and Muslim traditions. In other words, paganism is usually contrasted with monotheism, or belief in a single God. Most Arabs before the rise of Islam were pagans, worshipping a wide variety of gods, though some were Christians and a few tribes were Jewish.

You'll find detailed information about Saudi Arabia's geography in Chapter 12, but here's a good rule of thumb: In general, the parts of the Arabian peninsula that don't belong to Saudi Arabia have most of the rainfall and most of the arable land. Er, that's arable as in agriculture, not as in Arab.

All this trade meant that the camel caravans running—well, plodding, actually—up through the Hijaz had to have the ancient Arabian equivalent of service areas. The richest such stopping points were at the northern end, nearest to the Mediterranean markets, but smaller cities also sprang up in Arabia itself. By the mid sixth century C.E., the largest of these was Mecca, in the Hijaz. Mecca was also an important religious site for *pagan* Arabs, since it held the Kaaba, an ancient black rock (probably a meteorite) believed to have come from the gods. The shrine built around the Kaaba was the most popular goal of pagan Arab pilgrims, many of whom visited the site each year from all over Arabia.

Because of its religious significance, Mecca also played the part of a sanctuary, a place where refugees could find safety from the constant tribal raids and feuds that marked Arab society. The desert Arabs had evolved a rigid code of honor, in which disputes were settled by means of vendetta and counter-vendetta. By the sixth century this code had gotten out of hand, with entire tribes becoming embroiled in endless rounds of revenge over some long forgotten offense. Equally disruptive were the raids that tribal warriors mounted with impunity on the caravans trading with the north.

Mecca offered a refuge from this bloody spin-cycle of violence and retribution. Yet as Mecca's commercial prosperity grew in the sixth century, traditional social values seemed to be breaking down there as well. Where egalitarian desert traditions called for charity to the poor, for example, in Mecca a wealthy class now openly put greed ahead of generosity. At the head of this class was the powerful merchant tribe of the Quraysh, into which Muhammad was born around the year 570 C.E.

A Tale of Two Empires

The summary I've just given tells you a little about Arabia before the advent of Islam. But there's a bigger picture to consider, one that includes important events going on in the world outside Arabia. These events have their roots in something that is likely to be a little more familiar to you than Arabia: the ancient Western civilizations of Greece and Rome. They also have roots in something that's probably less familiar, the epic clash of Greco-Roman civilization with the equally ancient Eastern civilization of Persia. That confrontation between East and West went back to the Greek classical age (the fifth to third centuries B.C.E.). It continued, with various ups and downs for each side, into the period when Greece was part of the Roman Empire (starting around the second century B.C.E. and into the seventh century C.E.). And it plays a big role in the rise of Islam, so I'm going to take a moment to tell you something about it.

Byzantium

By now you're probably confused about something. At the beginning of this chapter I talked about the struggle between Persia and something called *Byzantium*. Now all of a sudden I'm talking about Persia versus Greece and Rome. What gives, you ask? There's an explanation. I wish I could say a simple explanation, but at least it's an explanation. Unfortunately, it's anything but simple—though at the risk of infuriating the experts I'm going to simplify it for you a bit. In fact, I'll start with something that may appear *too* simple, which I'll present as a mathematical equation:

Greece + Rome = Byzantium

Looks easy, huh? Yet beware. Behind this little equation lie some deep and complicated historical developments. Expanding the equation a little may give you a better idea:

Greece + Rome + Christianity = Byzantium

But even that only gives part of the picture. So I'll leave mathematical equations behind for the moment and put it in English, taking up the story at the beginning of the fourth century C.E., when one very influential man made two very influential decisions.

The man was the Roman emperor Constantine the Great, and here are his two decisions. First, he converted to Christianity. And second, he moved the capital of the Roman Empire to a Greek city called Byzantium, which he modestly renamed after himself, Constantinople.

Desert Dates

330 C.E.: Having converted to Christianity, the Roman emperor Constantine reinstates the ancient Greek city of Byzantium as Constantinople, making it the empire's new capital. A transformed empire gradually emerges, Christian in religion, Greek in culture, and Roman in political structure. The Byzantine empire will be the Arabs' biggest foe for centuries. It will last until the invading Ottoman Turks finally conquer the fabled city of Constantinople in 1453, renaming it Istanbul and making it the capital of the Ottoman empire.

Within a century or so, each of these choices had produced a whole set of consequences. On the religious front, Christianity (earlier subject to persecution by Roman emperors) became the empire's official state religion. On the imperial front, Rome itself, along with Italy and the Western Empire, fell to incoming barbarian tribes by the end of the sixth century. But the new Greek capital and the eastern Roman Empire continued to flourish—a case of "Rome without Rome." And since the capital was now in the Greek part of the Mediterranean, the new empire gradually became mostly Greek in culture, not "Roman" at all. So here's one last mathematical equation that gives a fuller picture:

Greece + Rome + Christianity – Rome = Byzantium

Mirage Ahead

When it comes to Byzantium, watch out for slippery names. First, there's the city of Byzantium, which became the empire's new capital, Constantinople, and which is now Istanbul. Historians use the city's original name, Byzantium, to refer to the whole empire after the city's name was changed. Some of them also use the terms "later Roman Empire" or "Eastern Roman Empire" when they talk about early Byzantium.

Lately the Byzantines have been emerging from the shadows to be recognized for their central place in world history. (Byzantium is the noun, Byzantine the adjective—not to be confused with "byzantine," small *b*, meaning "devious." That usage arose as, shall we say, a tribute to the Byzantines' often nasty and always Machiavellian diplomatic skills.) As I've said, they certainly played a major role in Arabic and Islamic history, so you'll be meeting them further in the story ahead. In fact, knowledgeable scholarly types have called Byzantium one of the "parents" of early Islamic civilization, which is why I've taken up valuable space to introduce you to it now.

Persia

Along with Byzantium, Persia is sometimes considered the other "parent" of the Islamic civilization that arose in the Middle Ages, after the Arab conquests of the seventh century C.E. And also like Byzantium, it helped shape the context in which Islam arose within Arabia. So it's worth taking a moment for a brief summary of Persia, too. Persia's long pre-Islamic history can be divided into three big chunks. Conveniently, each period has its own ruling dynasty (named after the dynasty's founder):

- **Achaemenids.** Under the Achaemenid dynasty, Persia first arrived as a major player around the same time as Greece (seventh to sixth centuries B.C.E.). The famous Persian Wars (immortalized by the Greek historian Herodotus, the "father of history") happened when Greece managed to repel an invasion by this powerful new empire in the fifth century B.C.E. Conflict and confrontation continued until the Greek conqueror Alexander the Great extinguished the Achaemenid state in the fourth century.

- **Arsacids.** Persia revived under the Arsacid dynasty from the third century B.C.E. until the third century C.E. During most of this period, it was the main opponent in the east of the Roman Empire, which now ruled Greece. In case you weren't confused enough, the empire ruled by the Arsacids is called Parthia, although it basically amounted to the same territory as old Persia. (Parthia had been a province of the Achaemenid state.)

- **Sassanids.** Finally, the Sassanid dynasty overthrew the Arsacids in 224 C.E. Viewing themselves as a revival of the ancient Achaemenids, the Sassanids ruled until they were conquered by the Arabs in the seventh century.

Of these three periods, the one you really need to remember (as far as Arabian history goes, anyway) is that of the Sassanids. They're the ones who were conquered by the Arabs. But they're also the ones who were in charge of Persia when the Roman Empire underwent its slow transformation into Byzantium. And just as the Byzantines were adopting Christianity as a state religion, so did the Sassanids have their own official faith, which is called Zoroastrianism. Named after its founder, Zoroaster (who may have lived around 700 B.C.E.), Zoroastrianism had been the state religion of the Achaemenids. Reviving it was part of the Sassanid propaganda effort to reclaim the glory of the ancient Achaemenid heritage.

The Mother of All Holy Wars

You've patiently waded through all of these unfamiliar names, so here comes the payoff. For reasons that should now be starting to grow clear, the late sixth and early seventh centuries C.E. turned out to be a huge turning point—and not just for the Arabs and other peoples who would be influenced by the rise of Islam, but for the Western world as well. It is this period that marks the transition from Antiquity (the ancient world—think Rome) to the Middle Ages (the medieval world—think Byzantium).

In that vein, the rise of Islam can be seen as the first globally significant event of the Middle Ages. (The next chapter, which covers the Arab conquests, will show this more clearly. Right now we're still on "deep background" for the rise of the new faith within Arabia itself.) Other medieval stuff, of course, was going on in Western Europe, where all those barbarians were taking over after Rome "fell." But the knights, lords, ladies, and peasants of feudal Europe were only one part of the emerging Middle Ages. Byzantium and Islam, though less familiar to us in the West, were equally important elements of the overall medieval picture.

By the early seventh century, the conflict between Byzantium and Persia was changing in a way that relates to all this. Having simmered along quietly on a back burner, that struggle was now suddenly coming to a boil, with newfound religious zeal on both sides adding fuel to the fire. The process of Christianizing the Byzantine empire was now complete. Christianity extended to nearly every level of Byzantine society. For example, religious icons were suddenly appearing everywhere. These stylized, haunting portraits of Christ and the saints were widely revered by the Byzantines (as by their modern descendants, the Orthodox Greeks). Giant icons were even on display now at the head of the Byzantine army as it marched into battle. One especially famous icon of the Virgin Mary was paraded along Constantinople's massive land walls to protect the city when the Persians besieged it in 626.

This sort of thing was new, and it shows that the ancient confrontation between Rome and Persia had taken on a fresh intensity. Once a chronic border dispute, it had changed into a holy war. Over future centuries, religious warfare would help define the Middle Ages, especially when it came to conflicts between Christians and Muslims.

The Persians were the first to step up hostilities, by invading and occupying large amounts of Byzantine territory. Up to this point, the Byzantines had ruled the entire eastern Mediterranean coast (and parts in the west as well). Between 614 and 620 C.E., however, the Persians conquered Byzantine lands in Syria, Palestine (including the holy city of Jerusalem), and Egypt (including the eastern empire's second city, Alexandria), as well as elsewhere in the east. Those lands remained under Persian control for a whole generation. Despite these staggering defeats, it was the Byzantines who ultimately won. They owed their victory to the genius and determination of their emperor, Heraclius. Heraclius spent the 620s mounting a desperate counteroffensive, which paid off with the complete defeat of the Persians in 631. Heraclius installed a Byzantine puppet on the Persian throne.

Desert Dates

630 C.E.: The Byzantines mark their recapture of Jerusalem with a massive celebration in which they restore the True Cross to its place in Jerusalem's Church of the Holy Sepulchre. (The True Cross was believed to be the cross on which Christ was crucified.) Earlier the Persians had gloated over their capture of the city, which is holy to Jews and Christians. They had deliberately humiliated the Byzantines by removing the True Cross, which Christians revere as a sacred relic. The ceremonial restoration of the True Cross is the high point of the war for the Byzantines. The whole episode perfectly illustrates the war's religious overtones.

It was a great victory for the exhausted Byzantines. Yet within a few short years, Heraclius would watch it all crumble to dust at the hands of the Arab armies of Islam. Before we get to that story, however, there's more background that I ought to fill in for you. It's time to shift gears for a moment, from politics and war over to the spiritual realm.

Questions About the Nature of God

Both the Persians and the Byzantines had had relations with the Arabs for centuries, with the Arabs playing the role of a half-civilized sideshow on the periphery of the two empires. Both had also involved the Arabs in their ongoing struggle, mostly by using northern Arab "client" tribes as allies. Like trade (which I talked about at the beginning of this chapter), these alliances helped expose Arabia to what was going on in the world outside.

I've already hammered home the point that much of what was happening in the outside world had to do with religion. And when it came to religion, Byzantium and Christianity were more influential in Arabia than Persia and Zoroastrianism. Not only were there Christian tribes in Arabia, but significant numbers of Arabs also lived under Byzantine rule in places like Syria and Palestine. Most Byzantine Arabs were Christians, but they were Christians with a difference. Where the official Byzantine church stressed the dual nature of Christ as both divine and human, Arabs and others in Syria, Palestine, and Egypt disagreed. They emphasized Christ's divine nature alone, and so are called "Monophysites" (after the Greek words for "one" and "nature").

In the fifth and sixth centuries, the Monophysite controversy bitterly divided the eastern church. (There were in fact many other such disputes among Christians in this period.) Revolts were staged, blood was shed, and the whole issue got very political. Because the emperors supported the official line, for Arabs and others the Monophysite doctrine became a way of resisting the Byzantine imperial authorities. So while it was no doubt a sincere religious belief, it was also a form of local protest against foreign rule.

The hard feelings that these Byzantine subjects had against their rulers in Constantinople would make it much easier for the Muslim Arabs to conquer these lands. (That same hostility had made it easier for the Persians, too.) Right now, though, I'm bringing up the Monophysites mainly to make a religious point. It's important to understand that Islam arose at a time when everyone in the known world was deeply preoccupied with the question of how to think about God. That certainly includes the Arabs back in Arabia, where the atmosphere of religious debate was seeping in from outside. So now let's return to Arabia itself. Having gotten the bigger picture, you're ready for the rise of Islam.

Muhammad

So far, all I've told you about Muhammad is that he was born in Mecca around the year 570 C.E., into Mecca's leading merchant tribe of the Quraysh. Other than being orphaned as a boy, Muhammad seems to have lived a fairly unremarkable life until about the age of 40. According to Islamic tradition, it was then that he began experiencing the religious revelations that ultimately led to the creation of the new faith. In those early visions, the tradition goes, the angel Gabriel appeared to Muhammad and told him that he, Muhammad, was to be the final messenger of God. Many subsequent revelations are held to have come to Muhammad directly from God. These mystical experiences would recur for the rest of Muhammad's life.

Sheik-Speak

Islam means "submission" (to God) in Arabic. It is related to the word **Muslim**, which means "one who submits." The words underscore the idea that Muslims are expected to be mindful of God's will in all of their behavior, always.

By the early 610s, Muhammad was sharing his experiences with a few others who accepted their validity. For about a decade, he slowly gathered a small group of followers in Mecca. Eventually they called themselves *Muslims*, and they called the practices and beliefs that grew out of Muhammad's visions *Islam*.

Escape to Medina

Before long, however, the other Quraysh began to resent the Muslims. Partly this was because they felt that Muhammad had turned his back on his own tribe and rejected their ancestral paganism. But Muhammad also angered the Quraysh by calling on the wealthy Quraysh merchants to restrain their rampant greed and give to the poor. Relations turned hostile and then violent. In 622 Muhammad and his followers—perhaps some 70 families—accepted an offer of refuge from the inhabitants of Yathrib, a town about 250 miles north of Mecca. In a daring flight called the *hijra*, they escaped from Mecca. Mecca had become dangerous, and Muhammad was nearly assassinated before he was able to slip away to Yathrib.

It's entirely appropriate that Muslims count their years starting with the year of the hijra, for it was the hijra that turned Muhammad and Islam into a force to be reckoned with. As for Yathrib, most of its people soon converted to Islam. Abandoning its former name, it would become known forever after simply as al-Medina, "the city." When open warfare broke out between the Meccan Quraysh and the Muslims in Medina, the Muslim forces were now strong enough to defeat the Meccans.

Sheik-Speak

The Muslims' escape from Mecca to Yathrib (Medina) is the **hijra,** a word that means "emigration" with a hint of "sanctuary." It marks the start of the Muslim era, just as the birth of Christ marks the start of the Christian era. All of history before the Islamic era is referred to as "the time of ignorance" (of God).

Medina also had three Jewish tribes, the Qaynuqah, the Nadir, and the Qurayzah, each with its own army. They allied with the Quraysh in opposing the Muslims, and after vanquishing them in battle, Muhammad dealt harshly with them. In the case of the Qurayzah, he killed the tribe's 700 men and sold its women and children into slavery. In those days this was not an unusual way of dealing with diehard opponents in Arab tribal warfare.

Mirage Ahead

Muhammad's treatment of Medina's Jewish tribes has given rise to charges by some modern observers that anti-Semitism (hatred of Jews and Judaism) is part and parcel of the Islamic faith. Others, however, dispute that interpretation. Obviously, in today's world this is a highly sensitive issue, as is the question of Islamic attitudes toward Christianity. You'll find out what Muhammad's basic take was on these two older faiths in the next couple of pages. But throughout the rest of this book, you'll see Arabs and other Muslims encountering Jews and Christians in many different contexts. I'll make it clear what I think about these encounters in Chapter 14. In the end, though, you'll have to make up your own mind.

Return to Mecca

In 628, having inflicted several major military defeats on the Quraysh, Muhammad signed a treaty with them. Under its terms Muslims would be allowed to go on pilgrimage to Mecca, and both parties were supposed to end hostilities. Nonetheless, violence broke out repeatedly in 629, and the following year Muhammad marched on Mecca with a massive army of 10,000 men. Realizing the game was up, the Meccans surrendered, and Muhammad entered Mecca without bloodshed.

Sheik-Speak

Ummah is the Arabic word that denotes the entire Muslim community. Where in the early days it referred to Muhammad's few followers, it now covers all one billion plus Muslims throughout the world.

The Triumph of Muhammad

Muhammad's success persuaded many of the Quraysh to become Muslims, and by now converts from other parts of Arabia were also steadily swelling the Muslims' ranks. By the time he died in 632, Muhammad had brought virtually all of Arabia under his direct control, either by conquest or by peaceful conversion. In a single decade, the *ummah*, or Muslim community, had grown from a handful of pitiful refugees to encompass nearly all of Arabia's tribes.

Islam: A Vision of Society

The most important thing to know about Islam is that it grew out of the Judeo-Christian tradition, the monotheistic belief system that started with the Jews and that also gave rise to Christianity. That means that the world's three great monotheistic faiths are closely related. Muhammad recognized this, and like other Arabs he had plenty of exposure to Christian and Jewish ideas. (Remember, there were Christian and Jewish tribes among the Arabs, as well as pagans.)

Muhammad viewed himself as the last of the line of prophets that began with Abraham, the founder of Judaism. Islam accepts all the Jewish prophets as valid, and includes Jesus Christ among those who have relayed the word of God to people on earth. Indeed, Muhammad demanded that his followers show special respect to Jews and Christians as "people of the book," a reference to the holy scriptures that give both faiths their content.

At the same time, their relations with Christians and Jews made the Arabs painfully aware that they had no special prophetic tradition of their own. No one had appeared to give *them* God's word. Muhammad addressed this sense of being on the margins, by putting the Arabs right at the pinnacle of the monotheistic heritage. Not only was he a prophet in the great tradition, Muslims believe, but he was the *last* prophet, and therefore has special relevance. In Islamic terms, Muhammad is "the seal of the prophets."

Islam parts company with Christianity over the matter of Christ's divinity, which Muslims deny. In other words, Muslims believe that Christ was a true prophet, but not the Son of God. They see that idea as an error made by Christ's followers. Remember the controversies wracking the Christian world at this time? The Arabs had seen these bitter divisions arise among Christians over complex theological issues like the nature of the Holy Trinity, and especially of Christ. Islam can be seen as an attempt to return to a simpler monotheism, by avoiding the subtle distinctions that divided the Christian world.

Unlike Christianity, Islam has no organized church or official hierarchy. Religious authority is based instead on the piety, knowledge, and exemplary behavior of those who would aspire to positions of leadership. Islam is meant to shape every aspect of one's daily life and of society, and worship doesn't end when a Muslim leaves the mosque. Accordingly, Muslim cultures traditionally don't make the firm distinctions between religion and politics, for example, that you'll find in the West.

The Koran

The *Koran* is Islam's sacred text. It's divided into 114 chapters called *suras*, which represent the revelations from God (*Allah*) that Muhammad received after the age of about 40. Muslims thus view the Koran as the word of God, as dictated through Muhammad. Its content ranges from stories of the prophets to commands concerning charity, marriage, social and business interactions, and religious ritual.

The Traditions of the Prophet

Soon after Muhammad's death, some Muslims began recording his reputed words and deeds. A body of writings eventually arose that came to act as a supplement to the Koran. Called the *Hadith* or "reports," it's commonly known in English as "the Traditions of the Prophet," and is Muslims' second most important source of religious authority. The Hadith make up the core of the *Sunnah* or "custom," which include other deeds and sayings attributed to Muhammad.

The Five Pillars of Islam

From the Koran and the Traditions are drawn the "Five Pillars of Islam," or the five basic religious obligations of all Muslims:

♦ **Declaration of belief.** Called the *shahada* or testimony, this simple statement defines Islam's core doctrine: "There is no god but God, and Muhammad is His Prophet." Say this sincerely, and you're a Muslim.

♦ **Prayer.** Muslims must pray five times a day, facing towards Mecca as they do so.

♦ **Charity.** Muslims who can afford it must give to the poor.

♦ **Fasting.** Adult Muslims must fast from dawn to dusk during the Muslim holy month of Ramadan.

♦ **Pilgrimage.** All Muslims who can afford it must go on one or more of the annual mass pilgrimages to Mecca. Islam basically took over the pagan Arabs' pilgrimage concept, adding a Muslim overlay to preexisting rites (much as Christians took over earlier pagan festivals at Christmas and Easter). The pilgrimage is called the *hajj,* and those who have made it are given the honorific title *haji.* You'll find out a lot more about the hajj in Chapter 15.

Islamic Law

Islamic law, called *sharia,* is based on the Koran and the Traditions, but has also come from consensus and from the opinions of religious authorities of the past. I'll talk about it in greater detail later, mainly in Chapter 14. For now just bear in mind that *sharia* law is meant to regulate not just religion, but all aspects of life.

Sheik-Speak _____

Here are Arabic words for a few of Islam's key concepts:

♦ **Koran**   Islamic holy scripture as revealed by God to Muhammad

♦ **Suras**   Chapters in the Koran (114 of them)

♦ **Allah**   Arabic for God

♦ **Hadith**   The Traditions of the Prophet, a sacred scripture that includes the words and deeds most authoritatively attributed to Muhammad.

♦ **Sunnah**   Larger body Muhammad's sayings and deeds that includes the Hadith.

♦ **Shahada**   A Muslim's credo: "There is no god but God, and Muhammad is His Prophet"

♦ **Hajj**   Pilgrimage to Mecca

♦ **Haji**   A Muslim who has made the pilgrimage

♦ **Sharia**   Islamic law

As you see, Islam is very simple in the beliefs it demands of its followers. Instead of giving them a long list of things to believe, it focuses more on telling them how to act and live. In this it resembles Judaism more than Christianity. But Islam goes further than Judaism in attempting to provide a complete plan for an ordered and devout society. Above all, Muhammad sought to quell the chaotic violence that dominated Arabia in his lifetime—and by the time he died in 632, he had succeeded totally.

> **CAUTION**
>
> **Mirage Ahead**
>
> In the past, Westerners have sometimes referred to Muslims as "Mohammedans," which erroneously implies that they worship Muhammad. Unlike Christians, Muslims do not worship the founder of their faith as a divine being. Avoid the term "Mohammedan." It's very offensive to Muslims (though it's old-fashioned now and you'll probably see it only in older sources).

The Least You Need to Know

- Islam was founded by Muhammad in the early seventh century C.E.

- Muhammad's visions are recorded in the Koran, Islam's sacred text, which Muslims believe to be the words of God.

- Muslims regard Muhammad as the last of God's prophets, not as a divine being.

- Islam arose from Jewish and Christian monotheism.

- Muhammad's teachings emphasize behavior, not belief.

The Arabs Shake Things Up

In This Chapter

- ◆ The Arabs found an empire
- ◆ Islam becomes a civilization
- ◆ The Turks take over
- ◆ The Ottoman Empire begins a long slow decline

It's the year 632. Having unified Arabia's tribes under the banner of Islam, Muhammad has died after a short illness. Peace prevails. But Muhammad died without naming a successor. So as the Arabs struggle to deal with their loss, a big question arises. What next?

It doesn't take long to find an answer. Unity has brought peace, but it also means that the restless tribal warriors—accustomed to raiding and plundering at will—have no outlet for all their aggressive energy. The leaders who take over after Muhammad base their authority on the ability to direct the tribes' aggression outward, rather than against other Muslims. The result is one of the greatest campaigns of conquest the world has ever seen. Within a century, the Arabs conquer a vast empire that stretches from Spain to India. Along the way, they absorb new influences, transforming Islam into a sophisticated civilization on the cutting edge of science and learning.

In this chapter you'll witness the explosive Arab conquests and the rise of the Arab empire, then watch leadership of the Islamic world pass from the Arabs to a new people, the Turks. Yet after centuries of striking fear into its enemies, the Turkish Ottoman Empire, too, will start to stagnate and decline, leaving Arabia again stranded outside the mainstream of history.

A Century of Arab Conquest

Remember how Byzantium and Persia, the two empires north of Arabia, fought that long and bitter holy war in the opening decades of the seventh century? The Byzantines' grueling victory over the Persians almost exactly coincided with Muhammad's triumphant rise to power inside Arabia. The crucial decade for both was the 620s, when Muhammad and the Byzantine emperor Heraclius were each battling the odds. By the end of that decade, both had prevailed. That was about all they had in common, however. While Muhammad led a people whose energy and zeal had yet to be tapped, Heraclius—even in victory—ruled a tottering empire that was pretty well tapped out. For their part, the defeated and demoralized Persians were in a state of near anarchy.

The extent of the Byzantine and Persian exhaustion soon became clear. For when Muhammad's successors led the armies of Islam out of Arabia, the first places to fall were some of the same lands the Byzantines had just so painfully won back from the Persians. And Persia itself wasn't far behind.

Having inflicted several disastrous defeats on the Byzantine army, the Arabs completed their conquest of Palestine and Egypt by the early 640s, forever ending Byzantine control there. Much of Persia's territory had fallen by the mid 640s, and by the end of the decade the Arabs had pushed the Byzantines back in Syria as far as Anatolia (today's Turkey). After this quick start, the Arabs continued their campaigns of conquest, but at a slightly slower pace. They went in two directions, east and west, and the campaigns lasted until about 750. To the east, they mopped up the rest of Sassanid Persia by about 660, and then pushed on as far as India and Central Asia. To the west, from their base in Egypt they conquered steadily along the coast of North Africa,

---

Desert Dates

636: The Arab general Khalid ibn al-Walid shatters Heraclius's Byzantine army at the Battle of Yarmuk in Palestine, north of Jerusalem. This major victory opens Palestine to Arab expansion. Far to the east, in the same year another important victory at the Battle of Qadisiyyah similarly opens up Mesopotamia and other Persian territory to the Arabs.

Desert Dates

732: After conquering Spain, the Arabs push into central France, where they are finally defeated at the Battle of Poitiers by Charles Martel, the grandfather of Charlemagne.

crossing the Strait of Gibraltar in 711 and rapidly occupying Spain, which remained under Arab control for centuries.

The goal that always eluded them was Constantinople, which they repeatedly but unsuccessfully besieged, including a five-year siege from 674 to 678. The well fortified Byzantine capital held out, and though the Byzantines were now on the defensive, they kept hold of their lands in Anatolia and the Balkans. This is something to think about, since if Byzantium had fallen, the Arabs would have been able to mount a two-pronged attack on Western Europe. In that case, you might well be reading this book in Arabic!

Mirage Ahead

The standard view of the Middle Ages says that they started when a bunch of barbarians from northern Europe invaded the Roman Empire, leading to the "fall of Rome" in the fifth century. Wrong on all counts!

First, as you now know, the Roman Empire didn't fall at all. It became the Greek Christian empire of Byzantium. It didn't fall, that is, until 1453—not an era that most of us associate with the Roman Empire.

Second, at least according to one influential view, it wasn't the barbarians who kicked off the Middle Ages at all, but the Arab conquest. The Arabs became the dominant Mediterranean sea power, thus cutting Western Europe off from the Byzantine east, and it was Europe's resulting isolation that really created the Middle Ages. This idea is summed up in the phrase, "Without Muhammad, no Charlemagne," coined by the famous Belgian historian Henri Pirenne, who came up with this interpretation of the Middle Ages (Charlemagne was the ninth-century Frankish ruler who conquered much of Europe after the end of Roman power).

Early Arab Dynasties

Long before this period of conquest ended, the center of power in the Arab world shifted out of Arabia. Under a series of rulers called *caliphs*, the Arabs governed their new empire first from Medina, but then established successive new capitals in Syria and Mesopotamia (modern Iraq). In general, Christians and Jews were treated with tolerance in the newly conquered lands. Since Muslims were not taxed, Christians and Jews provided the caliphs' tax base, though the taxes and other legal restrictions encouraged many to convert to Islam over time. Eventually, the Arab empire fragmented, and a number of regional power centers arose. The following map shows a few of these regional centers, like the offshoot Umayyad dynasty that arose in Muslim Spain to rival the Abbasids.

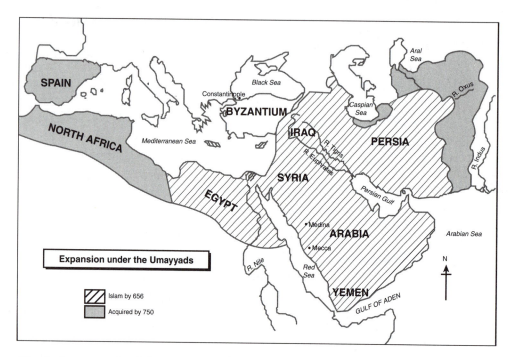

The Arab conquests founded an empire that stretched from India to Spain.

Sheik-Speak

Caliph, which means "successor" in Arabic, is the title given to the Arab Muslim rulers who succeeded Muhammad. Like Muhammad himself, the caliphs exercised both religious and political authority. The line of succession begun by Muhammad lasted until 1258, when the last caliph was overthrown by the Mongols. However, the title caliph was sporadically revived by later rulers.

Here are the highlights of this process, which lasted until the thirteenth century.

The "Rightly Guided" Caliphs

The first four caliphs, known as the Rashidun or "Rightly Guided" Caliphs, were either relatives or close associates of Muhammad, and like him, they ruled from Medina. They were the ones who kicked off the Arab conquest, and they ruled during its first, most energetic, phase. The four Rightly Guided Caliphs, in order of their rule, are ...

◆ **Abu Bakr,** ruled 632 to 634

◆ **Umar I,** ruled 634 to 644

◆ **Uthman,** ruled 644 to 656

◆ **Ali,** ruled 656 to 661

During their rule, a campaign of Arabization brought Muslim Arab immigrants from Arabia to places like Syria and Palestine, assuring that the populace there would be mostly Arab and Muslim. While some Christian Arabs had lived in these newly conquered lands before, Islamic Arab culture now became dominant there. This process also took place, though more slowly, in many of the other areas that the Arabs conquered, especially Egypt and Mesopotamia.

Keep the Rightly Guided Caliphs in mind, because they represent the last time that Arabia had undisputed leadership of the Muslim world. This period will later come to represent a "golden age" for the Arabian religious reformers called the Wahhabis, who will rise to power in the eighteenth century by calling for a return to the good old days of "pure" Islam and Arabian leadership.

Shiites and Sunnis

You probably noticed in the preceding summary that Ali only ruled as caliph for four years or so. Well, thereby hangs a tale. Ali, who is commonly believed to have been Muhammad's uncle, was also married to the Prophet's daughter (and only surviving child), Fatima. Ali had taken over after Uthman's murder. But for a number of reasons there was widespread resistance to Ali, leading to conflict between Ali's supporters and his opponents. His supporters called themselves the Shia or "Party" (of Ali) and have become known in English as Shiites. After Ali himself was murdered, the door was open for a powerful general named Muawiya to proclaim himself caliph. He won general acceptance, but the minority Shiites refused to recognize Muawiya and his successors, instead choosing to honor the descendants of Ali. In time the Shiites split further and further in their religious practices from mainstream Muslims, who are called Sunnis (for their adherence to the Sunnah; see the previous chapter).

Keep the Shiites and the Sunnis in mind, too, since this split has been Islam's deepest division. So the "golden age" of the Rightly Guided Caliphs of Medina also represents the last and only time Islam was whole and undivided. The division between Shiites and Sunnis plays an important role in the story ahead, and I'll be updating you on it as we go along.

The Umayyads Pack Up and Leave

Muawiya, the general who became caliph after Ali, was governor of Syria at the time, and the head of the Arabs' most powerful army. It was only natural for him to move the capital from Medina to Syria, and that's exactly what he did, establishing a new capital in the ancient Syrian city of Damascus. Arabia had been at the center of things for only a couple of generations, but no longer would the strings of the empire be pulled from the Arab homeland and the city of the Prophet. Muawiya established a new dynasty, the Ummayads (named for an ancestor of his), which ruled from Damascus until 750.

The Abbasids Fall to Pieces

At that point the Umayyads were overthrown by another dynasty, the Abbasids, who took the decisive step of moving the empire's center of gravity east to Mesopotamia. There, near the ruined old Sassanid capital of Ctesiphon, they built a magnificent new capital city from scratch. Called Baghdad, it would be a vibrant center of Arab and Islamic civilization for five centuries.

While technically the Abbasid caliphs lasted that long in power, in reality they had lost their grip on the empire before the first century was up. A whole slew of rival dynasties sprouted up around the empire, including a branch of the Umayyads in Spain and a Shiite dynasty called the Fatimids (after Muhammad's daughter, Fatima) in Egypt. Those two were exceptions in that they put forward their own claims to the caliphate, but smaller-scale local rulers also became adept at stealing power from the distant Abbasids.

The Golden Age of Islamic Civilization

While the Abbasids may not have been very good at ruling with an iron fist, they were pretty impressive patrons of the arts and culture. By now Islam was evolving into more than just the desert religion of ethnic Arabs. In the ninth century, Arabs still dominated politically, and Arabic—the language of the Prophet, of the Koran, and of the Traditions—remained the most prestigious language in the Islamic world. But you can't conquer so much land and so many people without being strongly influenced by them. Accordingly, Islam had absorbed many regional influences on the way to staking its claim as a world civilization.

Of all the cultural influences Islam absorbed, two stand out as the most important. I said in the last chapter that Byzantium and Persia are sometimes called the two "parents" of Islamic civilization, so it won't be a total surprise that they are the two influences I'm talking about now.

It's All Greek to Me

I explained, too, how Byzantium was basically Greek in culture, so it also shouldn't be a surprise that the most important part of the Byzantine influence on Islamic civilization came from Byzantium's Greek past. This may seem like a bit of a mystery at first.

But in a second you'll probably agree that, in fact, you already know roughly what I mean. After all, what do you think of when I say the word "Greek"? Socrates, right? Plato? Aristotle? All those guys. Philosophers and other intellectual pioneers that we've all heard of. Well, they were the ones who influenced Islamic thought. Most important was Aristotle, but the Arabs also took up the work of mathematicians like Euclid, physicians like Galen and Hippocrates, and scientists like Ptolemy.

These ancient Greek sages were still being studied in school when the Arabs conquered Byzantine lands in the Middle East. Eventually the Arabs realized they had a treasure trove of knowledge on their hands, and they began to promote further research on it. A leading example of this is the early ninth-century Abbasid caliph al-Mamun. He was once thought to have set up a research facility in Baghdad called "the House of Wisdom," especially to translate works on science and philosophy from Greek into Arabic. Historians have recently questioned whether the House of Wisdom actually existed, but we do know that these important works got translated one way or another.

Arabian Almanac

One of the scholars reported to have worked at Caliph al-Mamun's fabled House of Wisdom was the mathematician Muhammad ibn Musa al-Khwarizmi (c. 780– c. 850). Al-Khwarizmi took number theory from India, including the all-important idea of zero, which the Greeks had rejected. His new math eventually revolutionized Western math, too, which remains based on Indian numbers—known in the West, of course, as "Arabic numerals." And a garbled version of al-Khwarizmi's name comes down to us in the word "algorithm."

The Arabs didn't just copy these works mindlessly, however. Instead, Arab thinkers took the ideas of the Greeks and expanded on them, making valuable and original contributions to learning. Many words still essential to science and technology reflect Arabic origins, including "algebra," "alcohol," and "alkali." The "al" in these and similar words can be a clue: It means "the" in Arabic, and so is very common in scientific names. The greatest Arab contributions came in astronomy, and many stars take their English names from Arabic (for example, Aldebaran).

Kings and Things

At the same time, the second major influence on Islam—that of Persia—was also making itself felt. Persian literature, art, architecture, and music all made enduring contributions to the emerging Islamic civilization. But the most telling Persian influences came in the areas of law and politics. Don't forget that when the Arabs began their conquest they had very little in their own culture that prepared them to rule such a huge empire. Their basic technique was to let the old official institutions (tax collection, especially) continue to operate in the conquered areas. The only difference was that now everyone reported to the Arabs. Same management, but new ownership, you might say. While in former Byzantine lands the Umayyads had ruled using Byzantine power structures, when the Abbasids moved the center of power to Persian territory they took over Persian laws and institutions.

But the biggest thing the Persians had to offer was their traditional idea of kingship. When it came to kings, Persia had always specialized in awe-inspiring majesty. Indeed, ever since the Achaemenid dynasty, a Persian monarch had been styled "King of Kings." The Persians had come to think of a king as appointed by God to govern society using his own royal skill and wisdom. As the Abbasid caliphate declined in the eleventh and twelfth centuries, this idea of a divinely *appointed* ruler slowly replaced the original Muslim idea of a divinely *inspired* ruler. Slowly, in other words, the old unity of spiritual and political authority was replaced by a division of the two. More and more, Muslim rulers would exercise political power alone. And more and more, spiritual authority in the Islamic world would come to rest with the religious scholars, not the rulers.

Yet the old ideal would never disappear completely. After all, it's based on the example of the Prophet himself, as well as on the caliphate. In the pages ahead, you'll see how the ideal of combined political and spiritual authority still haunts the Islamic world today—especially Saudi Arabia.

The Turks Arrive

Towards the end of the Abbasid period a new group of people began to make their presence felt in the Islamic world. Tough nomads from the mountainous interior of Central Asia, the Turks had been pushed west across the Central Asian steppes by other peoples further east of them (such as the Mongols). During this time they had converted to Islam. At first they served as mercenaries and administrators to the ruling Arab dynasties, but the shoe would soon be on the other foot. By the mid-eleventh century, under the leadership of the Seljuk clan, the Turks had taken over the crumbling Arab empire in the east. Soon they would push further west. Technically, under the Ottoman dynasty Turkish dominance of the Islamic world would last into the twentieth century, though the Ottoman

> **Desert Dates**
>
> 1055: The Seljuk ruler Toghril takes over in Baghdad, styling himself "sultan," a title that encompasses political but not religious authority. The Seljuk sultans claim to act for the Abbasid caliphs, who remain in place as religious figureheads.

Empire began to decay as far back as the seventeenth century. During all of that time, Arabia—a poor, isolated province under the Ottomans—once again returned to the status of a backwater.

The Seljuks

Seljuk dominance eventually extended as far west as Syria and Palestine. The Seljuks also probed into Anatolia, and when the Byzantine army showed its weakness in a decisive defeat at the Battle of Manzikert in 1071, Turkish immigrants began flooding into that fertile region, too. This was when Turks first settled in what is now Turkey. Up to then Anatolia had been a Byzantine stronghold, and was mostly Greek and Christian. The loss of these lands prompted the Byzantine emperor Alexius I Comnenus to ask the Christian West for help against the Seljuks, resulting in the First Crusade (1095–1999).

Arabian Almanac

The Crusades lasted 200 years and had a huge impact on the development of Western European civilization, in part through exposure to the more advanced civilizations of Byzantium and Islam. Though Muslims today look back on them as a prime example of bloodthirsty Christian savagery, their impact on the Islamic world at the time was limited. There were five major Crusades (and many lesser ones):

- The First Crusade (1095–1099) was launched by Pope Urban II in response to the Byzantine emperor's plea for help. It sent some 100,000 Europeans to wrest the Holy Land from the grasp of the Turks. Only about 14,000 arrived, but in Jeru-salem and elsewhere the Crusade's leaders succeeded in establishing a number of "Crusader kingdoms."
- The Second Crusade (1146–1148) fizzled, basically. Afterward, the great Kurdish warrior Saladin led the Muslims in victories over the Crusader kingdoms.
- The Third Crusade (1188–1192) saved the Crusader kingdoms from being recaptured by Saladin's heirs.
- The Fourth Crusade (1202–1204) succeeded brilliantly—in capturing Constantinople, supposedly the Crusaders' ally. The Byzantines recovered their capital in 1261, but they never recovered their former strength.
- The Fifth Crusade (1217–1221) came close to capturing Egypt, but was defeated at the last minute by the Muslim defenders.

But the Seljuks never really got their part of the Islamic world under tight control, and even their own Turkish tribal leaders only obeyed them when they felt like it. The rest of the Islamic world, too, remained highly fragmented both politically and religiously, with Shiite regimes ruling over Sunni populations in many places. And the Crusades didn't help matters any, although in the end the Crusaders did more damage to the Byzantines, their fellow Christians and supposed allies, than to the Muslims.

The Seljuks' shaky grip on power was finally shattered by the Mongols. I've already mentioned the Mongols once or twice, but I'll introduce you to these fierce Asiatic horsemen properly now. Their restless raiding had been the engine behind centuries of migration westward across the steppes of Central Asia, including that of the Turks. But in the thirteenth century they formed a powerful tribal confederacy under their leader Genghis Khan and swept out of their Central Asian homeland. They stomped the Seljuks in battle several times, along with just about everyone else they met, and in 1258 they sacked Baghdad, bringing an end to the lame Abbasid caliphate. The city itself was destroyed. The Mongols reportedly put its leaders and intellectuals to the sword and made a mountain of their skulls. Over the course of the thirteenth century the Mongols pillaged and occupied much of Asia, Russia, the Middle East, and Anatolia. However, while their empire was extensive, it left little real imprint on history other than destruction.

Sheik-Speak

The **Mamluks** (also spelled Mamelukes) weren't an ethnic group, though at times they acted like one. Originally they were a branch of the Arab-led military made up of non-Muslim slave soldiers, most of whom were ethnic Turks. The Mamluks were such effective fighters that they evolved into an independent political power in places from Egypt to India, often taking control from their former masters.

Only in Syria were the Mongols firmly defeated, by an offshoot of the Turks called the *Mamluks*. These disciplined cavalry fighters proved more than a match for the fearsome charges of the Mongol horsemen. The prestige won by the Mamluks in defending Syria against the Mongol onslaught turned them into a regional power in their own right. In addition to Syria, they also ruled Egypt, where they set up a new line of figurehead Abbasid caliphs in Cairo. Their influence extended westward to Libya and eastward into Arabia. There they got the holy sites of Mecca and Medina to recognize their protection, dominating the Hijaz in the fourteenth and fifteenth centuries. Mamluk sultans ruled Egypt and Syria from 1250 to 1517, when the Ottomans took over those lands, and with them the Hijaz. But the Mamluks remained influential there well into the Ottoman era.

The Ottomans

The Ottomans arose in the early fourteenth century as a small Turkish dynasty in northwestern Anatolia, on the embattled border between the Turks and Byzantines.

Named for the dynasty's founder Osman I (c. 1258–c. 1326), they were the first group of Turks to regroup after the Mongols ravaged much of the Islamic world and finished off the wobbly Seljuks.

As the Ottoman sultans transformed their state from a tiny principality to mighty empire, they fulfilled Muhammad's prophecy that Muslims would one day rule "Rum," or Rome—the Arabs' term for Byzantium. Here's a timeline giving the highlights of Ottoman territorial expansion:

◆ **1307–1360:** The Ottomans conquer Byzantine lands in northwest Anatolia and establish their first footholds in the Byzantine Balkans.

◆ **1360–1400:** The Ottomans expand further in Anatolia and the Balkans, where they defeat the Serbs and absorb Bulgaria. Surrounded and forced to pay tribute, the Byzantine empire—now about the size of Vermont—is reduced to Constantinople, the area around it, and parts of Greece.

◆ **1453:** Sultan Mehmed the Conqueror takes Constantinople, the Byzantine capital. It becomes the new Ottoman capital, Istanbul.

◆ **1450–1490:** The Ottomans absorb Bosnia, Serbia, Albania, and mop up the last areas of Byzantine Greece. They now rule all of Anatolia and the Balkans, basically replacing the old Byzantine empire.

◆ **1512–1520:** Sultan Selim the Grim conquers Kurdistan, Syria, and Egypt and gains control of the Hijaz (including Mecca and Medina) in Arabia. Selim also defeats the Persian Safavid empire—the Ottomans' only rivals in the Muslim world—at the Battle of Chaldiran (1514).

◆ **1520–1566:** Sultan Suleiman the Magnificent conquers Iraq, Albania, and Hungary, and consolidates Ottoman control of North Africa. He forges the Ottoman navy into the Mediterranean's dominant fleet and reforms the Ottoman state. His rule represents the height of Ottoman power, despite his unsuccessful sieges of Vienna (1529) and Malta (1565).

Arabian Almanac _____

At its height the Ottoman Empire cast a long shadow over Europe. For centuries, the Ottomans were Christian Europe's feared enemy on land and sea. Twice they tried to capture the Austrian capital, Vienna. Yet Ottoman culture was highly cosmopolitan, and the Ottoman state was surprisingly tolerant of its Christian and Jewish subjects, who were essentially allowed to govern themselves. In this broadly multiethnic empire, non-Muslims and non-Turks could achieve great wealth and rise to influential positions in the army and government.

The Ottomans Lose Their Mojo

For a number of reasons (including an increasingly cumbersome bureaucracy and an inability to change with the times), the Ottomans started losing their edge sometime towards the end of the sixteenth century, although for a while they actually continued to add small pieces of territory to their already vast domains. The following map shows the Ottoman Empire when it ruled the greatest amount of territory, in the early seventeenth century. But even then decline was setting in. After Suleiman the Magnificent—who was indeed rather an impressive gent—future sultans were often decadent and lacking in leadership qualities.

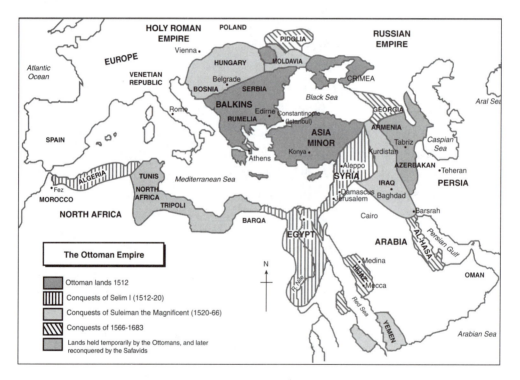

The Ottoman Empire reached the height of its territorial expansion in the early seventeenth century.

By the seventeenth century, Ottoman institutions were getting cumbersome and creaky. As European societies started to modernize their economic and state structures, and especially their armies, the Ottomans were slowly left behind, their government and economy proving incapable of reform. In a series of treaties starting in the late seventeenth century, the rising European powers whittled the Ottoman Empire away piece by piece. Elsewhere, local powers grabbed more and more autonomy from Istanbul, and by the nineteenth century—as European nationalism gathered steam—the empire's Christian subjects in the Balkans were demanding independence. Declaring the Ottoman Empire to be "the sick man of Europe," imperial powers like Britain and Russia calculatedly turned Ottoman weakness to their own advantage.

Here's another timeline, this one featuring major milestones of the Ottoman Empire's long, slow decline:

♦ **1571:** Combined European naval forces defeat the Ottoman navy at the Battle of Lepanto, destroying the Ottoman fleet and marking the beginning of Ottoman decline.

♦ **1683:** The second Ottoman siege of Vienna fails, with the Ottomans suffering a devastating defeat outside the city's walls.

♦ **1699–1739:** The Ottomans lose Hungary, Transylvania, and parts of Serbia to Austria, creating the Austro-Hungarian empire. Other losses include territory ceded to Poland and Russia.

♦ **1798:** A lightning French invasion of Egypt (led by Napoleon) demonstrates that Ottoman arms are totally outmoded.

♦ **1804–1833:** Revolts by Greeks and Serbs force the Ottomans to recognize their independence. By now Egypt, Mesopotamia, and Arabia have also all asserted themselves against Ottoman control. (More on this in the next chapter, when you'll get a closer look at how the Ottoman decline affected Arabia.)

♦ **1839–1876:** A series of Ottoman reforms called the Tanzimat (aimed largely at appeasing European critics) fails to reverse the decline.

♦ **1882:** Britain occupies Egypt, adding it to the worldwide British empire.

♦ **1920–1923:** In the wake of World War I, the Ottoman Empire is finally dissolved, and its Turkish core becomes the Republic of Turkey. The European victors of World War I divide Ottoman lands in the Middle East into, essentially, the Middle Eastern states that exist today.

Arabian Almanac

If the Ottoman Empire was "the sick man of Europe," by the mid-nineteenth century it was gasping on its deathbed. From that point on, European power politics focused more and more on the "Eastern Question"—which came down to who would get what territory when the Ottomans finally kicked the bucket. Russia wanted to gobble up as much as possible. This made Britain nervous, because it was worried about Russian encroachment on its empire in India. So the Brits plotted and schemed to prop up the Ottomans as long as they could. Russia and Britain fought the Crimean War (1853–1856) over this issue, which continued to fester.

So much for a bird's eye view of the Ottomans; as I've said, in the next chapter you'll get a view of the Ottoman Empire and its decline from the Arabian perspective. But that will also involve a closer look at colonial power politics on the part of the Europeans, and the emergence of the modern states of the Middle East. So keep in mind the basic problem of the "Eastern Question": what to do with all that Ottoman land and all those subject peoples. To the European colonial mind, self-rule was out of the question, at least until the various peoples under Ottoman rule had been properly "civilized."

On that note, perhaps the best way to close this chapter is to observe that of all Middle Eastern peoples, only the Saudis can look back and say that they were never under European colonial rule. I'll be reminding you of that later, too, because to this day it's a great source of Saudi national pride.

The Least You Need to Know

- ◆ Muhammad's Arab successors, called caliphs, lasted until the thirteenth century.

- ◆ Succession disputes over the caliphate led to the biggest split in the Islamic world, that between Shiites and Sunnis.

- ◆ Arabs led the way in science and learning at a time when Europeans had yet to rediscover the lost art of bathing.

- ◆ Around the eleventh century, leadership of the Islamic world passed from the Arabs to the Turks.

- ◆ The modern states of the Middle East emerged as European powers divided up the lands of the Turks' defunct Ottoman Empire.

The Rise(s) of the House of Saud

In This Chapter

- ◆ The Wahhabi-Al Saud alliance gets underway
- ◆ The ups and downs of the Al Saud
- ◆ The Europeans step in
- ◆ A desert warrior claims his inheritance

Darkness in the Arabian desert. Muffled sounds—the clink of steel on steel, the impatient rumbling of the hobbled camels—can barely be heard as a handful of men ready themselves. They move forward on foot, silently. Soon they pass the darkened shapes of buildings on the edge of town. It is the night of January 15, 1902, and Abdel Aziz Al Saud is about to take the city of Riyadh with little more than guts, cunning, and luck.

For Saudis, this is a familiar, breathtaking tale of adventure that combines the best of Robin Hood thumbing his nose at the Sheriff of Nottingham with George Washington crossing the Delaware. It is the founding myth of the modern Saudi state, and later King Abdel Aziz—better known to Westerners simply as Ibn Saud—would love to entertain visitors with gripping accounts of it. Never mind that each new version might differ widely in its details from the others, depending on the king's mood. They were all true, at least in the way that matters most for founding myths.

But the story really starts much earlier, in the middle of the eighteenth century, when the family of the Al Saud got its start. In this chapter I'll take you back to that time, filling in the background to Ibn Saud's remarkable career, and finishing up with the founding of Saudi Arabia.

The Emir Takes a Wife

Riyadh, the city that Ibn Saud would capture so boldly in 1902, is now the capital of Saudi Arabia and its leading city. It has historically been the chief city of Arabia's *Najd* region. Riyadh, the Najd, and other features are shown on the following map of Arabia in the eighteenth century.

But Riyadh (the name means "gardens" in Arabic) was not always the seat of Al Saud power. The founder of the Al Saud, Muhammad ibn Saud, originally ruled a small oasis principality called Dariya, a few miles north of Riyadh. The family is thought to have come to Dariya from eastern Arabia sometime in the fifteenth century, and by the late sixteenth century they had risen to leadership of the little community. The original family name has fallen by the wayside. Muhammad's father's first name was Saud, and so the son was Muhammad ibn Saud, "Muhammad son of Saud." Since Muhammad was the one who made the family into something, "ibn Saud" is the family name that stuck.

Sheik-Speak

The **Najd** is the name for the desolate region that lies in the center of the Arabian peninsula. The name means "plateau" in Arabic, and refers to the large plateau that is the area's dominant feature.

Muhammad was born around 1703, and he took over from his father as *emir* of Dariya when he was close to 40. Most likely that would have been that, and no one ever would have heard of Muhammad or his family, except for what happened next. The next town over from Dariya was another small oasis settlement called Uyayna, where a local teacher, or *sheik*, was making himself highly unpopular among the townspeople with his strict, puritanical preaching.

For a while the villagers put up with the preacher's railing against their religious laxness. But when he had his followers stone a woman to death for adultery—as provided for by strict Sharia law—they kicked him out of town. His name was Muhammad ibn Abdel Wahhab, and luckily for him his preaching had caught the ear of Muhammad ibn Saud, who offered him refuge in Dariya. The two Muhammads hit it off, and Wahhab became Dariya's *qadi*, or judge.

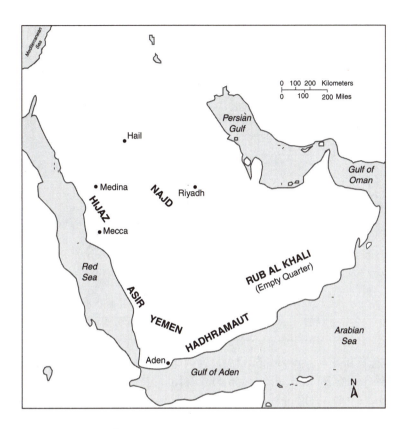

Here's a map of Arabia around the time the House of Saud got going, in the mid-eighteenth century.

Sheik-Speak _____

Three important Arabian titles:

- An **emir** (also spelled "amir") is a petty local ruler. This hereditary title is sometimes translated as commander or governor. An emir rules an emirate, as in "United Arab Emirates," a state on Saudi Arabia's eastern border.

- **Sheik** (also spelled "sheikh" or "shaykh") means teacher or elder, and refers to someone who has earned a position of authority or respect. It's not a hereditary title, but more of an informal sign of respect. Leaders of tribes have been sheiks, as have religious figures. Today, you might refer to your boss as a sheik, and the title is also offered to many figures in public life, especially the wealthy.

- A **qadi** is a religious judge who administers the Sharia, or Islamic law (see Chapter 2).

In addition to having the same first name, the two Muhammads were also the same age. To seal their friendship, in 1744 Muhammad ibn Saud married the daughter of Muhammad ibn Abdel Wahhab, marking the beginning of the close alliance between the two families. Wahhab eventually became known simply as the Sheik, so just as ibn Saud's descendants are known as the Al Saud, Wahhab's are called the Al al-Sheik, or House of the Sheik. The partnership between the Al Saud and Al al-Sheik remains very important today, and members of the two houses continue to intermarry.

> ### Mirage Ahead
>
> It was their detractors who first gave the name Wahhabis to the followers of Muhammad ibn Abdel Wahhab. They themselves find the term offensive, as it might imply that they worship Wahhab, a man, rather than God. For convenience you might as well call them Wahhabis, however, because that's how they're always known in the West. In addition, since it's probably impossible to avoid offending the Wahhabis anyway, frankly I see little point in trying! Just be aware that (in their view) the name goes against what they believe in. Their own name for themselves illustrates that belief: *Muwahiddin*, or "Unitarians," a reference to the oneness of God.

Wahhabism's central idea is that there's one God and only one God. Wahhabis thus reject the veneration of saints, prophets, holy men, the dead, and angels. Also, like fundamentalists everywhere, the Wahhabis insist on a literal interpretation of religious texts such as the Koran and the Traditions of the Prophet. (Learn more about Wahhabism in Chapter 14).

Muhammad ibn Abdel Wahhab's puritanical teachings proved more popular with hard-bitten nomadic Bedouin warriors than they had been with the settled townspeople of Uyayna. And the emir of Dariya proved to be not only an enthusiastic convert, but also an effective military leader of his fellow converts among the Bedouin. Just like the Prophet's successors, Muhammad ibn Saud used religious zeal to unify the feuding desert tribesmen and direct their aggression outwards. Also as before, the zeal of the desert warriors was a potent force.

For the next two decades, through a campaign of unending war and conquest under the Wahhabi banner, the emir constantly expanded his territory. By the time he died in 1765, Muhammad ibn Saud ruled most of the Najd—including Uyayna, where the Sheik oversaw the execution of the same official who had earlier exiled him.

The Ottoman Empire Strikes Back

The expansion continued under the emir's son Abdel Aziz (1765–1800) and his grandson Saud (1803–1820), until by the early nineteenth century the Al Saud controlled most of Arabia. In the east they expanded all the way to Oman, forcing Oman's ruler to pay tribute. With access to the well-traveled waters of the Persian Gulf (which Arabs call the Arabian Gulf, by the way), the Wahhabi warriors took to the sea, turning to piracy.

This irritated the British, who were the major sea power and who wanted to keep the Gulf shipping lanes open to vessels bound for their empire in India. In the west, more significantly, the Al Saud conquered the Hijaz, including Mecca and Medina, Islam's two holiest sites. In doing so, they also irritated the Ottomans, because the Hijaz had been under Ottoman control since the early sixteenth century. No one in the outside world really cared about the Najd, but the Hijaz was a different matter altogether. The holy cities of Mecca and Medina were vital to the Muslim world, and so who ruled them mattered to all Muslims.

Adding injury to insult, the Saudi conquest of the Hijaz also hit the Ottomans in their pocketbook, since money spent by pilgrims has always provide a revenue windfall to whoever rules the holy cities. So the Ottomans asked their viceroy in Egypt, whose name was Muhammad Ali, to take care of the problem. A dynamic and ambitious ruler who was eager to expand his own power, Ali was only too, happy to oblige. And like his boxer namesake, this Muhammad Ali, too, could float like a butterfly and sting like a bee—as the Al Saud soon found out.

In 1811 Ali sent his son Tusun into the Hijaz at the head of a large invasion force. It took a few years of warfare for Tusun to recapture the Hijaz, and even in defeat the Wahhabi warriors remained defiant. But Saud died in 1814, and his son and successor Abdullah withdrew with the Wahhabis back into the Najd. Abdullah may have thought he would be safe there, but two years later Muhammad Ali sent another of his sons, Ibrahim Pasha, with a second army into the Najd. Ibrahim razed Dariya to the ground, captured Abdullah, and sent him to Cairo, where Muhammad Ali turned him over to the Ottomans in Constantinople. There, in 1818, Abdullah was beheaded. On top of that, the following year the British navy annihilated the Wahhabi pirates in battle in the Persian Gulf.

> **Desert Dates**
>
> **1805:** Muhammad Ali (1767–1849) is appointed viceroy in Egypt by the Ottomans. Six years later, in 1811, he secures his position by massacring the Mamluk aristocracy, whose rule in Egypt had grown stagnant and corrupt. Over the next few decades, Muhammad Ali will use Western advisors and techniques to modernize the Egyptian army, turning Egypt into the Middle East's most powerful state.

Return of the Saud-i

Their ruler executed, their capital destroyed, the Wahhabis in tatters—that might well have been the end of the Al Saud and their tribal fighters. Yet only a few years later, in 1824, Abdullah's great-uncle Turki once again rallied the Wahhabi faithful and reconquered the Najd. Leaving Dariya in ruins, Turki set up his capital in Riyadh, which was then little more than a dusty village.

Turki was assassinated a decade later by an ambitious relative, a usurper who was in turn overthrown and killed by Turki's son Faisal. Faisal ruled until 1838, when Muhammad Ali sent another invasion force into the Najd and again captured the Saudi ruler. But the Ottomans didn't execute Faisal, and after other problems forced Muhammad Ali to withdraw from the Najd, Faisal returned to power in 1843. This time he would rule for more than two decades, once again expanding Saudi domains. Faisal brought the second Saudi state to its height of power and prosperity before his death in 1865.

Exile in Kuwait

Faisal's death brought another downturn in the family fortunes, for three of his sons—Abdullah, Saud, and Abdel Rahman—fought among each other bitterly for years over the succession. As they did so they weakened the dynasty's control of its hard-won lands, and local leaders took the chance to reassert themselves. One of them, Muhammad ibn Rashid, had acted as governor for Faisal in the Rashid power base of Hail, in the northern part of Najd. When Abdel Rahman finally outlasted his older brothers and succeeded to his title, he found Rashid firmly in control of the whole Najd. And when Rashid contemptuously made Abdel Rahman governor of Riyadh, all he could do was say yes, and bide his time.

In 1891, after failing in an attempt to overthrow Rashid, Abdel Rahman was forced to flee with his family to Kuwait. With him was his 11-year-old son, Abdel Aziz, later to be known as Ibn Saud. There the Al Saud would survive in humiliating exile for just over a decade, until Abdel Aziz was old enough—and bold enough—to make his move on the Rashids.

Ibn Saud Steps Up to the Plate

Ibn Saud (as I'll call him from now on) has been described as the twentieth century's greatest Arab leader. It's hard to disagree with that assessment. A man of action and at times cruelty, he was also a handsome, charming ladies' man and an entertaining companion to his male friends. As a statesman he combined shrewdness with principle (though critics have said he was heavier on the shrewdness than the principle).

Most important, he possessed a long-term vision for his country. That vision turned out to be remarkably resilient, given the totally unpredictable geological accident that would start to transform Saudi Arabia during the last years of his rule. All in all, he was a fascinating and attractive character, even a compelling one, and certainly one I'll enjoy introducing you to in the pages that follow.

Arabian Almanac

Abdel Aziz ibn Abdel Rahman ibn Faisal Al Saud (1880–1953), better known to the world as Ibn Saud, was the father of modern Saudi Arabia. Married numerous times, he also fathered some 80 children. He was the first of his family to take the title "king." All of the kings who have ruled Saudi Arabia since his death have been his sons.

The Capture of Riyadh

We last saw Ibn Saud and his merry men at the beginning of this chapter, in January 1902, as they stealthily made their way into Riyadh under the cover of darkness. Ibn Saud had left Kuwait several weeks earlier with 40 carefully chosen fighters, cutting south of Riyadh and approaching the city from the south. Leaving most of his men with his brother Muhammad, he had taken a small band of 10 with him into Riyadh. They climbed over the city's wall and snuck into the house of a sympathizer. The house lay opposite the Misnak, the massive fortress where the Rashid's nervous governor had decided to sleep. In the morning, when the governor warily emerged to go home, they rushed him and his guards. In hand-to-hand fighting Ibn Saud repeatedly blocked the governor's slashing sword with his rifle butt. The governor was slain as he desperately tried to scramble to safety back inside the gate of the fort.

It was never totally clear who killed the man. Ibn Saud always gave credit to his brave cousin, Abdullah ibn Jaluwi, who had stood out for his courage in the fighting. The fort surrendered immediately, the rest of Ibn Saud's men entered the city, and Riyadh was once again in the hands of the Al Saud.

Playing Politics with the British

Taking Riyadh, however, was only the first step on the long road to restoring the influence and prestige of the Al Saud. Soon afterward, recognizing Ibn Saud's potential, Abdel Rahman abdicated as emir in favor of his son. Yet Ibn Saud's new authority was mostly on paper. The Rashids still commanded the rest of the Najd, and it would take Ibn Saud some 20 years to break their power completely. As legend has it, he did so on a diet of little more than dates and camel's milk, the traditional Spartan fare of the desert Bedouin.

Ibn Saud started by using the conventional means that Arab rulers had always relied on to win allies among the notoriously fickle tribes. First was his own charisma and his now proven leadership, always crucial factors in the highly personal world of Arab politics. He also made a number of strategic marriage alliances, both for himself and for other members of the Al Saud.

Sheik-Speak

The **Ikhwan** or "Brotherhood" amounted to a whole new class in society—a class of disciplined Wahhabi fighters fanatically dedicated to conquest in the name of God's unity. To spread them out yet keep them ready at a moment's notice, Ibn Saud settled the Ikhwan in small oasis farming communities throughout his domains. Distinguished by special uniforms, the Ikhwan numbered some 11,000 by 1912.

It was going to take more than that, though, to get rid of the Rashids. So Ibn Saud decided to take a page from his ancestors' book and resurrect the Wahhabis as a military force. In fact, he went his ancestors one better. Before, the Wahhabi fighters had operated as traditional, loosely knit tribal units. Now, however, Ibn Saud organized them in a single large but tightly structured unit of their own. Known as the *Ikhwan*, they would prove to be an immensely effective weapon.

However, that weapon turned out to be more like a double-edged sword. As you'll see in a moment, the Ikhwan's appetite for conquest would make them violent, unpredictable, and in the end uncontrollable. Eventually their fanatical zeal would threaten Ibn Saud himself, and he would be forced to disband them.

As for Ibn Saud's own religious feelings, by all accounts he was an extremely pious man, and sincere in his devotion to Wahhabi ideals. And yet it appears that he also had a more worldly side as well. For example, Wahhabi clerics forbade the use of Western technological developments like radios and phonographs. The reason given was that such things were the work of Satan. Later, in establishing a radio system in Saudi Arabia, Ibn Saud outflanked the clerics by getting them to declare that Satan would never carry the word of God. He then had passages from the Koran read over the radio. The clerics were defeated. Perhaps they had already heard that Ibn Saud enjoyed relaxing alone by listening to music on his phonograph.

In addition to organizing the Ikhwan, Ibn Saud also began courting the British, whose interest in the region got stronger in the years leading up to World War I. In some ways it was a natural alliance, as the savvy Ibn Saud was well aware. The Ottomans, who still resented the Al Saud, were supporting the Rashids. And the

Ottoman Empire was moving in the direction of an alliance with Germany, an alliance that would in fact shortly become official with the outbreak of World War I in 1914. Since Britain and Germany were becoming stronger enemies every day, it seemed to make sense for the British to oppose the Ottomans—which meant opposing the Rashids, which meant supporting the Al Saud. (Whew. Talk about Byzantine.)

On top of all that, the British hoped to counter recent German moves to secure Arab allies for the war that everyone knew was coming. This was all very complicated diplomatically, and even more Byzantine than it might appear at first glance. For example, the British didn't want to oppose the Ottomans *too* strongly, because then the Russians would benefit. (See the previous chapter for an explanation of this strategic point.)

The British already had a strong colonial presence in Kuwait, and in 1910 their agent there, one Captain William Shakespear (yes, that's right), got in touch with Ibn Saud. They got along well, and on one occasion the British officer took the first known photo of Ibn Saud. Several years later, in 1913, Shakespear met with Ibn Saud at an oasis in the Najd. He was shocked to hear that the Arab ruler had plans to invade the Hasa, the wealthy region on the Persian Gulf coast. The Hasa was ruled by the Ottomans, and Shakespear warned Ibn Saud that he would be foolish to provoke them, even in their weakened state. But Ibn Saud went ahead and conquered the Hasa, which the Ottomans did not, in fact, try to recover. Later, the Hasa would turn out to have the richest oil fields in the Gulf.

The following year, as World War I was about to break out, Shakespear journeyed through the desert to Riyadh. There this acting official of the British empire joined up with an armed raiding force that Ibn Saud was leading out against the Rashids. Despite Ibn Saud's repeated warnings of the danger, Shakespear insisted on going.

What a sight it must have been—Shakespear in his splendid British uniform, mounted on his camel amid the robed warriors of the desert. Sadly, he was killed in action, and immediately passed into legend. Shortly afterward, the new British agent in Kuwait recognized Ibn Saud as "Sultan of Najd and Dependent Territories." Still, it wasn't until 1921 that Ibn Saud finally captured Hail, the Rashid stronghold in northern Najd.

Hashing Things Out with the Hashemites

As far as a potential Al Saud alliance with the British went, there was only one fly in the ointment—but it was a big one. The British already had an Arab ally, and they weren't sure they wanted another. In fact, the British government ended up being divided into two camps on the issue. One camp came to support the Al Saud, while the other put its money on another, more powerful clan, the Hashemites, who controlled the Hijaz.

British support for the Hashemites reached its height during World War I. In 1916 the colorful British officer T.E. Lawrence helped Husayn ibn Ali, the Hashemite ruler of the Hijaz, rebel against Ottoman rule. Husayn rather grandly called this campaign the Arab Revolt; he even more grandly declared himself King of the Hijaz. In his name, Lawrence planned and executed a number of daring attacks on the Turkish railway that ran south through the Hijaz from Syria to Medina. Lawrence's classic account of the Arab Revolt, *The Seven Pillars of Wisdom*, became an international bestseller. His exploits were later glorified by Hollywood in David Lean's Oscar-winning 1962 film *Lawrence of Arabia*.

Arabian Almanac

The Hashemites enjoy special status in the Arab and Muslim worlds, because they belong to the same clan as the Prophet Muhammad, that of the Hashim. As *sharifs* or descendants of the Prophet, Hashemites had ruled in Mecca since the eleventh century. All descendants of the Prophet are entitled to be called sharif, but the Hashemite Emir of Mecca was called the Grand Sharif. In the early twentieth century, that title belonged to Ibn Saud's Hashemite rival Husayn ibn Ali. Since Ottoman times the Hashemites and the Wahhabis have despised each other, each group viewing the other as dangerous heretics.

The popular story of the underdog Sharif Husayn of Mecca dramatized in the movie only tells one side of things, though. In the long run, Husayn proved to be a less than stable ally. Shortly after World War I, for example, he styled himself "King of the Arabs," greatly offending other Arab leaders, including Ibn Saud. Following a number of other blunders on his part, the last straw came in 1924, when the worldly Husayn proclaimed himself caliph. (This religious title had been vacated by the recent demise of the Ottoman Empire, whose sultan had also styled himself caliph.) The move was thought by Muslims and Westerners alike to be arrogant and unjustified. And as Ibn Saud predicted, it finally induced the British to drop Husayn.

> **Desert Dates**
>
> **1923:** After the defeat of the Ottoman Empire in World War I, the international community recognizes the Republic of Turkey, formed out of the Ottoman Empire's Turkish core.

As Ibn Saud's territory grew he had begun to think more and more about how he could return the Hijaz, with its two holy cities of Mecca and Medina, to the dominions of the Al Saud. The holy cities, after all, were the jewel in the Arabian crown—and they belonged to Husayn. Given the longstanding enmity between the

Hashemites and the Wahhabis, the Ikhwan were burning to wrest the holy cities from what they saw as Husayn's impure hands. Yet Ibn Saud owed much of his success to modern arms and equipment supplied by the British, so he was reluctant to anger the British by attacking their ally. This was especially true during World War I. He clashed with the Hashemites soon after the war, sharply defeating them at the Battle of Turaba in 1919. That, however, was essentially a dispute over the border between Najd and the Hijaz.

Arabian Almanac

After World War I, under the aegis of the League of Nations, the victors Britain and France split up the lands of the old Ottoman Empire into areas called "mandates." As you can see on the following map, the borders of most of today's Middle Eastern countries reflect the mandates, which in turn reflect lines drawn on a map almost at random by the victors. Britain took the mandates of Palestine, Transjordan (later Jordan), and Iraq, while France got Lebanon and Syria.

Since Britain already ruled Egypt, all that left was the Hijaz—which Ibn Saud took from Husayn. Meanwhile, the British had installed Husayn's sons as the kings of Transjordan and Iraq. Although the Hashemite king of Iraq was overthrown in 1958, the present king of Jordan, Abdullah, is Husayn's direct descendant.

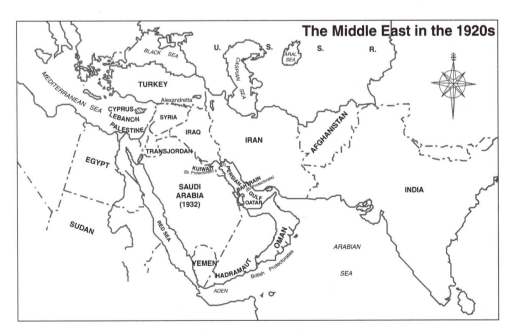

The "mandates" reflect the borders of the modern Middle East, essentially as it is today (Israel would later be carved out of Palestine).

In 1924, however, with Husayn's most recent blunder, Ibn Saud felt that the moment had come for him to make his move on the Hijaz without fear of reprisal from the British. As it turned out, he was right. He sent the Ikhwan into the Hijaz, sacking the city of Taif in 1924 and occupying Mecca more peacefully that same year. The next year he took the important Hijazi coastal city of Jiddah (where many pilgrims arrived by ship), and the year after that he took Medina.

In 1925, the year he captured Jiddah, Ibn Saud adopted the title of king for the first time, calling himself King of Najd and the Hijaz. Two years later, in the Treaty of Jiddah (1927), the British recognized him as "King of the Hijaz and Najd and Its Dependencies," and in 1932 Ibn Saud changed the country's name to the Kingdom of Saudi Arabia.

Here's a timeline of Ibn Saud's major campaigns:

- **1902:** Ibn Saud takes Riyadh and begins winning control of Najd.

- **1913:** Ibn Saud conquers the wealthy region of Hasa, on the Persian Gulf coast, from the Ottomans. This is where the bulk of the Saudis' oil would later be found.

- **1919:** In his first conflict with the Hashemites, Ibn Saud destroys a Hashemite army in the Battle of Turaba, on the border between Najd and the Hijaz. Only pressure from the British holds him back from advancing further against the Hashemites.

- **1921:** Ibn Saud finishes off the Rashids and occupies their power base, Hail, finalizing his conquest of Najd.

- **1924–1925:** Ibn Saud occupies the Hijaz (with Mecca and Medina).

- **1930:** Ibn Saud annexes the southern region of Asir, which his son Faisal (the future King Faisal) had conquered from Yemen in 1924.

Getting Tough with the Wahhabis

Throughout the 1920s Ibn Saud had a harder and harder time controlling the Ikhwan. By the end of the decade, the boundaries of his kingdom had pretty much taken the shape they have today (though some border disputes remained to be settled, and there would be one more land grab that I'll talk about in the next chapter). But the Ikhwan grew impatient with peace. In 1928, under their leader Faisal Dawish, they openly revolted against Ibn Saud's authority and raided Iraq and Kuwait, favorite targets for their plundering activities. The following year—employing non-Ikhwan soldiers—Ibn Saud annihilated the Ikhwan rebels at the Battle of Sibila. The Ikhwan were disbanded, and the Wahhabis' tribal warriors never again threatened the rule of the Al Saud.

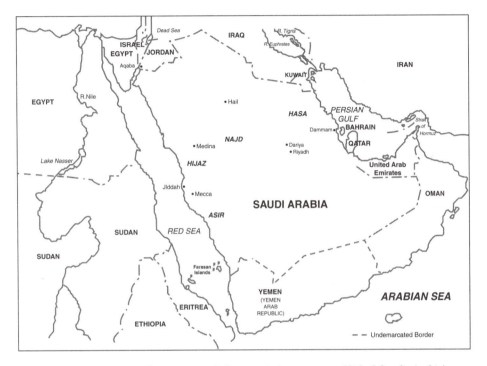

Ibn Saud's conquests in the first quarter of the twentieth century established Saudi Arabia's borders.

Money Troubles

Ibn Saud was now firmly in control, and the 1930s proved to be a relatively calm and peaceful decade for the new country. But a new problem soon reared its ugly head: money. One reason everyone was always eager to control the Hijaz, don't forget, was the income that could be derived from its huge pilgrim industry. Ibn Saud was no different. But with the arrival of the worldwide Great Depression starting in 1929, he watched receipts from the annual hajj decline to less than half, and then dwindle still further. From 130,000 pilgrims a year in the late 1920s, the number had fallen to fewer than 40,000 by 1931. During the 1930s, the growing political tensions that would soon lead to the Second World War further cut in to the numbers of pilgrims making the hajj.

At the same time, the more powerful Ibn Saud became, the greater his debts became, too. The key to understanding this paradox lies in the way traditional Arabian culture and politics work. In Arabia, a leader is measured by how much he gives away, and Ibn Saud had always been careful to create a buzz about his generosity.

Traditional desert etiquette requires that all visitors be welcomed into your household for three days. You've got to feed them and see to their every comfort. If you are known as a man of means and aspire to be a leader, you must bestow an appropriate gift. For much of his reign, Ibn Saud received a steady stream of his subjects, and according to all reports, he literally never sent anyone away empty-handed. Of course, that meant he had to give a lot of things away. His food bills alone were enormous. Often his cooks fed thousands of people at a sitting.

By the middle of the 1930s, Ibn Saud was turning desperate in the face of mounting debts. He urgently needed to find a reliable source of income.

On the other hand, he had always been a pretty lucky guy. And who knew what lay around the corner?

The Least You Need to Know

- The Saudi royal family has been allied with the Wahhabis since the middle of the eighteenth century.

- Ibn Saud owed his conquest of much of Saudi Arabia to fanatical Wahhabi soldiers and British arms.

- Despite being a pious Muslim and a devout Wahhabi, Ibn Saud didn't hesitate to break the Wahhabi soldiers when their fanaticism got out of hand.

- After founding Saudi Arabia, Ibn Saud faced huge debts that he had no realistic hope of repaying.

Drilling for Dollars

In This Chapter

- ◆ Prospecting for black gold
- ◆ The Americans arrive
- ◆ Ibn Saud finds buried treasure
- ◆ The beginning of the Saudi oil economy

In the mid 1930s, Saudi Arabia was one of the poorest countries in the world. Its royal government was in a state of chronic financial distress. Twenty years later, it was one of the wealthiest countries in the world. And its royal government was still in a state of chronic financial distress. Yet when oil was discovered in 1938, Ibn Saud thought his problems were over. A rosy future seemed to lie ahead. At last he'd be able to bestow endless riches and largesse on his beloved subjects.

Alas, nothing is ever so simple. The rich will tell you that money doesn't solve every problem (naturally, no one believes them). It certainly makes some things more fun, and Ibn Saud's rapidly growing family soon learned how to enjoy themselves at the king's expense. But money also has a way of creating new problems of its own. As the generous king found out, the more you have, the more you seem to spend. Or in his case, give away.

The bewildered patriarch wondered again and again how the debts could keep piling up when so much oil was being pumped.

In this chapter you'll discover oil along with the Saudis, sharing in the excitement of sudden riches. You'll also watch the aging Ibn Saud struggle with the burdens of new-found wealth, as he lays the foundations of Saudi Arabia's oil economy. In addition, a digression on the founding of Israel will fill you in on how Saudi Arabia fits in with this thorny issue.

The Discovery of Oil in Saudi Arabia

By the mid 1930s Americans were looking for oil in Saudi Arabia, but they hadn't had much luck. Nor had they persuaded Ibn Saud that they were likely to. He was much more interested in the modest fees they were paying him for the privilege of looking, than in the promise of larger amounts in the unlikely event that they succeeded. After all, the British had been there already and had told him quite firmly that there was no oil in Saudi Arabia.

Oh, there was oil in the Middle East, all right. Since the early 1900s, the enterprising British had been pumping it steadily out of the ground in Persia. But as for Saudi Arabia … terribly sorry, and all that, it just wasn't on.

Hang on a minute. In the early 1900s there were no freeways and hardly any automobiles. Cars were still the playthings of a few wealthy daredevils. Henry Ford and the assembly line didn't inaugurate the technique of mass production until 1913, when cars finally became affordable to the average Joe. Even then it took a while to get the ball rolling. So what brought the British to Persia in the first place? Who wanted the oil and why? What was it about oil that made it so desirable in those early days?

A Brief History of Oil

It all started with a shortage of whales. Yes, whales. Ultimately, a whale shortage was behind the rise of Saudi Arabia's great wealth. Remember *Moby Dick*? Around the middle of the nineteenth century, when Herman Melville wrote his great masterpiece of vengeance and, well, whales, the big blubbery denizens of the deep were a highly prized commodity. They were sought mainly for the precious oil that could be extracted from their blubber. By the 1850s, though, overhunting was causing the great whaling fleets to come up short.

In countries like the United States and Britain, with growing cities and growing industry, whale oil was the most popular fuel for lighting. As it became more scarce and thus more expensive, people started looking for alternatives. They came up with kerosene, which the British call "paraffin," and which you might know better as paint thinner or even jet fuel. Long before its aviation application, however, this versatile liquid replaced whale oil as the best fuel for lamps. Kerosene was already being re-fined from coal (it's also called coal oil). Soon techniques were developed to refine it from *petroleum*, or "rock oil," as well.

The first oil well was drilled in Pennsylvania in 1859, and before long the United States was the world's leading oil producer, followed by Russia. (Both still have significant oil re-serves, by the way.) By the late 1870s, John D. Rockefeller had bought up virtually all the American refineries, giving his company, Standard Oil, an effective monopoly on the oil market. Unfortunately for the burgeon-ing oil industry, however, in 1877 Thomas Edison invented the light bulb, and that was that. No more need for lamps, so no more mass market for oil.

Sheik-Speak

Petroleum comes from the Latin words *petra* ("rock") and *oleum* ("oil"). The word was coined in 1556 by the German mineralogist Georgius Agricola. Petroleum and coal come from the same thing, dead organic matter (like leaves) that's been buried for millions of years and fossilized. Hence, they're called "fossil fuels."

Arabian Almanac

"Rock oil" has long been used for various purposes. Before modern drilling began, oil was found in seeps, places where it oozed up out of the ground. Oil pitch (black sticky stuff) could be slathered on to patch the seams of boats. Both the Egyptians and the American Indians reportedly used oil for medicinal purposes (yuck).

The Persians, Byzantines, and Arabs all used the highly flammable stuff to make vari-ous nasty incendiary weapons. The Byzantines were the masters. Their secret weapon was "Greek fire," a sticky napalm-like substance that burst into flame when it got wet. They used it to great effect against the wooden ships of the terrified Arabs. The recipe was a state secret, so hush-hush that we don't know exactly what went into it, but it almost certainly included pitch and sulfur.

Or so it seemed. Yet just the year before, in 1876, a German named Nikolaus Otto (no kidding) had invented a little thing called the internal combustion engine. It would take this dirty, smoke-belching contraption several decades to catch on. But the upshot was that just as oil was being phased out for lighting, it was being phased in for transportation and other uses. The new demand would soon dwarf the earlier market for lamp oil.

Desert Dates

August 27, 1859: Edwin L. Drake finishes drilling the first oil well in Titusville, Pennsylvania. This feat ushers in the modern oil industry. By the end of the cen-tury, hundreds of wells have been drilled in 14 states from coast to coast, and from Wyom-ing to Texas and Louisiana.

First in line was the oil-fired engine, which got a huge boost in 1912 when the British decided to replace coal with oil as fuel for the ships in their mighty navy. That's what brought the British to Persia, where the first oil concessions were signed in 1901 and the first oil fields found in 1908. Don't think the British would have switched their navy over without a ready supply, especially with war looming.

Arabian Almanac

Since the start of the Industrial Age, the burning of fossil fuels has accounted for an estimated 90 percent of human energy consumption. Fossil fuels will probably run out in 100 years or so, if we survive global warming and all the other effects of the pollution they cause. But this flexible, powerful, and highly portable energy source has changed virtually every aspect of human life—for better, and for worse.

By the time World War I broke out in 1914, therefore, oil had already become a strategic commodity. Shortly afterward, of course, the automobile vastly increased demand, along with all the other applications for the internal combustion engine. (Before the gasoline-fired internal combustion engine, gasoline was viewed as a useless waste product of the kerosene-refining process, and was usually thrown away or burned off.) In addition, there would be a growing need for industrial lubricants and eventually synthetic materials like plastic, all of which are based on products derived from refining petroleum.

The Americans Stake Their Claim

The corporation that controlled the Persian oil concession was called the Anglo-Persian Oil Company, later to be renamed the Anglo-Iranian Oil Company and finally British Petroleum (B.P.). It was largely owned by the British government. Britain's foothold in Persia gave it a dominant position in the Middle Eastern oil industry that would last until the 1960s. With America's ample oil reserves, both the U.S. government and the American oil companies were slower to start looking elsewhere for oil than the British. But in the end it was the Americans who got things going in Saudi Arabia—though by an unlikely route.

Inspired by Anglo-Persian's success, a prospector from New Zealand named Major Frank Holmes came to Arabia in 1922. Putting out a story about adding to his butterfly collection (he didn't fool anyone), Holmes really wanted to locate some oil seeps he had heard about in the Hasa region. Although he never found them, he did succeed in getting Ibn Saud to sell him an oil concession, outmaneuvering British Anglo-Persian operatives (who were also sniffing around) with great dexterity. Irritated at being outmaneuvered, Anglo-Persian soon decided that there was no oil in Arabia anyway. If they hadn't been outmaneuvered by Holmes, however, things might have turned out very differently.

Holmes wasn't a very tenacious prospector. He was really more interested in the concession as an investment. Finding no buyers for his concession in Arabia, he allowed it to lapse in 1928. Meanwhile, he had moved on to nearby Bahrain, the little island emirate just off the coast of Arabia in the Persian Gulf. He got Bahrain's emir to sell him an oil concession there, and this time he did find a buyer, because at long last the Americans had begun taking an interest. Holmes sold his Bahrain concession to Gulf Oil, which in turn sold it to Standard Oil of California (Socal, later Chevron). In 1932, Socal struck oil in Bahrain.

This success got Socal very interested in Saudi Arabia, which had similar geography, and where an American geologist named Karl Twitchell had recently been prospecting. In fact, Twitchell had already crossed to Bahrain and been run off by Socal's representatives there. But Twitchell had established a relationship with Ibn Saud, and so now Socal hired Twitchell to help the company land a concession from the Saudi king. Socal won the concession in 1933—outbidding the Brits, who still didn't think there was oil in Saudi Arabia, but who didn't want the Yanks to get their foot in the door there, either.

Dammam No. 7 Goes Down in History

To execute the concession, Socal created a wholly owned subsidiary called the California Arabian Standard Oil Company, or Casoc, which later became the Arab-American Oil Company, or Aramco. (Gotta love those cute oil company acronyms. Come to think of it, why didn't Standard Oil of New York become Sony?) Casoc's geologists pointed to the Dammam Dome, a massive geological feature, as a likely place to start. It was located in the Hasa region, near the coast opposite Bahrain and also near where Holmes had earlier been looking for those seeps he'd heard about. Casoc crews began drilling in the Dammam Dome in April 1935.

Well, they drilled once. And they drilled twice. And … but you get the idea. Six times they drilled, going down each time to the level at which they'd struck oil in Bahrain. Finally, in December 1936, they started the seventh well. When they got to the Bahrain

> **Desert Dates**
>
> **March 3, 1938:** The famous oil well known as "Dammam No. 7" suddenly starts flowing, to the tune of more than 1,500 barrels of oil a day. Some days, more than 3,000. In the nearly seven decades since, it's kept right on flowing. Oil wells in the United States are considered good if they hit 10 or 20 barrels a day.

level, they decided the heck with it, let's hit Brazil (or something to that effect), and kept going down. A lot farther down—more than 5,000 feet. And you'll never guess what happened. Hey, you guessed!

The War Years

You can imagine the rejoicing, all the more so when Casoc geologists brought the news that, as far as they could tell, Dammam No. 7 was just the beginning. It quickly became obvious that Saudi Arabia was sitting on top of one of the Middle East's—one of the world's—greatest reservoirs of oil. Casoc gave Ibn Saud a handsome loan of around a million dollars worth of gold, with promises of plenty more where that came from. Things started looking up. In 1939 the kingdom—which meant Ibn Saud—collected $3.2 million in oil revenues.

War Intervenes

And then, on September 1, 1939, Hitler invaded Poland, and it all came grinding to a halt. World War II had begun. Shipping was disrupted, markets went haywire, and suddenly there was little capital available for developing new oil resources. The Americans folded their tents and went home, leaving barely a skeleton crew in Saudi Arabia. Six years would pass before Ibn Saud would see any further significant income from oil.

Cozying Up to Uncle Sam

At first Casoc tried to tide Ibn Saud over with loans against future oil earnings, but in 1941 it began to pressure the U.S. government for help. The official U.S. policy was still one of neutrality in the war, but in private most American officials assumed that sooner or later the United States would be entering the war against Germany and Japan. In contrast with their relaxed attitude during peacetime, the American planners realized that during wartime Saudi Arabia's oil could be of major strategic importance.

In 1943 U.S. Secretary of State Cordell Hull declared that Saudi Arabia was eligible for American aid under the Lend Lease program, by which supposedly neutral America was already supplying money, arms, and equipment to Britain and the Soviet Union. Over the next two years, the United States provided Ibn Saud with over $33 million in cash and material, including steel—a scarce wartime resource—for the construction of new pipelines and refineries.

World War II thus marks the beginning of the ongoing strategic alliance between the Saudi and U.S. governments. The new relationship was sealed in February 1945, in a secret meeting between Ibn Saud and President Franklin Delano Roosevelt. The two met on board an American destroyer, the USS *Quincy*, at Great Bitter Lake in the Suez Canal, just a few days after Roosevelt's historic conference with Winston Churchill and Joseph Stalin at Yalta. When Churchill heard about it, the British leader scrambled to arrange his own meeting with the Saudi king.

He was too late. As the photo of the president and a relaxed and smiling king suggests, F.D.R. had hit it off with Ibn Saud in a way that Churchill did not. For one thing, F.D.R. had cannily avoided smoking or drinking in front of the abstemious Wahhabi king, to the extent of sneaking cigarettes on the ship's elevator. In contrast, the always irreverent Churchill couldn't have cared less about the king's desert puritanism, puffing away on his trademark cigar and drinking whisky with gusto in the royal presence. The king was not amused.

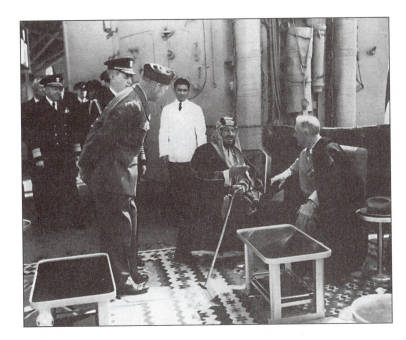

King Abdel Aziz (Ibn Saud) responds to F.D.R.'s famous charm at their meeting aboard the USS Quincy *in 1945.*

(Photo courtesy of the Roosevelt Library)

Pay Dirt, Sort Of

While the U.S. Navy started buying some oil from the Saudis during the war, it wasn't till after the war ended in 1945 that Saudi oil really began to come online. Aramco (Casoc's new name as of 1944) worried about the effect of additional oil entering the already glutted postwar oil market. Nevertheless, development and exports proceeded rapidly. In 1948 Aramco geologists found the Ghawar oil field, which has turned out to be the largest oil field in the world. See the following map for the location of Ghawar and other Saudi oil deposits.

Most of Saudi Arabia's oil is located in the parts of the country nearest the Persian Gulf, with much of it in the Hasa region.

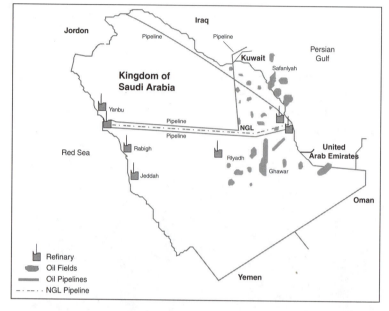

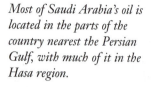

Arabian Almanac

Saudi oil revenues rose sharply and quickly after World War II as the kingdom's oil output jumped dramatically:

- ◆ $10 million in 1946
- ◆ $53 million in 1948
- ◆ $57 million in 1950
- ◆ $212 million in 1952

Saudi oil revenues jumped by a factor of more than 20 in the years between 1945 and Ibn Saud's death in 1953. Yet in the end, all the new wealth simply encouraged the king to borrow more and more heavily from Western banks, since he was now able to do so quite easily against his future revenues. Each year Ibn Saud borrowed significantly more than he made, and of course that meant that each year more and more of his income went to servicing the growing debts. This vicious circle became the pattern, and by the early 1950s each year brought the kingdom closer to the edge of financial collapse.

Where did all the money go? One place it didn't go was public works. That would have to wait until after Ibn Saud's death. Virtually the only major improvement made to the country's infrastructure during Ibn Saud's reign was a railway he built from the Persian Gulf port of Dhahran to the capital, Riyadh. He also built some wells and paved a few roads. But improvements like schools, housing, airports, water, and sewage systems—none of that sort of thing featured prominently in the king's thinking. When his son Talal proposed building a public hospital in Riyadh, Ibn Saud just stared at him in surprise. Why on earth would he want to do that?

Instead, Ibn Saud continued to do as he had always done, only more so. He distributed cash payments to the tribes to keep them loyal, he fed thousands of his people every day, and in general he bestowed gifts and largesse with an open hand. And the king's 40-odd sons, many now old enough to have expensive children of their own, learned all about luxurious foreign cars and vacations to the south of France. In addition, Ibn Saud was now aging, growing frail and often hazy. More than ever, he had a hard time saying no to anyone.

Ironing Out the Details

I've been talking in general terms about the *concessions* bought by the Western oil companies, but so far I haven't explained much about the financial arrangements behind the exploitation of Saudi oil. Now it's time to focus on those arrangements for just a moment.

Ibn Saud's original concession (which included loan agreements) was based on a small yearly fee and a very small royalty—remember, he didn't really think oil would be found. In 1949, however, Ibn Saud granted another concession to Pacific Western (later Getty Oil), an American competitor of Aramco, who gave him better terms than Aramco. This helped him negotiate better terms from Aramco the following year, when he got the company to agree to a 50–50 split in the net profits. Immediately, Saudi oil revenues roughly quadrupled.

Sheik-Speak

In the context of the oil industry, a **concession** is the temporary purchase of exploration and development rights to a specified area. The seller receives an annual fee that maintains the concession, plus a royalty or percentage of the profits. Loans against future royalties are not unusual.

It didn't occur to Ibn Saud that Saudi Arabia might own and operate all of its own oil wells and refineries, and keep 100 percent of the profits that way. Like the idea of building hospitals and other services, that was something that would have to wait for a later generation of Saudi leadership. Indeed, it appears that Ibn Saud preferred to keep oil production in U.S. hands, so that the Americans could do the dirty work and let him get on with the job of running the country. One reason he chose American companies over British, reportedly, was that he thought the American companies less likely to promote an imperialistic political agenda than British ones. Of course, they also had more money to throw around, which didn't hurt either.

A Brief Digression: Israel

I've also been holding back on another important subject, one that's so complicated and sensitive that it seemed best to address it separately. This is the subject of Zionism, the international movement to found a Jewish state in Palestine and Israel, the new Middle Eastern state that finally resulted from that movement. The reason I waited to talk about it is that Israel wasn't founded until 1948, in the aftermath of World War II. However, to understand the issues at work in Saudi perceptions of Zionism and Israel, I'll have to take you back to a period we talked about in the last chapter.

Too Many Promises

You'll recall that Britain, with its worldwide empire, was the major player in the Middle East in the early part of the twentieth century. This meant, basically, that anyone (or any group) who wanted anything had to appeal to Britain to get it. Britain was in a position to make promises, in other words, and during the desperate years of World War I (1914–18) it had strong motives for making them. As is often the case in such circumstances, the British ended up making too many promises to too many people, as the following list demonstrates:

- **Promises to the Arabs.** Remember Ibn Saud's Hashemite rival, Sharif Husayn of Mecca, and his Arab Revolt against the Ottomans? The British encouraged the revolt, because at the time they were fighting against the Ottomans in World War I. The carrot they held out to the Arabs was independence. Although the British engaged in a lot of doubletalk, they deliberately led the Arabs to believe that if they rose up against the Ottomans, they would be rewarded with independence in places formerly under Ottoman rule, like Syria and Palestine.

- **Promises to the Jews.** At the same time, the British held out similar hopes to the thousands of Jews who had emigrated to Palestine as part of the Zionist movement. In November 1917, Britain issued the Balfour Declaration, which stated that the British government "will view with favour the establishment in Palestine of a national home for the Jewish people." Britain would rule Palestine under the League of Nations mandate from 1922 to 1948, and the Balfour Declaration would play a major role in encouraging Jews to immigrate there during the 1920s and 1930s.

- **Promises to Britain's allies.** Also in November 1917, a secret accord called the Sykes-Picot Agreement came to light between Britain and its allies France,

Russia, and Italy. Under its terms, in the event of an allied victory over the Ottoman Empire, Ottoman lands would be divided up among the victorious allies. France would get Syria and Lebanon, Russia would get what is today northern Turkey, Italy would get today's southern Turkey, and Britain would get everything else. The Sykes-Picot Agreement never went into effect, but when it was uncovered it deeply angered the Arab world. Like the Balfour Declaration, it clearly went against the promises of Arab independence Britain had earlier made.

Of course, Britain was under a lot of pressure, and its first concern was to win the war. And it is true that if you looked at the fine print of these promises, there was so much hedging that little actual commitment was made. Yet the effect was there anyway, especially among Arabs and Jews. Both groups felt that they had been promised an independent nation in Palestine. In addition, based on their ancient scriptures, the Jews also felt that this Promised Land had been reserved for them by God.

Israel's War for Independence

Jewish immigration into Palestine during the 1920s and 1930s created deep resentment among the generally poor Arabs who lived there. Between 1933 and 1936, some 200,000 Jews arrived, many of them fleeing Nazi persecution (or the threat of it) in Europe. In 1936 the Palestinian Arabs exploded in a round of violence that's also (confusingly) called the Arab Revolt, in which they attacked both Jews and the ruling British. Their main grievances were the loss of their land to Jewish immigrants and the lack of democratic institutions under British rule. With a democratic system, the majority Arabs would have been able to prevent further Jewish immigration.

The situation was already tragic for all sides, but it was about to become a lot more so. As World War II (1939–1945) drew to a close and the full horror of the Holocaust was revealed, most of those among the tattered remnants of Europe's Jews had only one thing to give them hope: a Jewish state in Palestine. Only with the foundation of such a state, they believed, could the Jewish people ensure that such a catastrophe would never again befall them. Western nations, many feeling guilty over their own refusal to admit Jewish refugees before and during the war, now swung in favor of a Jewish state in Palestine, adding impetus to the groundswell.

Jewish immigration to Palestine quickened after the war, and fighting again broke out in Palestine between Jews and Arabs. The British, for their part, were exhausted by the war. Their empire was finished, and they wished only to go home. Britain could barely maintain a semblance of order in the region, and even that fell apart in 1947, as the clashes between Jews and Arabs turned into outright warfare. In May 1948, having defeated the Palestinian Arabs, the Jews declared the existence of the independent state of Israel. The next day, six Arab countries—Egypt, Jordan, Iraq, Syria, Lebanon, and Saudi Arabia—declared war on the new state. The war resulted in a humiliating loss for the disunited Arab forces. Saudi Arabia played a minimal role in the war, for reasons that help explain why the Arabs were so disunited. The territory claimed by Israel, in effect, took land from Jordan's Hashemite king, and Ibn Saud wasn't about to fight too eagerly on behalf of the Hashemites. He couldn't turn his back on them completely—they were fellow Arabs and fellow Muslims, after all—but he wasn't going to help them too much either. That sort of rivalry has continued to stand in the way of Arab unity ever since. It's been a source of great frustration among Arabs, both in Saudi Arabia and elsewhere.

The Palestinians

The establishment of Israel caused a whole new problem, that of the estimated 500,000 to 1,000,000 Palestinian Arabs who either fled or were driven out of the new Jewish state. Most (perhaps 300,000) went to the West Bank, others (perhaps 150,000–200,000) went to the Gaza Strip, and most of the rest went to Jordan, Lebanon, Syria, and Iraq. In the West Bank, the Gaza Strip, and elsewhere, generations of Arabs grew up in refugee camps. The camps were meant to be temporary, but with the passage of time many have become permanent homes to an ever-growing population of refugees.

This sequence of events has cast a shadow over everything that's happened since in the Middle East and the Arab world. It's an almost unbelievably complicated and controversial problem, and obviously I can only sketch the basics for you here. But overall it remains the most urgent political issue in the Arab world to this day, and I'll be referring to it often in the rest of this book.

Like the rest of the Arab world, the Saudis (predictably enough) have been sympathetic to the Palestinian cause. In fact, before Israeli independence, concern over the plight of Palestinian Arabs was the main reason why Ibn Saud was interested in meeting with F.D.R. Ibn Saud understood the world's horror at the Holocaust, he told the president. But the Holocaust was a European crime, not an Arab crime. Why, he wondered, should the West expect Arabs to pay for it by giving up their land? It made more sense, in his view, to make the criminals pay by giving up their land. Give the Jews a homeland on German soil, he suggested, rather than in the Arab villages of Palestine. Why should poor and relatively powerless Arabs be pushed aside to pay for the crimes of the West?

Needless to say, that's not a position that has won much agreement in the West. However, in one form or another it has pretty much been the position taken by many Arabs ever since. It will have to be addressed if Western leaders wish to heal the divisions between the Arab and Western worlds. Equally, however, the Arabs will have to address some issues of their own, and we'll be exploring a few of those later in the book.

The Passing of a King

In the mid 1930s, Saudi Arabia faced the illness of national poverty. Oil was the cure. But by the time Ibn Saud died in 1953, the cure was threatening to do more harm than the illness. As the king's growing bewilderment suggested, oil was setting the pace, not him. The aging Ibn Saud simply did not have the ability to keep abreast of the new world he found himself in.

As the old king weakened, oil had already commanded the state's foreign policy on one notable occasion. While the borders of the Saudi state reflected Ibn Saud's earlier campaigns of conquest, in 1949 the Saudis made one last land grab. In a move dictated by the American oil companies, the Saudi government attempted to claim some 50,000 square miles of desert on the border with Oman and Abu Dhabi. The resulting dispute lasted 25 years, until the Saudis agreed to give up their claim to the land in 1974. It was one of the most unpleasant aspects of Ibn Saud's legacy.

> **Desert Dates**
>
> **November 9, 1953:** Ibn Saud dies at age 77. His oldest son, Crown Prince Saud, becomes the new king.

Despite his many limitations, though, it shouldn't be forgotten that Ibn Saud left behind a country that he had created himself—with the strength of his personality and the fanatical edge of his Wahhabi faith. The fact that the country's official name contained his name reflected the very real truth that Saudi Arabia was essentially *his*. Ibn Saud drew no distinctions between his royal self and the Saudi state. And that meant that its finances were his finances. The truth was that his finances were a complete mess, and the country was bordering on bankruptcy. Like so much else, fixing that would be up to his successors.

The Least You Need to Know

- An American oil company discovered oil in Saudi Arabia in 1938.

- The oil companies paid Ibn Saud a percentage of their profits in order to drill and export Saudi oil.

- Ibn Saud gave the money away to his subjects rather than investing it in infrastructure and services.

- Saudi Arabia's strategic relationship with the United States began during World War II.

- On his death in 1953 Ibn Saud left a major financial mess for his successors to clean up.

Chapter 6

Saudi Arabia Takes the Driver's Seat

In This Chapter

- ◆ Ibn Saud's successors take over the country's oil production from the Americans
- ◆ A Saudi-led oil embargo stuns the West
- ◆ Modernization Saudi-style
- ◆ An oil boom fizzles out

Ibn Saud has laid the foundations of the modern Saudi oil state, but now it's up to his successors to build the structure itself. This chapter tells that story, taking it from Ibn Saud's death in 1953 up to the early years of the current king, Fahd, who took over in 1982.

It begins with a false start, however—the reign of Ibn Saud's oldest surviving son, Saud. Saud's rule is so ineffective that in 1964 the Al Saud get together and throw him out, replacing him with his half-brother Faisal. Faisal turns out to be a much more competent ruler, and under his skillful guidance the kingdom starts to make real progress. When Faisal is assassinated in 1975 by a disgruntled relative, modernization continues under his half-brother Khalid, who rules until his own death in 1982.

The three decades between Ibn Saud's death in 1953 and Fahd's accession in 1982 brought great changes to the kingdom. As you watch that story unfold in this chapter, you'll also see a fresh set of complex challenges arise—along with new wrinkles on some knotty old problems.

Saud's Reign of Error

The career of the hapless Saud reflects some of the same shortcomings that had left his father, Ibn Saud, so bewildered at the end of his life. Saud's personal courage was never in doubt. In 1935 the burly prince had thrown himself in harm's way to protect his father during an assassination attempt, taking a nasty dagger wound to his shoulder. But courage and good intentions were about all the amiable Saud had going for him.

Though his heart was in the right place, his head was in the clouds. Saud proved totally unable to grasp the complexities of ruling the nation that his father had created.

The first fiasco in Saud's reign came in 1954, the year after he took over. An ambitious scheme to put the shipping of Saudi oil in Saudi hands, it sums up his unfortunate mix of good intentions and poor execution. The plan foundered when top-secret negotiations between the Saudis and shipping magnate Aristotle Onassis leaked to the press, angering Aramco, which ran the tankers that handled the oil. And when Aramco—backed by U.S. Secretary of State John Foster Dulles—refused to load the oil on board the ships, the whole plan collapsed. The Al Saud were deeply embarrassed by the publicity, and for the moment, at least, Saudi oil remained fully under American control.

Other royal screw-ups soon followed, in both domestic and foreign policy. For example, after unhappy Saudi workers at Aramco held strikes in 1953 and 1956, Saud simply issued a royal decree forbidding further strikes, an inept response that (naturally) only angered them further. Then there was Egypt. In 1958 Egypt and Syria declared their political union as the United Arab Republic, a development that stunned the world. Yet even more shocking were the subsequent allegations that Saud had hatched a conspiracy to undermine the union and assassinate the dynamic and popular Egyptian president, Gamal Abdel Nasser. I'll go into more detail on the Egypt-Syria union and other international developments in the next chapter, but you get the idea.

Those sorts of scandalous messes were bad enough, especially since Arabian culture considers the public airing of dirty secrets to be among the greatest evils that can befall anyone. But the real problem remained money. When it came to finances, Saud was very much his father's son—only more so, if such a thing is possible. He upped the traditional cash handouts with which Ibn Saud had kept the tribes loyal, and in general went on a massive spending spree that resulted in a lot of gaudiness and waste but little real development. One of his favorite things to do was to drive around in one of his many Rolls-Royces scattering gold coins from the open window. Corruption, favoritism, and petty intrigue ran rampant in his administration. And as the debts mounted despite steadily growing oil income, the kingdom edged closer than ever to bankruptcy. By 1958, Saud was forced to devalue the riyal, Saudi Arabia's main currency unit, by close to 80 percent.

Faisal Straightens Things Out

In addition to his royal ineptitude, Saud also worried other members of the family by passing over his experienced brothers and putting his own young sons in important government positions. The family was afraid that Saud planned to establish his own dynasty, with the throne going to his descendants alone, rather than being passed from brother to brother (as Ibn Saud had wished).

In 1958 they pressed Saud to name his half-brother, Crown Prince Faisal, prime minister. The experienced Faisal, next oldest of Ibn Saud's surviving sons, had been foreign minister since 1930. Their father had known perfectly well that he was better monarch material than Saud, and on his deathbed he had made the two promise to support each other. Though Saud kept the title of king, Faisal now took over the reins of power.

Balancing the Royal Checkbook

Faisal's first step was an austerity program that stabilized the currency and sharply reduced allowances to the royal family—including the king's household. This angered Saud, who now had second thoughts about the arrangement. In 1961 he forced Faisal out of power, just when Faisal was making real progress towards balancing the country's budget for the first time. But Saud's erratic judgment and lavish spending once again got him in hot water, and he had to bring Faisal back the following year. Faisal resumed his austerity measures, making a balanced budget his first priority. He would succeed in this, but only after further cuts to Saud's personal budget in 1964.

You're Out!

Peeved once more by the cuts, Saud again tried to oust Faisal, but this time the attempt backfired on him. Backed by the *ulema* or religious leaders, the royal family united in support of Faisal. When the ulema issued a *fatwah* proclaiming Faisal king, Saud realized

Sheik-Speak

The **ulema** are Muslim scholars, who act as authorities in legal and religious matters.

A **fatwah** is a formal legal or religious decree issued under traditional guidelines by a member of the ulema.

the game was up. On November 3, 1964, Saud abdicated in favor of Faisal. He then left Saudi Arabia for Greece, where he died in 1969.

Faisal's Reign: Building the Oil State

Humble, honest, hardworking, and austere to the point of severity, King Faisal proved to be the capable leader that the Al Saud needed in order to build upon the foundations laid by Ibn Saud. It was during Faisal's 11-year reign that the basic institutions that define modern Saudi Arabia were put in place, including the structure of its oil economy. Before I get to some of those institutions, however, I want to bring you up to speed on the biggest crisis Faisal faced on his accession to the throne.

Civil War in Yemen

Earlier I mentioned that, as a young man fighting on behalf of Ibn Saud, Faisal had conquered the southern region of Asir in 1924, and that Ibn Saud had annexed Asir to Saudi Arabia in 1930. Asir borders Yemen, and in the past Yemeni rulers have claimed it as their territory. Indeed, when Faisal conquered it the Yemenis didn't give up their claims. Yemen's rulers challenged Ibn Saud, and Saudi Arabia fought and won a major war with Yemen in 1934 over Asir and other borderlands.

I've opened a can of worms here, so I'd better take a moment to fill you in on the situation. There were two Yemens, actually, and the Yemen that the Saudis fought with over Asir was North Yemen. South Yemen at the time was under British colonial rule, like other Gulf states such as Oman, the future United Arab Emirates, and Kuwait. By the 1950s, North Yemen's rulers were looking for ways to strengthen themselves against both the British and the Saudis, and they naturally turned to Egypt's Gamal Abdel Nasser. In fact, North Yemen was the third partner in the short-lived United Arab Republic formed by Egypt and Syria in 1958. But Nasser's socialist-flavored Arab nationalism helped inspire a revolution against North Yemen's hereditary monarchs. In 1962 the revolutionaries proclaimed the Yemen Arab Republic, and for the next eight years civil war raged between their forces and the royalists.

None of that would matter much for this book, except that the civil war in North Yemen immediately took on international overtones. The Egyptians aided the socialist revolutionaries, while the Saudis figured they had to help their fellow monarchists. Both sides sent in arms and other war supplies. So the war became a major irritant in the relationship between Egypt and Saudi Arabia. And not too far behind the scenes were Egypt's and Saudi Arabia's superpower allies, the Soviet Union and the United States respectively. North Yemen's civil war thus threatened to become a flash point in the Cold War. I'll be mentioning it again in the next chapter, where I'll talk about the larger geopolitical background of the post-World War II period.

Yet partly because of Faisal's statesmanship, the war didn't blow up into the major disaster it might have. In 1965 Faisal and Nasser met to discuss a compromise, and both agreed to dial down their participation. Then, in 1967, the whole Arab world was shaken by another catastrophic defeat at the hands of the Israelis. Called the Six Day War, that conflict will also play a big role in the next chapter. At the same time, a far more radical socialist movement than North Yemen's drove the British out of South Yemen, which in 1967 became the People's Democratic Republic of Yemen. Meanwhile, in North Yemen the socialists and royalists agreed to form a joint government, the Yemen Arab Republic, in 1970. It was an uncomfortable union, and flare-ups of violence continued through the 1970s. By the mid 1980s, though, the Yemen Arab Republic was largely at peace.

Confused? Here's a timeline that'll give you the upshot on Yemen:

- **1962:** Civil war begins in North Yemen between the socialists (supported by Egypt) and the royalists (supported by Saudi Arabia).

- **1967:** South Yemen boots out the British and becomes the radically socialist People's Democratic Republic of Yemen (P.D.R.Y). It does not have good relations with Saudi Arabia.

- **1970:** After eight years of civil war, North Yemen becomes the Yemeni Arab Republic (Y.A.R.). A compromise mix of the socialist and royalist elements, it gets a lot of support from a friendly Saudi Arabia.

- **1990:** The two Yemens merge warily. This newly unified Yemen will come up again when we get to the Gulf War, since the Yemenis decided to support Saddam Hussein and Iraq against the Saudis and the U.S.-led coalition.

Aramco Goes Saudi

Like the civil war in Yemen, the oil industry also has an international dimension, of course, and that, too, will be part of the next chapter. In this chapter, I'm more concerned with sketching out the story from the point of view of Saudi Arabia's internal development. This chapter will end Part 1, the "Historical Background" section, while the next chapter will kick off Part 2, the "Recent History" section. Naturally, there's some overlap. So for the rest of this chapter keep in mind that many of the things I'm mentioning briefly will come up again later, when I'll put them in the larger context of oil and recent geopolitics.

From both perspectives, however, the big story of Faisal's reign was the Saudi takeover of Aramco. This gave the Saudi monarch new power and prestige in the international community, and it also led to stronger pressures towards modernization within Saudi Arabia. It didn't happen in a vacuum, though. Other Middle Eastern countries were gaining control of their own oil resources from Western corporations during this era. (I'll give examples in the next chapter.) Many of these governments simply grabbed their nations' oil processing facilities by "nationalizing" them, or claiming them as government property. Saudi Arabia took a more conservative approach known as "participation," by which the Saudi government stepped up its ownership of Saudi oil production gradually, according to a plan carefully negotiated with the oil industry.

The mastermind of the participation idea was Sheik Ahmed Zaki Yamani, Faisal's ablest advisor and Saudi Arabia's petroleum minister from 1962 to 1986. Yamani saw the way nationalization had backfired on some Middle Eastern countries, by alarming the West, causing capital flight, and isolating the governments that practiced it. Yamani announced his idea in a speech in 1967, but no one in the oil industry took it seriously at the time. The following year, however, Yamani managed to get the concept endorsed by the *Organization of Petroleum Exporting Countries* or OPEC, where he represented Saudi Arabia. And in 1971, OPEC passed a resolution calling for his plan to be implemented immediately.

Sheik-Speak

The Organization of Petroleum Exporting Countries (OPEC) was founded in 1960 by leading oil exporters in order to counteract the oil companies' control of the petroleum market. The founding members were Saudi Arabia, Venezuela, Kuwait, Iraq, and Iran.

By the end of 1972, Saudi Arabia had negotiated a participation agreement with Aramco, and its smaller neighbors Qatar and the United Arab Emirates had concluded similar arrangements with the companies that controlled their major oil concessions. Under a series of agreements with Aramco, Saudi Arabia acquired 25 percent ownership of the company in 1973, 60 percent in 1974, and 100 percent in 1980. The company's name was eventually changed to Saudi Aramco, although for years it continued to employ mostly Americans. The first Saudi CEO didn't take over until 1984.

But don't let the smooth pace of the participation process fool you into thinking it was all fun and games during this period. In the very first year, 1973, the Saudis' 25 percent of Aramco gave them control of company policy. They wasted no time before throwing their weight around in a big way.

The Arab Oil Embargo: A Preview

In 1973 Saudi Arabia led OPEC in a total oil embargo on the United States. Overnight, it seemed, Americans were lining up at the pumps for gas, with prices going through the roof. Panic reigned and tempers flared. The Saudi-led Arab oil embargo struck fear into the hearts of Cadillac-drivers from coast to coast, and put Japan on the map of big-time auto manufacturers forever. Why on earth would the Saudis do such a thing, you might ask?

Desert Dates

October 1973: Saudi Arabia leads OPEC in an oil embargo on the United States that lasts until March 1974. The embargo's effects are far-reaching for both Saudi Arabia and America. In Saudi Arabia, the resulting higher oil prices cause a massive jump in revenues, forcing modernization and development at an unprecedented pace. The embargo also raises Saudi Arabia to a leadership position within both OPEC and the Arab world. In the United States, the higher prices spur research into alternative forms of energy and ways of achieving greater energy efficiency. They also overturn the auto industry, letting Japanese companies—which reacted faster than Detroit in turning out fuel-efficient cars—into the U.S. market, where they retain a dominant position.

The answer can be summed up in one word: Israel. In 1973, two Arab countries, Egypt and Syria, went to war with the Israelis once again, and it was America's support of Israel that so angered Faisal. Where the 1967 war had been an unmitigated disaster for the Arabs, this time things didn't turn out quite so badly for them. They started off strong, and finished with essentially a draw—which felt like a victory over the formidable Israelis. Again, I'll cover all this in more detail in the next chapter. This is just a preview. But the 1973 Arab-Israeli war and the 1973 to 1974 Arab oil embargo gave many in the Arab world a taste of the powerful feeling they had been hungering for. And the embargo itself transformed Faisal into the Arab world's most respected statesman and political leader.

Faisal's Approach to Modernization

Even before the oil embargo, Faisal had begun to devote much of his attention to modernizing the country. Because Faisal's approach to modernization has been faithfully followed by his successors, it's worth taking some time to describe it for you. Understanding Faisal's modernization philosophy is essential to understanding how the Saudis view this important issue today.

The author and former diplomat David E. Long has coined the phrase "modernization without *secularization*" to sum up Faisal's basic approach. In other words, Faisal wanted to bring the Saudis into the twentieth century without undermining the dominant place of Islam in society. And in Saudi Arabia, of course, Islam means Wahhabism. It's worth pointing out that Faisal is the only one of Ibn Saud's sons who's also a direct descendant of Muhammad ibn Abdel Wahhab, the founder of Wahhabism.

Faisal's mother, whose name was Tarfah, came from the al al-Sheik, the House of the Sheik, as the descendants of Muhammad ibn Abdel Wahhab are known. (For background on this, see Chapter 4.) She died shortly after giving birth to Faisal in 1906, and Faisal was raised in the home of his maternal grandfather, a strict Wahhabi. Faisal's upbringing no doubt helps to explain his pious austerity, which stands in stark contrast to the spendthrift ways of most other members of the Al Saud.

Sheik-Speak

"Secular" refers to areas of life outside of religion, and so **secularization** and **secularism** mean the general exclusion of religion from government and other public institutions. American political life offers a strong form of secularism, enshrined in U.S. constitutional law as "separation of church and state." But to some extent most Western countries are secular democracies. Secularism does not mean doing away with religion, but merely limiting it to private life. The American tradition insists on this in order to ensure religious freedom, a concept totally alien to the Saudi outlook.

Another way of looking at Faisal's modernization philosophy is to say that he wanted to use the kingdom's oil revenues to give his people all the benefits the West had to offer, without letting them be "corrupted" by Western culture. One of the big questions I'll be addressing later is whether such an approach can actually work.

Mirage Ahead

At first glance, "modernization without secularization" may seem like a simple idea. Indeed, secularism itself may look like a side issue. But don't be fooled. It lies at the heart of the most challenging problems facing the Saudis today. Indeed, the Arab and Muslim worlds as a whole are also grappling with it, and so is much of the rest of the globe.

Some observers have argued that many of the tensions currently wracking Saudi society have arisen precisely because Faisal's approach may in the end be unworkable. Ditto, in fact, for tensions in the larger Arab and Muslim worlds. In Chapter 10, I'll ask you to consider whether it's truly possible to have "modernization without secularization." With all due respect to the memory of King Faisal—a fine leader and a worthy successor to his father—my own answer to that question will be a firm "no."

Infrastructure at Last

Interesting as such questions may be, let's leave them for later, though. Right now I want to give you a look at some of the results of Faisal's modernization efforts. And here's something to keep in mind as you go. While Faisal certainly wanted to modernize Saudi society to some extent, the embargo forced his hand. By pumping almost unimaginable amounts of money into the kingdom (from higher oil prices), the embargo made him go faster than he wanted. This was something that worried him, and it also caused opposition from Wahhabi religious leaders. For example, remember how Ibn Saud had to outmaneuver Wahhabi naysayers who wanted to ban radios in the kingdom? Faisal had to repeat that trick for TV. Only when he showed how it could be used for readings of the Koran was he able to go ahead with television broadcasting in the kingdom.

Before the embargo, annual oil revenues stood at something below $5 billion. In 1974, the year after the embargo, they spiked to over $40 billion. In 1981, the peak of the oil boom, they were reported at $227 billion. That's an increase of more than *45* times in seven years. Something had to be done with all that money. Sure, it could be put in Western banks—and slowly lose its value with inflation. Sure, it could be invested in Western economies—ensuring that Saudi Arabia would continue to be dependent on those economies for basic assistance. Sheik Yamani, the architect of participation, laid it out for Faisal very simply: The only way to make the money work for the kingdom was to make it *work*—in other words, to make it productive. And that meant infrastructure. At last.

Here's a breakdown of the modernization effort that began with Faisal and has been continued by his successors, Khalid and Fahd. It came in a series of "five-year plans," starting in 1970.

- **Industry.** Oil production and processing leads the way here, obviously. Massive industrial complexes were built at sites such as Jubail on the Persian Gulf and Yanbu on the Red Sea. They included facilities for refining crude oil and other petrochemical products, as well as exploiting natural gas (which had been largely wasted up to then by being "flared" or burned off). Agriculture and non-oil industries have also been tried, with mixed success.

- **Construction.** In addition to putting up all those industrial complexes, the Saudis went on a general building spree. Huge gleaming new airports went up in Riyadh and Jiddah, and each government ministry got a state-of-the-art office building. Hospitals, housing, hotels, roads, railways, and other facilities sprouted up as cities like Riyadh mushroomed. Electricity, sewage, water, desalination, and telecommunications systems were built. From overwhelmingly rural, the population became overwhelmingly urban in just a few short decades. Everyone in Saudi Arabia discovered air conditioning in a big way.

- **Education.** Faisal increased government spending on education to about 10 percent of the annual budget, where it has pretty much stayed. Schools and universities were founded at a dizzying rate. The student population rose from about 35,000 in the mid 1950s to some 3 million by 1990. Largely owing to the efforts of Faisal's wife Iffat al Thunayan, almost half of Saudi students are girls. Each of the Al Saud monarchs has at least one university named after him, and other family members do, too. Large numbers of religious universities were also established. (More on Saudi education in Chapter 14.)

- **Subsidies.** Faisal also created the comprehensive subsidy program that institutionalized the government's most important activity: handing out money to the kingdom's citizens. We're talking about a welfare state paid for by oil. Utilities, fuel (naturally), health, education, and many other services are free or close to it for Saudis. Cheap loans, technical assistance, and other incentives are also available to spur non-oil development in the private sector. And don't even think about taxes—there are none. Taxes would be seen as an outrage. In fact, Saudis view the idea of paying for services like utilities as an unfair "tax."

Khalid, Fahd, and Abdullah: Successors and Partners

Another thing that got ironed out—at least temporarily—during Faisal's reign was the process of choosing a new king. This stood the Al Saud in good stead when King Faisal was assassinated by a deranged nephew in 1975, and the crown passed smoothly to his designated successor, Crown Prince Khalid. In choosing Khalid as Crown Prince, Faisal and the family had passed over several of Khalid's older brothers, who graciously removed themselves from consideration. A precedent was thus established for arriving at a consensus within the family, and above all avoiding the sort of public mess that had embarrassed everyone in the transition from Saud to Faisal. With the family's approval, Khalid designated Fahd as the new Crown Prince. Again, several brothers were passed over by common consensus.

Khalid Carries On

Khalid was 63 years old when he became king, and not in the best of health. Though pious, he was by nature both less severe and less vigorous than the dynamic Faisal. Fahd, at 52, was more energetic and more experienced, having served for many years as education minister and interior minister. They ruled in partnership, with many of the kingdom's day-to-day responsibilities falling on Fahd's shoulders.

Yet Khalid was anything but the figurehead that the Western press widely assumed him to be. He was very much in control, and Fahd deferred to him without hesitation. Under Khalid's rule, many of the development programs begun by Faisal came to their full fruition. Indeed, Khalid's six-year reign represents the most intense period of modernization the kingdom has seen.

Oil Boom

That's because Khalid's reign coincides almost exactly with the great oil boom, which started with the embargo in 1973 and began tailing off in 1981, the year before Khalid's death. During this time Saudi wealth became legendary in the West. At home, the economy was thriving and the people were now among the best educated in the region. But the nature of the oil economy limited the amount of capital that it could absorb. The bottom line: It just wasn't possible to spend all the oil money in Saudi Arabia. By the early 1980s, therefore, the Saudis' foreign investments totaled about $200 billion, much of it in U.S. and British holdings. Still, they had spent about $500 billion developing and modernizing the country—even if critics complained that much of that expenditure represented corruption and waste.

Fahd and Abdullah

When Khalid died of a heart attack in June 1982, Fahd, Saudi Arabia's current king, assumed the crown in the smoothest transition so far. According to the family's prepared plan, he quickly named his half-brother Abdullah, head of the National Guard, as Crown Prince, and his full brother Sultan as second in line of succession. When Fahd suffered a debilitating stroke in 1995, Crown Prince Abdullah took over the day-to-day responsibilities of running the kingdom. Today, he is, in effect, the Saudi monarch.

Despite Fahd's experience and his smooth succession after Khalid, he never enjoyed the esteem given to the forbidding Faisal or the kindly Khalid. From the start, his rule has been marred by his early reputation as a playboy, and by his indulgent and extravagant lifestyle.

The Bottom of the Barrel

At the same time, oil boom turned to oil glut, as increased conservation and efficiency combined with greater reliance on other fuels to reduce international demand for oil. As a result, oil prices declined from $35 a barrel in 1979 to less than $13 a barrel a decade later. Saudi production had to be cut, and yearly oil revenues fell back from 1981's high of $119 billion to a low of $26 billion in 1985. Eventually, they would hover around $50 billion. Not chicken feed, but it all depends on what you're used to—and what expectations you've built up. Don't forget, this is a land where people have been conditioned to view the idea of paying for electricity as an unjustifiable "tax."

At first, as prices began their long slow fall, the Saudis decided to keep on spending and wait for things to get better. It took a few years for them to realize that things weren't going to get better any time soon. The oil glut lasted and lasted—it's still going on as this is written, more than two decades later. The Saudis' massive foreign investments are a thing of the past, worn down by year after year of deficits. As the population has mushroomed from about 7 million in 1981 to nearly 20 million today, per capita income has fallen from almost $30,000 per year to less than $8,000. The once shiny new infrastructure is now cracked and peeling. And the people are starting to lose patience.

The Least You Need to Know

- The architect of the modern Saudi oil state was King Faisal.

- The Saudis carefully negotiated their takeover of their oil production rather than grabbing it.

- Modern Saudi Arabia is essentially a taxless welfare state, in which the government's main job is to distribute oil revenues to the people.

- Since the 1980s an oil glut has drastically cut the government's revenues.

Part  Recent History: The Gulf War and Its Aftermath

Congrats! You've mastered the basics of Saudi Arabia's historical background. Unfortunately, however, the world's peoples and their stories don't come with clear dividing lines between historical background and current events. History is always unfolding, and today's headlines can't be understood without a clear picture of what happened yesterday—and so on and so on, all the way back.

So I suggest a compromise: a bridge between historical background and current events. That turning point is the Gulf War of 1991. Pretty much everything going on today in the Arab world was influenced by it in one way or another. Because it was both recent and influential, the Gulf War offers a perfect bridge between historical background and current events. I've called that bridge "Recent History," and it makes up Part 2 of this book. It ought to set you up nicely for the snapshot of today's Saudi Arabia that will come in Part 3.

Chapter 7

Prelude: Oil and Global Politics

In This Chapter

- ◆ Two superpowers square off after World War II
- ◆ The Arabs and Israelis fight a series of wars
- ◆ A revolution in Iran alarms the Americans and Saudis
- ◆ Iran and Iraq fight a long, bloody, and expensive war

This chapter begins the "Recent History" section of the book, by filling you in on the international and strategic backdrop to the Gulf War. It covers pretty much the same time period as the last chapter. The difference is that before I was focusing mostly on things going on inside Saudi Arabia. Now it's time to step back a bit and take in the same era with a wider lens.

But, as I'll remind you regularly, it's all connected in the end. Wars and revolutions have a way of spreading their shock waves in a kind of ripple effect, especially when strategic commodities like oil are involved. So while this chapter focuses on things that were going on outside Saudi Arabia, the Saudis themselves will also have a significant role to play.

A Brief History of Oil Revisited

Let's start by going back to that huge subject we last looked closely at in Chapter 5: oil. At that point, I was talking about oil mostly in relation to the birth of Saudi Arabia under Ibn Saud. But I also wanted to give you a rough idea of the way that oil rose to dominate the world's political struggles. Now it's time to expand on that a little.

Oil and World War I

Given its economic importance, it's hardly surprising that oil has played and continues to play a big part in global politics. Earlier I mentioned one important turning point, when the British switched over from coal to oil as the fuel for their powerful navy. That came in 1912, two years before World War I broke out, and was enabled by British access to Persia (soon to be called Iran) and its oil. At that time there were many who warned that dependence on such a remote source was risky. Britain had plenty of coal, but no known oil deposits. Yet Britain's fast new oil-fired ships outperformed Germany's old coal-burning fleet, helping her win the war.

World War I (1914–1918) turned out to be the proving ground for a number of new weapons that relied on petroleum, including the airplane and the tank. But perhaps most valuable was an offshoot of the automobile, the truck, which introduced a whole new speed and flexibility when it came to moving men and supplies. Again, the British got the jump, relying on trucks heavily where the Germans stuck to the more traditional railway. For that reason, World War I has been described as the victory of the gas-powered truck over the horse-powered cart and the coal-powered locomotive.

Oil and World War II

If World War I was the proving ground for oil power, World War II (1939–1945) was fought to a large extent over oil itself. When the Japanese attacked Pearl Harbor, it was after the United States—their major oil supplier—imposed an oil embargo on them, and they decided they needed a new supply in the Pacific. The sneak attack on Pearl Harbor was meant to safeguard that new supply from American military interference. Similarly, with no oil deposits of its own, Germany, too, made securing oil a top priority. Hitler's fatal strategic mistake in the war, his failed invasion of Russia, was aimed largely at conquering the rich oil fields of the Caucasus.

Petroleum also determined the outcome of the war. Oil tankers on the North Atlantic run from North America to Britain were the most sought-after targets for U-boats, the German submarines that stalked the North Atlantic. The U-boats sank so many tankers that often three would be sent with identical shipments, to increase the chances that one would get through. Throughout the war, Britain relied on fuel shipped from the United States, and would not have been able to stay in the war without it. Conversely, both Japan and Germany were defeated only when the Allies managed to cut them off from the oil supplies needed to power the new mechanized armies, navies, and air forces.

Arabian Almanac

In World War II, Hitler's greatest tank general, Erwin Rommel, was at the mercy of his gas supplies during the North Africa campaigns that won him the nickname "the Desert Fox." "Shortage of petrol," he wrote to his wife as he was forced to retreat by lack of it, "It's enough to make one weep." Later in the war, Rommel's American counterpart, George Patton, had similar frustrations. Stalled near the German border when his tanks ran out of gas, Patton firmly believed he could have hastened the German surrender if he had been allotted a gasoline ration that went instead to his British ally (and rival), Bernard Montgomery.

Oil and the Cold War

While oil took on new importance during World War II, that new importance was magnified a thousandfold during the Cold War. This long ideological contest came after World War II, as that war's two major victors, the democratic United States and the Communist Soviet Union, squared off against each other. In the West, the Cold War coincided with an almost unbelievable boom in auto sales and a surge in general economic prosperity, both of which steadily increased the demand for oil.

The Cold War was fought largely by proxy, as each side sought influence through networks of alliances around the world. In the United States, fear of communism gripped the nation. The main U.S. foreign policy objective became making sure that "friendly" regimes around the world were able to resist Communist "subversion." The Cold War lasted until the Soviet Union fell apart between 1989 and 1991, when its constituent republics (like Russia, the biggest one) went their separate ways.

When it came to the Middle East, America's growing reliance on imported oil after World War II added special urgency to fears that oil exporters like Iran (formerly Persia) or Saudi Arabia might "go Communist." And those fears seemed justified in 1946, as the first real confrontation of the Cold War came in Iran. It happened when the Soviet dictator Joseph Stalin refused to withdraw his troops from northern Iran, which they had occupied in the course of World War II. In the end Stalin did withdraw, but the British quickly decided to shore up their interests in Iran by inviting two American oil companies to take a share in Anglo-Iranian. (The British oil company had changed its name from Anglo-Persian, reflecting the country's name change from Persia to Iran in 1935.)

Iran became one of the major pieces in the Cold War chess game between the two superpowers, the United States and the Soviet Union. For most of the period, like Saudi Arabia, Iran was on the U.S. side of the board. In State Department parlance, Iran and Saudi Arabia were the "twin pillars" of U.S. support in the Middle East. This situation contributed to rivalry between the Iranian and Saudi governments.

In Saudi Arabia, as you know, the Americans entered a strategic alliance with the Al Saud. In Iran, the Americans supported the increasingly dictatorial Muhammad Reza Shah Pahlavi, known as the Shah, until the Shah's overthrow in the Iranian Revolution of 1979. I'll get to that hugely important event shortly. Before I do, however, there are a few other aspects of Cold War oil politics I ought to cover.

Whose Oil Is It, Anyway?

In the last chapter I mentioned the spate of nationalizations that occurred as developing nations with big petroleum reserves decided to take over their own oil industries. Many nationalizations were performed by leaders who overthrew monarchies that had been put in place by the Europeans. The revolutionary movement these leaders were part of has become known as *Arab nationalism*. It arose as the old European colonial order dissolved after World War II. Arab nationalist leaders were proud of overturning the old colonial order and reclaiming their countries' oil from Western corporations. In general they stood on the Soviet side of the Cold War chessboard, and many of their regimes became Soviet clients.

 Sheik-Speak _____

Arab nationalism (also called "pan-Arabism") refers to a rising sense of solidarity that swept the Arab world as the British and other European empires crumbled after World War II. In the 1950s and 1960s, a number of Arab states were taken over by regimes in which socialism, secularism, and Arab nationalism went hand in hand.

The movement looked beyond mere borders to espouse unity in a larger, transnational Arab identity. It gave rise to several attempts to unify various Arab nations under a single government. Most notable was Egyptian president Gamal Abdel Nasser's attempt to unify Egypt and Syria in 1958 as the United Arab Republic. Unity proved elusive, however, and Syria left the United Arab Republic in 1961. Arab nationalism basically lost steam after the death of Nasser, its strongest proponent, in 1970.

Inspired by Marx, Lenin, and Mao, many Arab nationalist leaders used revolutionary rhetoric in which they claimed to act for the "people" against the Western "oppressor." In its heyday, Arab nationalism was highly popular—in the late 1950s, an idolized Arab leader like Egypt's Gamal Abdel Nasser drew bigger crowds on a visit to Saudi Arabia than the Saudi monarch. Though several of these regimes remain in place, Arab nationalism lost much of its credibility by the 1970s. Arab nationalist rulers who stayed in power often ended up feuding with each other as bitterly as they condemned Israel and the West. (Syria's Haffez Assad and his bitter enemy Saddam Hussein are good examples.) These regimes have generally been brutal and authoritarian, and the sad fact is that Arab nationalist rulers have oppressed far more Arabs than Israel and the West put together.

Earlier I promised some examples of states that nationalized their oil industries. Here's a quick rundown on the largest Middle Eastern oil states during the Cold War period, including nationalization info and whether they lined up with the Soviets or the Americans (with the important exception of ethnically Persian Iran, they are all Arab states):

◆ **Saudi Arabia:** The Al Saud remained closely allied with the United States, choosing the conservative option of participation in the oil industry over nationalization (see the previous chapter). The Al Saud generally tried to oppose Arab nationalism as much as they could without tainting themselves as disloyal to the Arab cause. As a royal family in partnership with Wahhabism, they clearly had to reject its secular, anti-monarchy message.

◆ **Iran:** This major non-Arab state nationalized its oil industry in 1951, under its militant nationalist prime minister Muhammad Mossadegh. In 1953 Mossadegh tried to oust the Shah—but with U.S. backing the Shah ousted him instead. After Mossadegh's departure from power, the Shah retained government ownership of the oil industry. Along with Saudi Arabia, Iran under the Shah was a pillar of support for the United States—at least until 1979. Stay tuned!

◆ **Egypt:** A populous Arab country, Egypt doesn't have a lot of oil. What it does have, however, is the Suez Canal. Purchased by Britain in 1875, the canal cuts between the Red Sea and the Mediterranean, saving ships the long journey around Africa. With its heavy tanker traffic, the canal was viewed by Western states as an essential part of the Middle East oil picture. In 1952, a group of army officers overthrew King Farouk, and by 1954 one of them, Gamal Abdel Nasser, had emerged as the country's leader. Taking Mossadegh as a model, Nasser claimed the mantle of leading Third World nationalist ruler. Unlike Mossadegh, however, he also adopted a socialist platform, and in 1955 he turned to the Soviet Union for aid. And the following year, Nasser nationalized the Suez Canal—leading to a major Cold War crisis. More on that in a moment, too.

♦ **Iraq:** With a large Arab population and oil reserves second only to Saudi Arabia's, Iraq has played a key role in the Middle East since World War II. Until 1958 it was firmly aligned with the United States, under its pro-Western leader Nuri es-Said. In 1958 the Arab nationalist feelings unleashed by Nasser swept Nuri aside in a Communist/nationalist coup led by General Abdul Karim Kassem. The next two decades saw turbulent political instability until Saddam Hussein took over in 1979. Like the earlier regimes, Saddam's government was a major Soviet client. Originally British-owned, the Iraq Petroleum Company was fully nationalized by the mid-1970s.

♦ **Libya:** This North African Arab state has large oil reserves. Libya's oil was nationalized by another militant Arab nationalist, Colonel Muammar Qaddafi, after he and his group of young army officers overthrew King Idris in 1969. Qaddafi severed the country's ties with the West, supported international terrorism, and aligned himself with the Soviets, who were Libya's main arms suppliers. Libya has been considered a rogue state by most of the international community.

> **CAUTION**
>
> **Mirage Ahead**
>
> Though they both come from the word "nation," nationalism and nationalization are not necessarily connected, and they're certainly not limited to the Arabs. Nationalism is a sense of ethnic or patriotic fervor, and it's often directed against a perceived enemy (like the West, for example). Nationalization is a political and economic maneuver by which a country's government takes over ownership of one of its important industries.

Four Arab-Israeli Wars

So far I've sketched out the basics on how the early decades of the Cold War played out in the Middle East. I've also related the Cold War to the rising tide of Arab nationalism that swept the Arab world in the 1950s and 1960s. Now it's time to bring another big topic into the discussion: Israel, and its ongoing friction with the Arab world. U.S. support for Israel has also been the biggest source of friction between the United States and the Arabs, including Saudi Arabia.

I last touched on Israel at the end of Chapter 5, when I filled in the background on the Zionist movement and Israel's War for Independence in 1948. That was only the first of four wars that Israel fought against its Arab neighbors. Like Israel's treatment of the Arab Palestinians, these conflicts remain a source of great tension and hostility within the Arab world, including in Saudi Arabia. They also played a major part in the Cold War and contributed in a very big way to the rise of Arab nationalism. Israel was the focal point for Arab nationalism, and the chief reason for its hostility to the West.

Arabian Almanac

Earlier I recounted the story of Ibn Saud's meeting with FDR in 1945, near the end of World War II. At that meeting, the American president promised the Saudi king U.S. protection in exchange for access to Saudi oil for American companies. This simple arrangement was complicated by FDR's successor Harry Truman, who angered the Saudi king in 1948 by supporting the newly independent state of Israel. Some observers have argued that Truman needed to court American Jewish voters by supporting Israel, but that he also needed to court the Saudis for their oil. What's certain is that ever since then, these two conflicting interests have been at the heart of the tensions in the U.S.–Saudi relationship.

Here's a timeline with the essentials on the four Arab-Israeli wars:

- **1948–1949:** The Israeli War for Independence. After declaring independence, Israel is attacked by six Arab countries: Egypt, Jordan, Syria, Lebanon, Iraq, and Saudi Arabia. Israel wins a stunning victory over the disunited Arab forces.

- **1956:** The Suez Crisis. A moment ago I mentioned Nasser's 1956 nationalization of the Suez Canal. This act prompts the Suez Crisis, which results when Britain, France, and Israel get together secretly and cook up a plan to invade Egypt and "liberate" the canal. Their joint attack is a military success but a year-long diplomatic disaster. Under strong international pressure (including from the United States), they are forced to withdraw by the end of 1957.

- **1967:** The Six-Day War. Rising tensions between Israel and the Arab states culminate in military preparations by Egypt, Jordan, and Syria, which mass troops on their borders. In a preemptive lightning attack, the Israeli air force wipes out the Arab air forces on the ground. The Israeli army also invades Egypt and Syria, occupying the Sinai peninsula, the Golan Heights, and the Gaza strip. From Jordan the Israeli army also takes the West Bank and East Jerusalem (the city had been partitioned between Israel and Jerusalem in 1949). The Israeli occupation of the West Bank and East Jerusalem, both areas with majority Palestinian populations, will remain a major bone of contention between Israel and the Arab world. For the moment, though, Israel is exultant, and the Arabs are once again humiliated. His strongman image shattered, Nasser offers to resign, but the demoralized Egyptian people turn him down.

- **1973:** The October (Yom Kippur) War. After Nasser's death in 1970, his successor Anwar Sadat secretly organizes a joint attack on Israel with Syria's Haffez Assad. Taken by surprise on the Jewish holiday of Yom Kippur, Israel loses some of the territory gained in 1967 before digging in and repelling the Arab advance. It's the Arabs' turn to exult, and the Israelis' turn for troubled self-examination.

The 1973 war sets the stage for negotiations between Egypt and Israel, culminating in the Camp David peace accords of 1979—the first peace treaty between Israel and an Arab state. (The peace accords outraged many in the Arab world, including in Saudi Arabia, and Egyptian fundamentalists would assassinate Sadat in 1981; see Chapter 10).

All of these conflicts tied in with the Cold War and also with oil. For example, the Suez Crisis was the only time that the Soviet Union openly threatened Western Europe with a missile attack. And the British and French concern with the canal arose in large part because of the canal's role as a conduit for oil tankers. Indeed, Nasser closed the canal in 1956 by sinking ships in it, which ultimately helped spur the development of supertankers and lessened reliance on the canal. Similarly, the 1967 and 1973 wars brought the Soviets and Americans closer to pushing the nuclear buttons than any other incident save the Cuban Missile Crisis of 1962. And of course the 1973 war changed everything, by revealing the fearsome power of the "oil weapon."

Embargo!

There's a saying that timing is everything, and in the case of the 1973 Arab oil embargo, it couldn't be more true. The Arabs had been making noises about the "oil weapon" since the 1950s. The Saudis had embargoed Britain and France in 1956, and all the major Arab exporters had embargoed the United States and other allies of Israel in 1967. Both times had resulted in an "oil crisis" accompanied by higher prices and lots of hand wringing. But both times the embargoed countries had been able to find the oil they needed, as the major oil companies redistributed it among themselves. Non-embargoed countries simply upped their imports, with the extra amounts going to the embargoed countries. Plus, the United States—the world's "swing producer"—could always increase its own production to help make up the shortfall. The end result was that the embargoes only hurt the exporting countries, by reducing their revenues.

> **Desert Dates**
>
> **1970:** The United States becomes a net importer of oil rather than a net exporter. In other words, for the first time it imports more for its own needs than it has on hand for export. U.S. production capacity hits 100 percent, and oil prices slowly start to rise. The stage is set for the Arab oil embargo three years later.

In 1973, however, things shaped up very differently. There were a number of reasons why the 1973 embargo was more effective than its predecessors. Global demand had already begun to outstrip production, for example, leading to higher prices even before the embargo. Changes in the oil industry (like nationalization and participation) had also given the exporters more control.

But here's the clincher. The United States had topped out its own oil production sometime around 1970, the year in which it became a net importer for the first time. In other words, U.S. production was already at full capacity when the embargo hit. No longer could Texas, Oklahoma, and Louisiana increase production to make up the oil that the Arabs had stopped exporting. At the same time, the Saudi slice of the world oil market was larger than ever, and getting bigger all the time. So the Saudis, not the Americans, were now the "swing producer." It was this change more than any other factor that made the 1973 embargo so effective.

Arabian Almanac

When the October War between Israel and the Arab states broke out on October 6, 1973, U.S. president Richard Nixon promised King Faisal that the United States would remain impartial. On October 19, however, Nixon announced plans to give $2.2 billion in military aid to the Israelis. King Faisal took this as a personal betrayal, and initiated the embargo the next day. The embargo had two parts: first, an absolute cutoff of all oil exports to the United States and the Netherlands (also seen as pro-Israel); second, ongoing production cutbacks designed to make sure that other customers didn't have extra oil to sell to the Americans and Dutch.

For Americans, the oil embargo is almost like the assassination of President Kennedy—one of those cultural and historical watersheds that is clearly remembered by anyone who was around when it happened. Yet because of export increases by some countries that did not observe the embargo, the actual hit wasn't really that bad. In December 1973 the shortfall amounted to less than 15 percent of the internationally traded oil, as compared with the amount available on the international market several months earlier. Gas prices climbed by some 40 percent overall, from October 1973 when the embargo began to March 1974, when it ended—steep, sure, but hardly the end of the world from today's standpoint.

Panic at the Pump

It was the shock—the sudden and totally unexpected sense of vulnerability—that did it. And once the initial shock wore off, fear and uncertainty kicked in and did the rest. At the time, few Americans even knew that their country imported any oil at all, much less how dependent on those imports it had grown. Suddenly, however, their whole way of life seemed under threat. Motorists saw gas stations raise prices on a daily basis. As rumors spread, people who normally waited till the tank was nearly empty started "topping off" whenever they could, adding to growing gas lines. Others hoarded gas, exacerbating the shortages. Some gas stations rationed their gas, according to the day of the week or whether your license plate ended in an odd or even number. Many closed completely, putting up hand-scrawled "No Gas" signs.

The End of Plenty

For nearly three decades—the most prosperous period in American history—Americans had taken cheap, plentiful gas for granted. Never again would they be able to do so. This is why Americans who were alive at the time still recall the embargo so vividly. It marked the passing of prosperity and ushered in an era of inflation, unemployment, and stagnation (the "stagflation" of the mid 1970s to early 1980s). The embargo's success made OPEC an overnight powerhouse, and its ascendancy lasted nearly a decade, until the oil glut of the 1980s set in. For much of that time, the American media was dominated by fearful talk of "Arab oil sheiks," OPEC *price hawks*, and *production quotas*. For America, the oil embargo was the end of plenty—and in the eyes of many Americans, the Arabs were the culprits.

Sheik-Speak

Price hawks were those OPEC members (like Libya and Iran) who consistently pushed for price increases. The oil embargo was carried out by Arab oil producers within OPEC, under Faisal's leadership, but the OPEC price hawks enhanced its effects. OPEC's basic method is for its members to seek agreement on **production quotas** for each member country. The idea is that setting fixed production levels will help determine favorable prices, by controlling market pressures.

Saudi Arabia and Iran: Price Rivals

Throughout the 1970s, two of the biggest beneficiaries of higher oil prices were the Al Saud and the Shah of Iran. But these two U.S. allies had very different agendas. For the Saudis, with a relatively small population and lots of oil still in the ground, economic logic said to resist letting the price get too high. Higher prices, as they learned after the embargo, spurred conservation and other measures that would only hurt them in the long run. Lower prices today meant more revenues in the future. For Iran, however, with a much larger population and diminishing oil reserves, economic logic said the reverse. Keep prices high while the oil lasts—in other words, get it while the getting's good.

Consequently, Saudi Arabia and Iran frequently found themselves at loggerheads in the OPEC boardroom during the 1970s. Obviously, the economic logic of the Saudis' situation was favorable for the U.S.–Saudi relationship. But the Saudis had a lot of trouble understanding why the United States was so blindly set on supporting a price hawk like Iran.

On top of that, by the 1970s the dictatorial Shah was behaving more and more like a power-crazed megalomaniac. Sheik Yamani, the Saudi oil minister, warned as early as 1975 that if the Shah were overthrown, the new regime in Tehran might be violently anti-American. American planners paid no attention. But while Americans were getting used to energy conservation, small cars, and higher gas prices, further shocks from the Middle East were waiting just around the corner.

Revolution in Iran

In 1979, the Iranian Revolution toppled the man who had been seen as America's most stable, permanent ally in the Middle East. Right away, there was another oil crisis, as Iranian oil went off the market. But within months this unpleasant surprise was followed by a far deeper national trauma for the United States, when Iranian fundamentalists held 52 Americans hostage for more than a year. Like the events of 1967 and 1973, the Iranian Revolution was one of those periodic upheavals that seem to overturn everybody's basic assumptions about the Middle East on a regular basis. And the hostage crisis proved an even more painful national disaster for Americans than the oil embargo.

Here's a timeline with the sequence of events.

◆ **1978:** Opposition to Iran's U.S.-supported dictator, the Shah, crystallizes around the exiled religious leader Ayatollah Khomeini.

◆ **January 1979:** Mass demonstrations against the Shah's brutal regime lead to his overthrow and exile. Ayatollah Khomeini returns from exile to become the ruler of Iran's new Islamic fundamentalist government.

◆ **October 1979:** President Jimmy Carter admits the Shah to the United States for medical treatment.

◆ **November 1979:** Enraged anti-American demonstrators storm the U.S. Embassy in Tehran, Iran's capital, and take 66 Americans hostage (14 are later released). The resulting hostage crisis drags down Jimmy Carter's presidency.

◆ **January 1981:** The hostage crisis ends after more than a year, when the hostages are released on the day that President Ronald Reagan is inaugurated.

The hostage crisis was deeply traumatic for the United States, and it continues to influence U.S. policy in the Middle East. At the same time, by standing up to and humiliating "the great Satan" (as they called the United States), the Iranian fundamentalists won immense prestige in the Muslim world. Indeed, partly through the Iranian example, fundamentalist Islam now began to replace secular Arab nationalism as a rallying point for the Arab world. During the 1980s this led to a new stage in the old rivalry between Iran and Saudi Arabia, which now became a contest to see who could be more "Islamic."

The Iran-Iraq War

Iran was now perceived as a major enemy of the United States. So when Saddam Hussein, long a Soviet client, sent Iraqi armies into Iran in 1980, U.S. planners decided that he deserved America's support. Saddam's main goal was control of the disputed Shatt-al-Arab waterway, which allowed access to the oil tankers plying the Persian Gulf. Despite Saddam's massive and well-equipped army, however, the Iran-Iraq War settled into a bloody stalemate in 1982, after Iran drove back the initial Iraqi offensive. For the next six years, in grinding trench warfare reminiscent of World War I, Iran's new fundamentalist government hurled its young men to be slaughtered as cannon fodder against the Iraqi line.

Arabian Almanac _____

The Iran-Iraq War (1980–1988) threw a shadow over the Muslim world in the 1980s. There was a lot of propaganda from both sides. The war of words had an ethnic dimension, since most Iraqis are Arabs, while Iranians are ethnic Persians. It also had a religious dimension, since Iran is almost entirely Shiite, while Iraq is dominated by a Sunni Arab minority, which lords it over the Shiite Arab majority. A further religious angle came from the fact that Saddam Hussein's aggressively secular regime was a natural enemy of the Islamic fundamentalists who had come to power in the Iranian Revolution. From this perspective, the war can be seen as a clash of old-style secular Arab nationalism (Iraq) with new-style Islamic fundamentalism (Iran).

Though the years of the oil glut had started, the war periodically sent jitters through the oil market. Both combatants regularly attacked tankers in the Persian Gulf that they thought might be carrying oil exported by the enemy. This led to involvement by the West, as the United States and other nations sent their navies into the Gulf to protect shipping. Several incidents occurred, among them an Iraqi missile attack on the USS *Stark* in 1987, killing 37 U.S. sailors, and the accidental downing of an Iranian airliner by the USS *Vincennes* in 1988, in which all 290 passengers perished.

By the time it ended in 1988, the Iran-Iraq War had claimed more than a million lives and had brought neither side any significant gains. It had also saddled Saddam Hussein with an estimated $80 to $100 billion in war debts. While many Arab states had lent money, the bulk of the debt was owed to Kuwait and Saudi Arabia, which had been Iraq's most loyal supporters in the war. None of it would ever be paid back—except in bullets, bombs, and bluster.

The Least You Need to Know

- ◆ Oil played a crucial role in both World Wars, as well as in the Cold War.

- ◆ Arab nationalism dominated much of Middle Eastern oil politics in the 1950s and 1960s.

- ◆ Arab nationalist regimes mostly sided with the Soviets in the Cold War.

- ◆ America's three big Cold War allies in the Middle East were Israel, Saudi Arabia, and (until 1979) Iran.

- ◆ American support for Israel has been the biggest problem in U.S.–Saudi relations.

The Persian Gulf War

In This Chapter

- Saddam's war machine stomps a tiny neighbor
- The Saudis face the Iraqi threat over the border
- An international coalition defeats the invader
- Iraq's tyrant lives to fight another day

It's the summer of 1990, and from the American perspective things are looking pretty rosy. The Berlin Wall, the harshest symbol of Cold War division, fell the previous winter. The once-feared Soviet Union is in the process of breaking up under its own cumbersome weight. By the following summer, it will have dissolved itself completely. The Cold War is over, and the Americans have won. Seemingly invulnerable, America stands alone as the last superpower.

From the Saudi point of view, things also seem promising. Israel and the Palestinians have begun working towards a negotiated peace settlement. Oil revenues are still down, but (for reasons explained in the last chapter) this isn't necessarily such a bad thing in the long term. The Iran-Iraq War has been over for two years. Peace is welcome, and the costs of the war to its two combatants have left the Saudis stronger than ever. Prosperous and stable, Saudi Arabia leads the Arab and Muslim worlds in overall wealth, religious influence, and general prestige.

When trouble arrives, it's a complete surprise to nearly everyone. Saddam Hussein's invasion of Kuwait sends out shock waves that will still be rocking the Arab world more than a decade later. In this chapter, you'll watch the initial crisis unfold: invasion, war, and victory. You'll also see victory come without satisfaction or security for the victors, as the war itself sets the stage for more than a decade of turbulence and terror.

Brave New World Order

The end of the Cold War had important consequences for the balance of power in the Middle East. As the main backer of radical Arab nationalist states like Syria, Libya, and Iraq, for example, the Soviet Union left a huge void when it began withdrawing from the scene in the late 1980s. These states had been among the region's most bellicose and aggressive, but now they were forced to tone down their rhetoric. For many observers, it seemed like the dawn of a peaceful new era.

One benefit of the Soviet collapse was that it speeded up the peace process between the Palestinians and Israelis. The radical Arab nationalist states had always been the most adamantly opposed to peace with Israel. With the Soviets gone, the Americans could put more pressure on the radicals, and on the Palestinians themselves, to stop undermining the peace process. At the same time, Israel's support as a precious Cold War ally against Soviet influence was now less important for the Americans. The world's last superpower could also now put more pressure on Israel to make peace, too.

> **Desert Dates**
>
> **1988:** The Palestinian Liberation Organization (PLO) officially recognizes the state of Israel. The main organization representing the Palestinian Arabs, the PLO had formerly relied on the Soviets for support. That same year the PLO and the Israelis began face-to-face talks that would culminate in their nearly reaching a comprehensive peace settlement in the mid 1990s.

So when Iran and Iraq announced that they were meeting in Geneva to finally bury the hatchet, it fit right in with the general mood of optimism. In July 1990, two years after a U.N.-brokered cease-fire ended the Iran-Iraq War, the two sides at last came together to work towards a peace treaty. Yet only a few weeks later, Saddam Hussein totally shattered this hopeful atmosphere by invading Kuwait and threatening Saudi Arabia. His overtures toward Iran, it was clear, had been inspired solely by his plans for new conquests. (Mental note to self: Be sure to make peace with one neighbor before executing a surprise attack on another.)

Iraq's invasion of Kuwait thus became the first international crisis of the post-Cold War era. The game of global politics had new rules—but the problem was, no one knew what they were yet. In a much-quoted speech given just hours after the U.S.-led coalition launched its effort to expel Iraq from Kuwait, President George Bush seemed to look forward to a victory that would define those new rules. "We have before us," he said, "the opportunity to forge for ourselves and for future generations a new world order, a world where the rule of law, not the rule of the jungle, governs the conduct of nations."

Similar words have been spoken by other American presidents, though, starting with the idealistic Woodrow Wilson, who was undone by such sentiments after World War I. Indeed, more than a few of Bush's predecessors could have warned him. Forging new world orders is easier said than done.

The Players

While the war that resulted from Saddam's invasion of Kuwait ultimately involved a list of nations as long as your arm, there were really just four main players: Iraq, Kuwait, Saudi Arabia, and the United States. In other words, we're talking about the three neighboring states directly affected by the events, plus the world's last remaining superpower. Before I give you the lowdown on the invasion and the war, it might be a good idea to introduce the subject with a few words about how these four players lined up before the war.

The events arranged themselves around one central military alliance, that between the United States and Saudi Arabia, and one central dispute, that between Iraq and Kuwait. So that's how I'll break the players down for you here, presenting them two-by-two, taking the alliance first and the dispute second.

America and the Saudi Military

I've recounted the story of how Ibn Saud and FDR cemented the strategic alliance between their two countries near the end of World War II. Now is the perfect time to tell you about the military side of that relationship.

It was FDR's successor as president, Harry Truman, who started military negotiations after the war. Truman met several times with Ibn Saud in the late 1940s. The U.S. president and the Saudi king agreed on the establishment of a U.S. air base at Dhahran, Saudi Arabia, which the United States leased until 1962. At the same time, the Americans made a commitment to protect Saudi Arabia (under the auspices of the newly formed U.N.) if the Saudis were attacked or threatened by another power.

In addition to the occasional presence of temporary U.S. bases and the U.S. commitment to defending the kingdom, the Americans also took on the role of training Saudi forces. These three elements would be the "tripod" that the relationship would rest on. Here's a timeline with the most important developments:

- **1950:** Ibn Saud enlists American support in establishing and training the country's first standing army. The result is the U.S. Military Training Mission for Saudi Arabia (USMTM), a permanent institution that becomes the backbone of U.S. training for Saudi forces. Arms and equipment will be supplied largely by U.S. and British manufacturers.

- **1956:** King Saud establishes the National Guard, partly as an insurance policy against a coup by the army (remember, this is the era of Arab nationalist army coups against monarchs). Stressing personal loyalty to the king, the National Guard essentially reconstitutes the old Ikhwan or Wahhabi Brotherhood, the tribal paramilitary force that Ibn Saud had disbanded in the 1930s (see Chapter 4).

Arabian Almanac

Despite its commitments to the Saudis during the early Cold War period, before about 1970 the United States still mostly relied on Britain as the guarantor of regional stability in the Middle East. The once-powerful British presence dwindled fast, however. British power had little credibility after the Suez Crisis in 1956, which popped Britain's overinflated imperial balloon with a loud, embarrassing bang.

- **1962:** Faisal appoints his half-brother Abdullah as head of the National Guard, a position he still occupies. (Abdullah, you'll remember, is now Crown Prince and is effectively in charge of running the country.) Abdullah brings in the British to train the Guard.

- **1965:** King Faisal negotiates a $400 million package with the British and Americans to modernize the Saudi air force, founded in the 1950s. The kingdom's geography and strategic requirements make the air force the most important and prestigious branch of its armed forces.

- **1972:** King Faisal puts the Saudi navy (founded in 1957) under the USMTM.

- **1972:** the Saudi air force receives the first of 114 American-made F-5 fighter planes. Saudi fighter pilots will go to the United States for training. Later the F-5s are replaced with more sophisticated F-15s.

- **1973:** Abdullah replaces the British with the Americans in training the National Guard. The Americans establish the U.S.-Saudi Arabian National Guard (SANG) program as a counterpart to the USMTM.

- **1974:** Saudi Arabia adopts a 10-year military expansion plan prepared by the United States, including construction of a massive base, King Khalid Military City, at Hafar al-Batin.

- **1981:** the Saudi air force orders five sophisticated AWACS (Airborne Warning and Communications System) planes from the American manufacturer Boeing. Congress approves the sale because of concerns over the new fundamentalist regime in Iran.

◆ **1985:** Saudi Arabia contracts with Boeing for the "Peace Shield" command, control, communications, and intelligence system, which is designed to coordinate the AWACS with other defensive systems.

Desert Dates

1979: The Iranian Revolution elevates Saudi Arabia, Iran's rival, to the role of America's top recipient of military aid in the Gulf region. Formerly, the Americans had put the Shah first when it came to military assistance. After the Shah's overthrow and replacement by a hostile fundamentalist regime, Congress bans military aid to Iran. True, the ban is violated in the early 1980s, when the Reagan administration secretly makes the illegal Iran-Contra deal with the Iranians. The deal offers Iran American arms in exchange for the freeing of American hostages captured by Iranian-backed terrorists during the Lebanese civil war. It was a major scandal for the Reagan White House. Such isolated skullduggery notwithstanding, however, Saudi Arabia now stands alone as America's big ally in the Persian Gulf region.

Though Saudi pilots flew defensive patrols during the Iran-Iraq War of the 1980s, the kingdom's armed forces had little combat experience before the Persian Gulf War. The Saudi armed forces' contribution to defeating Saddam Hussein—the largest after the American one—would constitute their trial by fire.

Iraq's Claims Against Kuwait

Though Iraq's invasion of Kuwait took the world by surprise, it didn't come completely out of the blue. Make no mistake, the invasion violated every standard of international law. Still, there was a history of old Iraqi claims against Kuwait, as well as a whole slew of new ones concocted by Saddam for the occasion. The Iraqi dictator made full use of both in the propaganda war that preceded the invasion itself.

To understand Iraq's historical claims against Kuwait you'll need to cast your mind back to Ottoman times. Under Ottoman rule, there were no such entities as Iraq and Kuwait. Instead, what is now Iraq comprised three distinct provinces of the Ottoman Empire. Each province was named after its principal city: Mosul in the north, Baghdad in the middle, and Basra in the south. The British took over these three provinces as the mandate of Iraq when the Ottoman Empire was dissolved after World War I. Iraq became independent in 1932, under its Hashemite monarch, King Faisal, the son of Sharif Husayn of Mecca. (Go to Chapter 4 if you want to review the end of the Ottoman Empire and the British mandates.)

Kuwait was originally part of the Ottoman province of Basra—at least until 1756, when the al Sabah, Kuwait's royal family, established it as an independent kingdom. On this basis, when Iraq became independent nearly two centuries later, its rulers repeatedly challenged Kuwait's right to exist. Their argument was that since it had been part of the old province of Basra, Kuwait belonged by rights to modern Iraq. Iraq's rulers went so far as to invade Kuwait twice, in 1961 and 1973. The second time, Iraq occupied a slice of Kuwaiti border territory for a decade before withdrawing.

The presence of oil, of course, added fuel to the fire (so to speak). As I mentioned earlier, Iraq borrowed an estimated $80 to $100 billion to wage war against Iran in the 1980s. Iraq's economy was ruined by the war, and at 1990 oil prices it would have taken about 20 years of oil income to pay that money back. The largest chunk of change was owed to Kuwait, and much of the rest to Saudi Arabia, Iraq's two staunchest backers in the war. Now, however, both countries refused to cooperate when Saddam Hussein tried to push for higher oil prices. Indeed, Kuwait was ignoring production quotas and consistently overproducing, helping to keep prices low. With its tiny population and large oil reserves, it followed the same long term economic logic as Saudi Arabia. (For an explanation of this, see the last chapter.) Iraq, by contrast, had big short-term financial problems, and needed higher oil prices to solve them.

Starting in early 1990, Saddam Hussein began threatening Kuwait, pressuring the Kuwaitis to forgive the war debts, lend Iraq more money, and stop pumping so much oil. He also complained that the Kuwaitis were drilling into Iraq's part of the shared border territory called the *neutral zone*, removing more oil than they were permitted under previous agreements. The Kuwaitis (who have a reputation among Arabs for arrogance and snootiness) ignored his demands—right up until the tanks rolled on August 2.

Sheik-Speak

The phenomenon of the **neutral zone** is another holdover from the random map drawing that followed the breakup of the Ottoman Empire after World War I. British planners had to draw up the borders separating Iraq, Kuwait, and Saudi Arabia, but they weren't sure exactly where to put them. Rather than make a potentially troublesome decision, they simply fudged it by creating vague buffer areas between the countries. Later, these neutral zones came in handy for dealing with the Bedouin, whose nomadic way of life had little room for things like borders anyway, and who were allowed to cross back and forth into the neutral zones without a lot of fuss. When oil was discovered in the region, the countries sharing the borders also agreed to share development costs and revenues from oil deposits found in the neutral zones.

The Invasion

The invasion itself was quick and easy, and was pretty much over the day it began. Outnumbered by more than ten to one, Kuwait's small military was in no position to offer much resistance to Saddam's heavily armed, battle-hardened invasion force. The al Sabah family—including Kuwait's ruling emir, Sheik Jaber al Ahmad al Sabah—fled over the border to Saudi Arabia. Saddam Hussein set up a puppet government in Kuwait City, and on August 8 he announced that Kuwait had been annexed to Iraq, as the country's nineteenth province.

By occupying Kuwait, Saddam Hussein apparently figured that he could solve all his problems at once. There were lots of reasons for him to think so—but in the end they all came down to oil. In adding Kuwait's reserves to Iraq's, by sunset on August 2, 1990, Saddam Hussein controlled a quarter of the world's known oil reserves, equal to those of Saudi Arabia.

As if that wasn't enough to cause migraines in Western capitals, Saddam's invasion force of 140,000 men was clearly bigger than was necessary just to occupy little old Kuwait. Indeed, U.S. military satellite photos soon showed at least six divisions moving towards the Saudi-Kuwait border. Behind this invasion force lay Saddam Hussein's much vaunted "million-man army," in sheer numbers the largest in the Middle East, and one of the largest in the world. Starting the day after the invasion, Iraqi troops made several "accidental" incursions into Saudi territory. It was clear that Saudi and U.S. troops on the ground in Saudi Arabia would not be sufficient to repel an invading Iraqi force. A successful invasion of Saudi Arabia would put fully half the world's oil in the hands of Saddam Hussein.

The Response

With U.S. leadership, the United Nations Security Council immediately began issuing a series of resolutions opposing the invasion, starting on the day of the attack itself. The first one, Resolution 660, called for Iraq to remove its forces from Kuwait. The second one, Resolution 661, imposed economic sanctions on Iraq. Passed on August 6, it called on all states to suspend trade with Iraq, except for humanitarian or medical purposes. Yet a few days later, at an emergency meeting of the Arab League, only 12 out of 21 member states voted to condemn Iraq. The split was a harbinger of the sharp and lasting divisions that Saddam's invasion would ultimately create in the Arab world.

> **Arabian Almanac** _____
>
> The Security Council is the U.N.'s most important agency when it comes to trying to keep international peace. It's essentially a committee, made up of the U.N. representatives from fifteen nations. Five of those nations have permanent membership on the Security Council: the United States, Britain, France, China, and Russia (which got the seat of the former Soviet Union). The other ten nations are elected by the U.N. General Assembly to two-year terms on the Security Council. All members of the Security Council vote on the issues before it, but a "no" vote from any of the five permanent members is enough to defeat a measure. (This is often referred to as a "veto" power.) Unlike the decrees of other U.N. bodies, the Security Council's resolutions and other measures are considered binding on all member states.

Within hours of the invasion, Prince Bandar bin Sultan, Saudi Arabia's ambassador to the United States and a nephew of King Fahd, began meeting with high-level American officials in Washington. President George Bush, meanwhile, froze Iraqi and Kuwaiti assets in the United States. Bush also joined the chorus of international leaders calling for Iraq's immediate withdrawal from Kuwait.

Unlike the others, however, the American president was actually in a position to do something about it. He would need help, but the recent end of the Cold War gave him a lucky assist. Saddam Hussein's biggest arms supplier, the Soviet Union, was no longer in the game of supporting rogue states. Soon it would cease to exist entirely. No longer could the Soviets, the Chinese, and other such countries be counted on to automatically oppose any actions by the Western powers. Indeed, both were now more interested in courting America than opposing it. They had either supported the Security Council resolutions or abstained from voting (allowing them to pass), which would have been highly unlikely only a few years earlier.

The end of the old Cold War divisions seemed to offer fresh hope of international solidarity. Okay, so maybe it fell short of being "a new world order." If the rest of the world appeared united, the Arabs definitely were not. Still, this accident of timing would be a great help in building a unified front against Saddam Hussein.

Desert Shield

Soon after Prince Bandar met with U.S. leaders in Washington, U.S. Secretary of Defense Richard Cheney was on his way to Saudi Arabia to meet with King Fahd and his advisors. Cheney showed the Saudis satellite photos of Iraqi troops approaching the Saudi border and moving to within striking distance of important Saudi oil fields. Fahd hesitated only briefly before consenting to the Americans' request that the United States rush 100,000 soldiers to Saudi Arabia to ensure its defense.

The United States immediately began deploying paratroopers of the U.S. Army's 82nd Airborne Division, giving the operation the code name Desert Shield. The troops were supported by fighters, fighter-bombers, and AWACS radar planes. At the same time, the U.S. Navy began moving aircraft carriers and battleships with cruise missiles towards the Persian Gulf. What would soon be a massive military buildup had begun.

Crown Prince Abdullah was one of those present at the discussions about Desert Shield. He supported the move, but suggested further consensus building among the Al Saud before giving it the final stamp of approval. Fahd overrode his brother's advice, an uncharacteristic act that shows how urgent he thought the situation was. Abdullah also expressed concern that a large U.S. military presence in the kingdom could damage its traditional position as a guardian of Islam, and might even undermine its stability. As you'll see in the next chapter, Abdullah's fears would prove justified.

In keeping with Crown Prince Abdullah's reservations, the Saudis did express some concerns about the troop buildup. In particular, they raised the following three potential trouble areas with the U.S. planners:

> **Desert Dates**
>
> **October 1986:** King Fahd assumes the title "Custodian of the Two Holy Places" in order to stress the Al Saud's role as guardian of Mecca and Medina—and by extension, Islam as a whole. The Gulf War would put Fahd's claims to be "Custodian of the Holy Places" in doubt among the Saudi public, by leading to the presence of large numbers of "infidel" U.S. troops in the kingdom.

- ◆ **U.S. staying power:** The Saudis sought assurances that the Americans would not put on a brave front and then leave if things got rough, exposing the Saudis to a vengeful Saddam. They remembered, for example, how the United States had quickly withdrawn from Beirut during the Lebanese civil war, after a terrorist bomb there killed 283 Marines in 1983.

- ◆ **A temporary presence:** While they wanted the Americans to stick it out, the Saudis didn't want them to overstay their welcome. They didn't want the infidels to turn into a permanent presence on Saudi soil.

- ◆ **Religious friction:** Christian and Jewish religious services are outlawed in Saudi Arabia, and the Saudis at first forbade the troops to bring Bibles or other non-Muslim religious texts into the kingdom. They finally agreed to allow Bibles on U.S. airbases in the kingdom, and to permit limited Christian services on the bases only if discreetly conducted as "private gatherings." They insisted that Jewish soldiers be flown to U.S. warships to conduct services.

Mirage Ahead

The Saudis' initial refusals to allow religious services for Christian and Jewish troops in the kingdom prompted a tough and provocative question from General Colin Powell. (At that time, Powell was serving as chairman of the Joint Chiefs of Staff.) As Powell only half-jokingly asked his longtime friend Prince Bandar, "They can die defending your country, but they can't pray in it?" I'll be discussing Saudi religious intolerance at length later on, so keep Colin Powell's question in mind. But here's a warning: Don't expect any easy answers to it. The Saudis may have compromised a bit over religious services for foreign troops, but if you think their token concessions ended, think again.

The issue of religious freedom for the troops protecting Saudi Arabia was never satisfactorily resolved. More significantly, it points to the sort of problem that would continue to dog the U.S.–Saudi relationship after the war was over. There's a whole web of related social issues, too, like standards of dress and behavior for women soldiers serving in the kingdom. Religious intolerance and social intolerance blend into one, because religious content can be such a big part of social customs. Later, I'll be focusing on such issues as I return to the question of whether it's truly possible to achieve King Faisal's ideal of "modernization without secularization."

Desert Storm

Further Security Council resolutions against Iraq followed, as summer turned to fall and Saddam Hussein steadfastly refused to withdraw Iraq's occupying forces from Kuwait. Meanwhile, the United States continued to deploy its military forces to the Persian Gulf. By November, U.S. forces in the region numbered more than 240,000 troops and some 1,600 combat aircraft. It became apparent that Saudi Arabia, for now at least, was out of danger.

Desert Dates

August 8, 1990: Declaring that Iraq's aggression "will not stand," President Bush indicates that U.S. aims included reversing Iraq's aggression, not just stopping it. By November, the troops in place are enough to defend Saudi Arabia, but not enough to drive the Iraqis from Kuwait.

November 8: After extensive talks with King Fahd, Washington announces plans to send as many as 200,000 more troops to the Gulf. This is the decisive move that begins turning Desert Shield, a defensive operation, into Desert Storm, an offensive one. Saddam Hussein responds by moving more troops into Kuwait, bringing the total number of Iraqi soldiers there to something over 650,000.

At the same time, the Bush administration was patiently building an international coalition that would ultimately include 37 member states. Their contributions to Desert Storm would range from sending troops and weapons to financial assistance. And on November 29, American diplomacy resulted in a key Security Council move, Resolution 678, authorizing member states "to use all necessary means" to uphold its previous resolutions demanding Iraqi withdrawal from Kuwait, unless Iraq withdrew by January 15, 1991. In other words, the Security Council was giving Iraq a deadline of January 15 to get out of Kuwait. The Security Council was also giving a green light to the use of military force against Iraq if it ignored the deadline.

Which, of course, it did. Accordingly, on January 16, the U.S.–led coalition officially opened Desert Storm with a massive air campaign against Iraqi targets in both Kuwait and Iraq. By January 23, General Powell declared that the coalition forces had achieved "air superiority," and for the next month they proceeded to bomb the Iraqis with near total impunity. Eventually, President Bush gave Saddam yet another deadline, February 24, by which to withdraw unconditionally from Kuwait or face a land war. When that deadline, too, passed without compliance, coalition forces launched a devastating ground attack. Within 100 hours, the Iraqis had been swept from Kuwait. The remnants of the Iraqi army who had not surrendered or been killed fled north towards Basra. On February 27, President Bush declared a cease-fire.

Total casualties from the Gulf War are hard to know for sure, with the uncertainty coming from the unknown number of Iraqi dead. Coalition forces suffered 243 fatalities (148 American), with about twice that number wounded. The bulk of Saudi casualties came as Saudi army and national guard units repelled the only Iraqi attack on Saudi territory, at the border town of Ras al-Khafji on January 30, 1991. After several days of heavy fighting, in which 18 Saudis were killed, the Saudis recaptured the town.

Initial estimates of Iraqi dead in the war ranged as high as 200,000, though the most recent ones suggest that between 21,000 and 35,000 Iraqis died, among them between 2,000 and 5,000 civilians, killed mostly during coalition bombing. In addition to the casualties from the war itself, as many as 10,000 Kuwaitis may have died during the Iraqi invasion and rape of Kuwait.

A Peace Too Early?

By ending the war after expelling Iraq from Kuwait, President Bush was sticking to the terms of the Security Council resolutions under which he had been able to gather such a strong and diverse group of allies. Still, he was criticized after the war for not pursuing Iraqi forces deeper into Iraq, as the U.S. commander of coalition forces, General Norman Schwarzkopf, and others had recommended. A survey one year later, for example, indicated that nearly two-thirds of Americans thought that the war should have been continued until Saddam Hussein was either removed from power or killed.

Saddam's Waiting Game

Iraq agreed to the coalition's terms for the cease-fire, including a formal annulment of the annexation of Kuwait and the restoration of seized Kuwaiti assets. On April 3, the Security Council imposed stiff conditions for peace on Iraq, including the destruction of all nuclear, chemical, and biological weapons. Saddam Hussein would spend the next decade dodging U.N. arms inspectors and biding his time. As the world's attention moved elsewhere, he knew that it would become increasingly difficult to again gather the kind of international support against him that had led to the coalition victory.

Indeed, to much of the Arab world at least, Saddam Hussein was able to portray himself as the victor. He had stood up to the West's mightiest armies, and he had survived.

The Saudi Gamble

For the Al Saud, the Persian Gulf War was a huge gamble, and the stakes went up sharply when Desert Shield became Desert Storm—in other words, when the defensive U.S. presence became an offensive one. The Koran forbids Muslims from attacking Muslims. Saddam Hussein had obviously violated that religious obligation, but that was one thing. He was a strictly secular ruler, though he could play the Islam card when it suited his propaganda needs. But no one seriously expected much from him in terms of piety and devotion. As the supposedly devout guardians of Mecca and Medina, however, the Saudis were a whole different kettle of fish. When it comes to Islamic values, the Saudis are held to a higher standard. To attack fellow Muslims, even when those Muslims themselves had invaded another Islamic country, was a very risky proposition for them—especially when they were doing so with the help of infidels.

It's still up in the air whether the Al Saud won or lost the gamble.

The Least You Need to Know

- The U.S.–led coalition was possible because the Cold War ended just before Saddam invaded Kuwait.

- Saddam's invasion of Kuwait was the first major international crisis of the post-Cold War era.

- The Persian Gulf War was about four things: oil, oil, oil, and oil.

- The war left Saddam Hussein with his most dangerous weapon intact—his public dignity.

Chapter 9

The Backlash (or Don't Forget the Wahhabis)

In This Chapter

- ◆ Some old alliances bite the dust
- ◆ Cash flow problems strike again
- ◆ Moderates and fundamentalists agitate for reform
- ◆ Driving while female becomes a crime

The Persian Gulf War is over. Saddam Hussein's vaunted million-man army has been driven from Kuwait, leaving Saudi Arabia's tiny neighbor in a shambles. Iraq, too, is in disarray as its armies retreat. Rebellions break out against Saddam Hussein's rule in both the northern and southern parts of Iraq, though Saddam soon crushes them. And within Saudi society, the war creates deep divisions, seriously undermining the Al Saud's authority and legitimacy.

The war also disrupts the patterns of power that have long shaped the Arab world. Most of all, the Saudis are surprised and hurt at how many supposed friends deserted them and sided with Saddam Hussein. The war leaves the Al Saud feeling somewhat like a rich kid who's been buying candy for other kids to make them like him. Then the neighborhood bully—who has also happily been taking the candy—starts to pick on the rich kid, and instead of rallying to his support, the other kids join in the bullying. The rich kid, of course, feels bitter, confused, betrayed, and more than a little insecure.

This chapter will focus on the problems—and the lessons—that emerged for the Saudis in the early 1990s. It wasn't a totally bleak situation. For example, it's in the war's aftermath that the Al Saud finally begin to take some long-promised steps toward democratic reform. The big question, in the end, is whether the rich kid will learn that it doesn't pay to keep handing out candy.

Money Troubles—Again

Speaking of rich kids and the lessons they have to learn, before I get to some of the social consequences of the war, I'd like to start by emphasizing its financial impact on the Al Saud. The Saudis basically paid for the war, and its price tag was partly responsible for bringing on a return of the Al Saud's old money troubles during the early 1990s. Since the family's rule depends so much on handing out money, the cash shortage potentially threatened the country's political stability.

Picking Up the Tab

The Gulf War was unusual in a few ways, but one of them was that the country that did most of the fighting, the United States, didn't pay for the war. In fact, it may even have come out slightly ahead on the deal. While building up the international coalition in the fall of 1990, the Americans were also busy passing the hat among their allies. U.S. Secretary of State James Baker went on a whirlwind "Tin Cup Diplomacy" trip around the world, winning pledges of financial support from wealthy allies like Germany and Japan. Not only did Saudi Arabia pledge the largest amount, but it also made arrangements with many of these countries to reimburse them indirectly for the money that they pledged. So in the end, though they did have a little help from Kuwait, the Saudis ended up pretty much picking up the tab for the war—to the tune of somewhere around $55 billion.

A Debt in the Family

Despite increased oil revenues as they took up the slack caused by the interruption of oil from Iraq, the Saudis were still bankrupted by the war. On top of that, their annual military budget—already one of the world's largest—rose even more in the years after the war, since they still felt threatened by Iraq (and to a lesser degree, Iran). So once again the Al Saud went into hock, running annual deficits in the neighborhood of $10 to $20 billion.

Arabian Almanac

One reason for the deficits of the 1990s was that the Saudi government continued, or in some cases even stepped up, its constant pumping of cash into the country's economy. There was a feeling that the people just wouldn't tolerate any lessening of their accustomed subsidies.

Looking on the bright side, however, one result was that in the early 1990s the Saudi private sector enjoyed a boom that in some ways surpassed even the halcyon years of the 1970s. Much of that economic strength came from the otherwise troublesome presence of the American military, which spent lavishly on goods and services.

Legacy of Discord

Now for the Gulf War's social and political consequences, which were dramatic and long-lasting. As I indicated at the beginning the chapter, the war sowed dissension and disunity right through the larger Arab world, as well as within Saudi Arabia itself. In this section, I'll summarize for you the Gulf War's legacy of discord in each of these arenas in turn.

A Wedge That Split the Arab World

As you've no doubt realized by now, the ideal of unity has always (at least in the modern era) been a very important emotional issue for the Arabs. In the past, no Arab politician or ruler could hope to survive for long without at least paying lip service to it. Saddam Hussein changed all that. While it still has great emotional appeal to Arabs, Arab unity no longer has pride of place in the public pronouncements of Arab leaders.

In this sense, the Gulf War was the last nail in the coffin of Arab nationalism. (You'll find background info on Arab nationalism in Chapter 7.) Instead of looking to some impossible-to-achieve ideal that transcended national borders, Arab leaders since the Gulf War have been more openly pushing the agendas and interests of their own states. One way of putting it is that after the Gulf War, Arab nationalism evolved into something more like just plain old-fashioned nationalism. Another way to put it is that Arab leaders have—very slowly and with great hesitation—started to become more pragmatic. In the long run, this may be the big hidden benefit to come from the Gulf War.

Mirage Ahead

Arab unity is not a dead issue. It's still got a huge emotional punch, as countless political speeches and newspaper articles in the Arab world easily show. What's changed is this: Arab leaders no longer feel bound to pretend that they're putting the interests of their own states second in order to pursue Arab unity. Upshot: Saddam Hussein strikes a blow for honesty in politics! Ironic, no?

Why did all this happen? It happened, basically, because the Gulf War drove a huge wedge into the Arab world that split it like a rotten log. Moreover, it did so *publicly*. Arab rulers have had their quarrels in the past, but they've always struggled to keep their disputes private. And just as Muslims are forbidden by the Koran from attacking Muslims, there was always an unwritten rule that no Arab state would attack another.

Arabian Almanac

Among the Gulf War's victims were approximately a million Yemeni "guest workers," who were booted out of their jobs and homes in Saudi Arabia in retaliation for Yemen's support of Saddam Hussein. Saudi Arabia also terminated all financial support for Yemen. Although Yemeni workers were later allowed to reenter Saudi Arabia, relations between the two neighbors remained strained.

By invading another Arab nation, Saddam forced the rest of the Arab world to choose sides. And he picked his victim well, since the wealthy and arrogant Kuwaitis were viewed as being well worth taking down a peg or two anyway.

How did it happen? The sharp end of the wedge was oil. Iraq's Arab supporters tended to be the poorer states that did not have a lot of oil, but did have a lot of poor people who resented the oil states' wealth. For example, the Northern African Arab states of Algeria, Morocco, and Tunisia sympathized with the Iraqi cause. Saudi Arabia's southern neighbor Yemen supported Iraq, too. (Although Yemen has some oil deposits, they didn't go online until 1986. As with Libya, another oil exporter that supported Iraq, Yemen's socialist history also came into play.)

Even though Iraq's oil reserves are greater than Kuwait's, Iraq has a far larger population and much lower per capita income. Kuwait's tiny population, in fact, had the world's highest per capita income, and flaunted it in everyone's face. So Saddam Hussein was able to play the role of oil underdog, pretending to be the champion of the poor and oppressed downtrodden masses.

Another part of the wedge was the Israeli-Palestinian conflict. It was no surprise that the Palestinians in general supported Iraq. But it sure surprised the Saudis and most other observers when PLO chairman Yasser Arafat publicly endorsed Saddam Hussein after the invasion of Kuwait. And when Saddam sent his Scud missiles flying, his two targets were Israel and Saudi Arabia—a novel combination to say the least. The Saudis found themselves, for the first time ever, feeling glimmers of sympathy for the Israelis and sparks of resentment towards the Palestinians. A further target of their surprised anger was Jordan. Swayed by Jordan's majority population of Palestinian refugees, Jordan's Hashemite King Hussein also supported Saddam Hussein (no relation) in the conflict.

For years, the Al Saud had generously supported these poorer Arab states, which tended to think of Saudi or Kuwaiti oil as belonging by rights to all Arabs. At the same time, ever since the Iranian Revolution of 1979, the Al Saud had been nervous that the United States might fail to help them in their hour of need, the way it had failed to protect the Shah. For the Al Saud, the big shock of the Gulf War was that it was their fellow Arabs, not the United States, who proved to be the unreliable friends.

Domestic Disturbances

On the domestic front, the most pressing problems arose from the sudden presence of thousands of American soldiers on Saudi soil. Just as oil was the wedge that split the larger Arab world over the Gulf War, so was the presence of numerous, highly visible, and heavily armed "infidels" the cause of growing unrest inside Saudi Arabia itself. For the first time, public criticism of the Al Saud by fundamentalist journalists and Wahhabi clerics became common. And it wasn't just criticism, but often bitter and stinging attacks on the ruling family's religious and political legitimacy. The royal family, and King Fahd in particular, was also pilloried as lackeys of the West.

Similar attacks had been made in the 1980s by Shiite fundamentalists in Iran, and by Saddam Hussein during the Gulf War. What was new was that now the Al Saud's Islamic credentials were being questioned at home. These new public reproaches were the most visible symptom of the stresses caused by the war—and, more specifically, by the presence of American soldiers in Saudi Arabia.

As the Americans had poured into the country, the Al Saud had done their best to keep them isolated from Saudi society. The soldiers were funneled straight into hastily erected tent cities in the desert. The Saudis tried to reproduce the system of segregation that had kept Western oil company employees and other workers safe in slapped-together desert housing compounds, largely cut off from outside contact. To minimize the impact on the devout population, for example, all army ambulances had to have their Red Crosses painted over. Chaplains were told to remove the crosses on their caps when leaving the bases, and soldiers had to conceal any crosses they wore under their clothing.

But these weren't Western workers, whom the Saudis could tell themselves were merely "servants." Instead, they represented the raw might of an obviously superior military power that the Saudis had called on to protect them. They were far more threatening than foreign workers, and could not be so easily reconciled with the Saudis' sense of honor. Their very presence seemed threatening and dishonorable to the Saudis and to Islam itself.

And most dangerous, most dishonorable, most heinously sacrilegious of all—there were women among them! Actual women soldiers, mixing freely and openly with the men and behaving like their equals! This was a bitter pill for Saudis to swallow. The American military brass—fearful of bad publicity in the U.S. media—dug in its heels when the Al Saud pushed to have female soldiers left at home. But the brass agreed that women soldiers would obey certain rules designed to prevent offending Saudi sensibilities. Hence, when off the bases, women were not allowed to appear in T-shirts, with their arms bare. Shorts were out of the question, nor could women jog when off the bases, or drive a car.

We're going to look more closely at Saudi social values in Part 3. But as you're probably already aware, when it comes to the role of women, people in traditional Islamic societies generally have very different attitudes from people in Western countries. In Saudi Arabia, the most conservative of all Islamic societies, the Gulf War made the role of women into a potent and divisive political issue. And for a while, tensions were at their highest over the question of women drivers.

In the West, if a man complains about women drivers, he's merely partaking of a hackneyed, sexist cliché. Not so in Saudi Arabia, where the same man might now be reporting a crime. Strict custom has always dictated that women weren't supposed to drive. During Desert Shield, some Saudi women were emboldened to demand their right to do so. However, the ulema reacted strongly against the demands. At the ulema's insistence, what had earlier been a custom was now, by royal decree, enacted into law. It became officially illegal for women to drive. And when 70 women took the wheel in a protest convoy to downtown Riyadh, they were, indeed, treated like criminals.

Desert Dates

November 6, 1990: At the height of Operation Desert Shield, 70 Saudi women drive their cars into central downtown Riyadh, in protest against the new law forbidding women to drive. In making their case, the women pointed to an Islamic precedent for women drivers: It was well known, they argued, that Ayesha, Muhammad's wife, rode her own camel. Despite strong support from moderates, in the resulting uproar the women were viciously denounced by the conservative Saudi press. Labeled "Communist whores" (a holdover from Cold-War-speak?), they were fired from their jobs and subjected to legal penalties.

Moderates and Fundamentalists

This whole business got a lot of publicity in the Western media, but that's only part of why I've focused on it here. I'm bringing it up now as an example of how the Gulf War sharpened the already-existing tensions between the moderates, who had long pushed for democratic reform and modernization, and the religious fundamentalists, who had resisted both as examples of corrupt, Western decadence. King Faisal had largely succeeded in maintaining a balance between the two sides, but the balance could only last so long. In the years since Faisal's reign, the moderates had edged ahead in public opinion, as the success of modernization added to their credibility.

CAUTION | **Mirage Ahead** _____

While it's helpful to use words like "moderates" and "fundamentalists" when talking about these issues, don't take these labels too seriously. I'll be examining the whole question of fundamentalism more closely in the next chapter. Until then, I'll ask you to keep in mind that such terms are not always precise.

Also, conflicting views can be held by the same people. Probably only a small proportion of the Saudi population has really strong views either way, say maybe 10 percent for the moderates and perhaps 15 percent for the extreme fundamentalists. Those are just guesses, so don't hold me to them. There's no way to poll a closed society like Saudi Arabia. But people everywhere are complicated creatures, and like most of us, Saudis seem to have contradictory feelings about things. For example, some talk about being both attracted and repelled by the "softness" of modern life and Western values. Similarly, they feel drawn by the certainty and reassurance offered by Wahhabism, yet sometimes impatient with its restrictiveness and narrow outlook.

But the women's defeat signaled the beginning of a shift in Saudi public opinion away from the moderates. Before the Gulf War, the moderates had the momentum, and the fundamentalists were on the defensive. After it, the fundamentalists began winning the upper hand, and their attacks worked to undermine the Al Saud's Islamic credibility. Since the middle of the 1990s the moderates have been mostly lying low in the face of the increasingly bitter—and ultimately violent—fundamentalist onslaught.

There were a lot of reasons for the shift, and most of them have to do with the war in various ways. But the biggest single factor was the Saudi public's allergic reaction to having thousands of infidel soldiers—especially women—present on Saudi soil. Speaking out against the Americans gave—and gives—the fundamentalists a strong and appealing platform. The moderates still exist, and from time to time they speak out. But since the fundamentalists, always louder and fiercer, have also become more numerous, the effect has been to raise the overall decibel level in what passes for Saudi Arabia's public discourse. Often the moderates simply get drowned out.

From Petitions to Bombs

As the women's protest suggests, the presence of the American troops initially encouraged both sides, moderates and fundamentalists, to become more vocal. At first, the moderates seemed to be holding their own, even gaining ground. It was only after a couple of years that it became clear that the fundamentalists were gaining an edge.

In part, the fundamentalists fought back by using techniques they had learned from the moderates. When the moderates pushed for liberal reforms, the fundamentalists pushed harder for conservative ones. Yet despite growing public support for the fundamentalists, the troops remained, and the government began jailing fundamentalist leaders. Soon some of the frustrated fundamentalists moved from demanding reform to calling for the overthrow of the Al Saud. And by the mid 1990s, a few had turned to terrorism.

Two Petitions

In February 1991, right in the middle of Desert Storm, a group of leading moderates presented King Fahd with a "Secular Petition" demanding democratic reforms. High on the list of their demands were a written constitution and the establishment of a *Majlis as-Shura*, or Consultative Council, that included members of the educated middle class.

Sheik-Speak

The institution of the **majlis** (council) is a traditional forum for interaction between Arab rulers and the public. Saudi monarchs and princes often hold a majlis as a way for the people to air grievances and be heard. An often casual audience at which Saudis address their king by first name, it's a major avenue by which the Al Saud keep in touch with the poor.

The fundamentalists quickly countered with a "Religious Petition" of their own, which Wahhabi critics of the government signed and presented to King Fahd in May 1991. The religious petition was designed to give the Wahhabis more control over the monarchy. It, too, called for a Majlis as-Shura, but the fundamentalist version was to be made up of members of the Wahhabi ulema. Its role, the petition suggested, would be to counteract the evil effects of Jews and Christians on the monarchy and the country as a whole, by making sure the king stuck to Wahhabi ideals in all his decisions. Implied in its rhetoric was the accusation that the main evil influence was coming from the presence of infidel soldiers.

Two Clergies

In addition to the two petitions of early 1991, there was another complication to the Saudi domestic picture as it emerged after the Gulf War. Before the war, the ulema had been pretty much united behind the Al Saud. At least in public, the regime enjoyed the general support of a basically unified Islamic clergy, although private scoldings were not unknown. Now, however, for the first time, the fundamentalists' attacks on King Fahd and the Al Saud created a growing rift within the Saudi religious establishment.

Arabian Almanac

In propping up their shaky religious legitimacy, the Al Saud relied heavily on a highly respected Wahhabi cleric, Sheik Abdel Aziz bin Baz. In 1993 they revived the old religious office of Grand Mufti, appointing bin Baz to the position. Until his death in 1999, bin Baz was the leading member of the "official" ulema, which attempted to defend the Al Saud's religious credentials. One reason for his effectiveness was his obvious independence, which gave his opinions great credibility with the public. For example, he had approved the 1991 Religious Petition calling for Wahhabi reforms.

In effect, the presence of the American soldiers split the ulema into two opposing groups. On the one hand, an "official" clergy echoed the Al Saud line with religious arguments that sought to justify the troop presence. On the other hand, an increasingly outspoken "popular" clergy criticized both the infidels' presence and the Al Saud with growing harshness. It was these fundamentalist views that jibed with public opinion, which more and more saw the "official" ulema as puppets of a corrupt, decadent, Western-dominated royal family.

The fundamentalists not only constantly preached their message in the mosques, the traditional forum for reaching the public. They also began taping their fiery speeches, which their followers then distributed on cassette tapes among the public. (Similar cassettes had been extraordinarily effective in helping the Ayatollah Khomeini topple the Shah in the Iranian Revolution of 1979.) By 1993, they had even begun organizing mass demonstrations, which before the Gulf War had been nearly unheard of in this tightly controlled society.

Two Bombs

Eventually, the government responded to the fundamentalists' agitation by turning to repressive measures. In September 1993, several hundred fundamentalist demonstrators were arrested in Buraidah, in central Saudi Arabia, along with their leaders, Salman al Auda and Safar al Hawali. The following year, a fundamentalist was publicly beheaded (Saudi Arabia's standard form of capital punishment) for allegedly assaulting a policeman.

The fundamentalists' answer was not long in coming. On November 13, 1995, a bomb exploded at a U.S. military training facility in Riyadh, killing 7 people (including 5 Americans) and injuring around 60. In April of the following year, the Saudi government announced the arrest of four Saudis in connection with the blast, and in May it declared that the men had been beheaded.

Then, on June 25, a much larger explosion rocked the American air base at Khobar, near Dhahran. This blast, caused by a truck bomb, killed 19 American servicemen and wounded nearly 400 Americans, Saudis, and others. It left a crater over 30 feet deep and blew out windows almost a mile away. The Khobar bomb was widely assumed to be in retaliation for the execution of the four Saudis in May.

Praise the Lord, and Pass the Admonition

I've just given a rough outline of the progression from petitions to bombs that reflects the fundamentalists' activities inside Saudi Arabia in the first half of the 1990s. Now that you have the basic outline, let's look at a few of the specific demands that the fundamentalists were making. A good way to do that is to focus on a second document that they presented to King Fahd, one that sums up their grievances nicely.

After receiving the two petitions for reform, King Fahd responded by finally establishing the long-awaited Majlis as-Shura, or Consultative Council, in 1992. But the king's choices of men to serve on the council pleased the moderates more than the fundamentalists. Over two thirds of the men were educated in the West, for example, mostly in American universities.

The fundamentalists reacted to this disappointment in September 1992, by producing a "memorandum of admonition." Like the petitions, the "admonition" falls firmly within Arabic tradition. It's a customary way for the ulema to warn a ruler that he is departing from Islamic principles. In addition to the issue of American troops on Saudi soil, the admonition listed the other grievances that the fundamentalists had against the Al Saud.

Here's a summary of the admonition's main points:

- The Al Saud should end their alliance with the United States, because of U.S. support for Israel.

- All relations with non-Muslim countries should be terminated immediately.

- Saudi Arabia should begin mandatory conscription for all Saudi citizens in order to beef up the army, so that the American troops would no longer be needed. (Believe it or not, with a straight face the authors cited the example of Israel's universal conscription as a model. Fundamentalists are not known for their sense of irony.)

- All laws and regulations should be brought into strict conformance with Islamic principles. (The major objection here was to the charging of interest by Saudi banks, which goes against the commands of the Koran.)

- Above all, the ulema should be given a larger, more powerful, and more independent role in the government.

"Legitimate Rights"

The Al Saud and the official ulema condemned the admonition, but it was clear that they were shaken by it. Encouraged, in May 1993 some of the admonition's signers established an organization known in English as the Committee for the Defense of Legitimate Rights. Its aim was to promote the Saudi fundamentalists' agenda not only within Saudi Arabia, but also in the outside world, and it did so by cleverly adopting the rhetoric of secular human rights prevalent in the West.

Western media reported approvingly on the committee's activities, not fully realizing that "legitimate" rights meant only those rights allowed by Wahhabi doctrine—not anything Western secular values would recognize as human rights at all. When the authorities threw the committee members in jail, human rights organizations like Amnesty International took up their cause. The publicity forced the release of the committee's Western-education spokesman, Muhammad Masari, who went into exile in London, where he revived the committee in 1994.

For the next two years, Masari mounted a highly publicized media campaign against the Saudi government from London, opening a website and sending out a steady stream of faxed press releases. Though Masari's campaign received much attention in the Western media, he lacked credibility in the Arab world. The committee's real effectiveness had been limited to the brief period in Saudi Arabia before the government clampdown.

The Upshot ...

As government repression stifled the Saudi fundamentalists' political efforts in the first half of the 1990s, some of them turned to terrorism to achieve their goal. At the same time, for some of the more extreme fundamentalists the goal itself shifted from reforming the Al Saud to overthrowing them completely. Like Masari, some of these would-be revolutionaries operated from outside Saudi Arabia, where they could avoid both censorship and imprisonment. As you'll see shortly, there was a global community of Islamic fundamentalists waiting to welcome them, and Saudi expatriates were already a big part of it.

The bombings of 1995 and 1996 helped transfer Western media attention away from Masari, towards another exiled fundamentalist critic of the royal family. This shadowy figure had been calling for the overthrow of the Al Saud since 1992.

His name was Osama bin Laden.

The Least You Need to Know

- The Gulf War drove a wedge deep into the Arab world and undermined the Al Saud's religious credentials at home.

- The presence of American troops in Saudi Arabia during and after the war offered Saudi fundamentalists a rallying point against the Al Saud and the United States.

- Before the Gulf War, the moderates had the edge in Saudi public opinion, but after it the Wahhabi extremists pulled ahead.

- Having failed to get the government to expel American troops by the mid 1990s, the extremists within Saudi Arabia began turning to terrorism against U.S. targets.

Chapter 10

The Fundamentals of Fundamentalism

In This Chapter

◆ A brief history of Islamic fundamentalism

◆ The Soviet Union gets spanked in Afghanistan

◆ The Saudis export fundamentalism in the 1990s

◆ Osama bin Laden and the rise of al Qaeda

I began Part 2 with a "big picture" chapter on oil and global politics, before moving on to look more closely at the Gulf War and its impact. Having tightened the focus, I'd now like to pull back again to another "big picture" theme, which will finish off this "Recent History" part of the book.

In this chapter, I'll give you a crash course on fundamentalism, which—like oil—has played a decisive part in shaping both global and Saudi history in the modern age. There are a lot of questions to ask about Islamic fundamentalism, and I'll be asking them and offering some answers as we go. One question, however, remains the most important one for the future of Saudi Arabia. It's the question I asked you to keep in mind earlier, when I challenged King Faisal's approach to modernizing his country. Is it possible to have "modernization without secularization," as Faisal assumed?

In the end, this is really a question about fundamentalism. My overall goal in this chapter will be not only to give you my answer, but also to help you arrive at an answer of your own. Your answer may agree with mine, or it may not. But in the end, your answer to this question will determine what you think about Saudi Arabia's future.

What Is Fundamentalism?

The word "fundamentalist" was first used in the 1920s, to describe a movement among American Protestants that arose in response to what they saw as the evils of the modern age. Secularism, religious skepticism, the growing influence of scientific ideas like evolution, and the frivolity of the Jazz Age were only part of what these religious activists objected to. Even more disturbing to them were the accommodations that liberal church leaders had begun making to some of the modern developments.

Sheik-Speak

There has been a lot of academic hair-splitting over terminology, but in the end **fundamentalism** is the label that most observers have settled on to describe the phenomenon, which cuts across all world faiths. Islamic fundamentalists are also commonly called "Islamists." The word "extremists" is generally (but not always) reserved for those fundamentalists who endorse violence in pushing their cause.

Rejecting such concessions to modernity, these religious activists sought a return to the "fundamentals" of their faith. For example, where religious liberals suggested that many parts of the Bible could be read allegorically, fundamentalists insisted on a strict literal reading, with no room for any interpretation at all. They painted a simple, black-and-white picture, one that offered attractive certainties in a time when the growth of secular rationalism increasingly seemed to call everything into doubt.

Since then, historians have observed similar movements in all the other major world faiths, and the word *fundamentalism* has been applied to them as well. In addition to the Christians and Muslims, the Jews, Hindus, Buddhists, Sikhs, Jains, and Confucians also have various fundamentalist strains.

So what is fundamentalism? Experts identify the following eight main points that most fundamentalist groups have in common:

◆ Fundamentalism reflects a group's attempt to preserve a religious identity that the group feels is under threat. In other words, fundamentalism is essentially *defensive*.

◆ However, to defend their identity, fundamentalists also fight back aggressively, in some cases even violently, and they don't compromise. So fundamentalism is also *offensive*—you could say that fundamentalists live by the old saying that the best defense is a good offense.

◆ Fundamentalists follow *a strict, rigorous code* that sets them apart from non-believers, including non-fundamentalist members of their own faith.

◆ Though they reject modern values, fundamentalists *adopt certain aspects of modernity* that they find useful in putting out their message.

◆ Fundamentalists reach back into an idealized "golden age" to *retrieve* parts of their tradition that they hold up as the purest and most faithful to the original message. Often this means a strict, literal interpretation of sacred texts.

◆ When they reach back into the past, fundamentalists *select* the parts of the texts and traditions that suit them in the here-and-now. They don't take everything available, only the elements that they like, ignoring the rest or dismissing it as inauthentic.

◆ When fundamentalists select the parts of the original message to embrace, they do so in order to further a *militant contemporary agenda*. So while fundamentalism appears to be about the past, it's really more about the present, and especially the future.

◆ Finally, with their eyes on the future, fundamentalists want to *reshape society* to reflect their own religious values.

Are the Wahhabis Fundamentalists?

The experts disagree on whether the Wahhabis qualify as fundamentalists. However, most would accept that the Wahhabis fit the requirements I just outlined. The four-volume academic monsterpiece called *The Fundamentalism Project*, published by the University of Chicago Press in the early 1990s and edited by Martin E. Marty and R. Scott Appleby, is now the standard scholarly work on the subject. Among its zillions of articles by many scholars on fundamentalist groups around the world, there's not a single article on the Wahhabis. At the same time, however, the Wahhabis are mentioned prominently as the inspiration for Islamic fundamentalist groups from Nigeria to Pakistan. The Wahhabis offer a model for these groups, as well as a major source of religious instruction and financial support.

The problem is that these scholars consider fundamentalism only as a strictly recent phenomenon that arose in the twentieth century, while the Wahhabis (as you know by now) have been around since the middle of the eighteenth. Yet that seems to me like a poor reason to count them out, when they meet the other requirements. The movement's founder, Muhammad Abdel Wahhab, traveled widely as a young man, and was clearly reacting to religious trends in the Ottoman empire that he saw as decadent, corrupt, and threatening. And hostility to the modern has always been a mainstay of the Wahhabis. At the same time, they've been quite happy to use modern tools like rifles (and more recently cassette tapes or the Internet) to achieve their goals, which definitely include reshaping society to conform to their puritanical ideals.

> ⚠️ **CAUTION**
>
> ## Mirage Ahead _____
>
> If you want to insist, like some, that fundamentalism only arose in the twentieth century, then I would argue that Wahhabism might be described as a sort of prototype. Personally, though, I think that's a little too complicated. To me, as to many other writers on the subject, Wahhabism smacks of fundamentalism from the get-go, and arbitrary time boundaries don't carry much water. What's important to me is the message, not the century. But you'll have to make up your own mind.

The Arabs' Sense of Failure

Fundamentalism may be primarily a religious phenomenon, but because fundamentalists pursue militant agendas in the world of the here-and-now, it has a political dimension, too. So having looked at fundamentalism in the abstract, now let's get down to the nuts and bolts.

And here we get into what seems to me like the best reason to set Wahhabism apart from other, later versions of Islamic fundamentalism. The later versions arose in reaction to a legacy of Western political and cultural dominance, but not Wahhabism. Wahhabism arose in the Najd, which was virtually the only part of the Arab world that did not come under European control during the colonial period. But this doesn't mean that the Wahhabis aren't fundamentalists. It just means their brand of fundamentalism initially arose under different conditions.

From North Africa to Pakistan and Afghanistan, the later versions of Islamic fundamentalism were born out of Muslims' sense of political failure and powerlessness against the West. This sense of failure was especially strong in the Arab world. But already there was another reaction against that sense of failure among the Arabs and other Muslims. The fundamentalists would have to wait until it had run its course before they would come to the fore.

The Decline of Secular Nationalism

That earlier movement was secular nationalism, which you're already familiar with from Chapter 7. It dominated the Arab and Muslim worlds in the 1950s and 1960s.

But at the same time, Islamic fundamentalism was taking shape underneath it. Like nationalism, fundamentalism reacted against the West. But it also reacted against the harsh and aggressive secularism of the nationalists themselves, especially that of Gamal Abdel Nasser in Egypt. Where Nasser and other nationalists blamed Islam for many of Muslims' problems, the fundamentalists instead saw Islam as a way out of those problems.

Islamic Fundamentalism's Three Founding Fathers

By the mid 1960s, three leading voices were taking a newly combative line against the rampant secularism of the nationalists. These three men were modern Islamic fundamentalism's "founding fathers." They were …

- ◆ **Abdul Ala Mawdudi** (1903–1979). A Pakistani Muslim, Mawdudi insisted that God alone should govern human behavior, and governments should be in accordance with the Koran and the Traditions of the Prophet (the Hadith). He was among the first to declare that jihad (holy war) is a central obligation of all Muslims, and to define it as an armed struggle to seize political power from non-Muslims. Considered a precursor to full-scale Islamic fundamentalism, Mawdudi founded the influential Pakistani Islamic group Jammaat i Islami in 1941.

- ◆ **Sayyid Qutb** (1906–1966). An Egyptian, Qutb was heavily influenced by Mawdudi, whose writings were widely read in Egypt in the early 1950s. He was also influenced by fellow Egyptian Hasan al Banna, who had founded another leading Islamic group, the Muslim Brotherhood, in Cairo in 1928. Qutb joined the Muslim Brotherhood in 1953, and along with many other members he was imprisoned and tortured during Nasser's offensive against the Brotherhood. Qutb took Mawdudi's ideas a step further, declaring that even Muslim rulers should be overthrown by jihad if they go against Islamic ideals. Released from prison in 1964, he was rearrested and executed by Nasser's government in 1966. But his ideas were taken up by a growing following in the 1970s, and Qutb is now considered the true founder of the Sunni branch of Islamic fundamentalism.

- ◆ **Ayatollah Ruhollah Khomeini** (1900–1989). You've already met this Iranian cleric in Chapter 7, where I covered the Iranian Revolution that he led against the Shah in 1979. But Khomeini was active against the Shah as early as 1963, when he came out in public against the Shah's secular regime. Khomeini was arrested repeatedly by the Shah in 1963 and 1964. Between jail terms he led mass demonstrations in Tehran and elsewhere, in which the Shah's secret police killed hundreds of demonstrators. While Qutb founded Sunni fundamentalism, Khomeini founded its Shiite counterpart. Shiite fundamentalism put more emphasis on social justice, which would eventually seep into the Sunni version prevalent in the Arab world.

The fundamentalists had the worst of it during the heyday of secular nationalism, but the nationalists' days were numbered. With Nasser's humiliation by Israel in the Six-Day War of 1967, secular nationalism began to decline. By the 1970s, many Muslims—Arabs and non-Arabs alike—were seeking another option. During those two decades, the Muslim Brotherhood had lain dormant, shattered by Nasser's oppression and well outside the mainstream of Arab public opinion. By the mid 1970s it had slowly re-grouped, becoming a flexible and international organization, revitalized by Qutb's fundamentalist ideology.

Arabian Almanac

Since the nineteenth century, many Muslim thinkers had called for modernizing Islam, suggesting various ways of adapting its traditionally flexible institutions to meet the requirements of the modern age. But these earlier figures can best be described as Islamic liberals, conservatives, or traditionalists. They generally sought accommodation and were willing to compromise. The true fundamentalist, by contrast, will only be satisfied with absolute victory.

Qutb predicted the failure of secular nationalism and offered fundamentalist Islam as an alternative. In his vision, the whole Muslim world should be a single nation, ruled under God, with the Koran as its constitution. The most revolutionary claim Qutb made was that jihad was permissible, even mandatory, against fellow Muslims who opposed the true faith—which (according to him) was embodied in this vision. That same claim would be taken up decades later against the Al Saud. It would be made by, among others, Qutb's most influential follower, Osama bin Laden, who studied under Qutb's brother Muhammad as a young man.

Desert Dates

October 6, 1981: Egypt's President Anwar Sadat is assassinated by a then little-known extremist group called Islamic Jihad. Sadat had angered the fundamentalists by making peace with Israel (see Chapter 7). Among the group's members arrested afterward was Ayman al Zawahiri, who was sentenced to three years in prison. Zawahiri would later serve as Osama bin Laden's close associate in Afghanistan, and one of al Qaeda's highest-ranking leaders. He was instrumental in helping Osama bin Laden transform the organization from a regional guerrilla group into a global terrorist network.

The Islamic Alternative

To most observers, secularism seemed invulnerable in the early 1970s. Religion, it was thought, had been kicked out of politics in the nineteenth century, and the triumph of secularism around the world seemed permanent. Nationalism might be on the wane, but no one took religious fundamentalism very seriously as a potential replacement for it. For many critics in both the Islamic and Western worlds, the Islamic fundamentalists seemed even more fascistic and totalitarian than the nationalists.

Yet fundamentalism was about to enjoy a major resurgence, both in the Islamic world and elsewhere. Islamic fundamentalism's biggest victory was the Iranian Revolution of 1979, when the fundamentalist dream of a radical Islamic state came into being. Throughout the 1980s, the Iranians tried to export their fundamentalist revolution to other Muslim countries. Iranian-backed terrorists, the Hezbollah or Party of God, wreaked havoc in Lebanon, during that country's bloody civil war. Islamic fundamentalism also seeped into the Arab-Israeli conflict, as fundamentalist rhetoric took over the PLO, which had earlier embraced the ideology of secular Arab nationalism.

> **Arabian Almanac**
>
> In the 1970s and 1980s, fundamentalism experienced its greatest period of world growth, not just among Muslims, but also among Christians, Jews, and others. One example is the rise of Christian fundamentalists to new prominence on the American political scene. Most powerful was the Reverend Jerry Falwell's "Moral Majority," which dominated conservative Republican politics in the Reagan era (1980–1988) and after.

Fundamentalism's Appeal

As a result of the Shiite-led Iranian Revolution, the social justice element entered Sunni fundamentalist rhetoric, too. Eventually, Islamic fundamentalism replaced the failed secular nationalism as an ideological rallying cry for the poor and oppressed Arab masses. Yet it also appealed to pious professionals in the middle classes, who had grown frustrated with the corruption of the authoritarian Arab governments. For all classes, fundamentalism had the advantage of feeling indigenous, native, authentic—in other words, not a Western import tricked up in Arab garb, which was how secular nationalism now appeared to many.

The pervasive sense of failure that had gripped the Arab world for decades had briefly lightened during the brief moment when Nasser looked like a hero. Then it came crashing back down, as the hero turned out to have clay feet. In its place, Islamic fundamentalism renewed the promise of reclaiming the strength and unity the Arabs had possessed when Islam was young and pure, and they were its brave and invincible conquerors. To the Arabs, that's the allure of Islamic fundamentalism in a nutshell. They're a people haunted by an idealized picture of past greatness, and desperately hungry to recapture it. If secular nationalism didn't help them do that, they hoped, maybe a return to religious "fundamentals" would.

Let's Make a Deal

As the Iranians tried to export their revolution in the 1980s, it fell to the Saudis to try to neutralize those attempts. In the end, the Iranian attempts to export the fundamentalist revolution failed. With a couple of temporary exceptions, no other Islamic states were established (the exceptions being Sudan and Afghanistan, which we'll get to in a moment). But virtually every Muslim country was forced to make concessions to its own fundamentalists, in order to stave off their anger. The concessions were meant to placate the pious middle classes, and so divide them from the radicalized poor. Otherwise, it was feared that these two classes would unite and overturn the governments.

Desert Dates

November 20, 1979: Apparently inspired by Iran's seizure of American hostages, some 500 armed Sunni extremists seize and occupy the Grand Mosque in Mecca, which holds the Kaaba, Islam's holiest shrine. Only after a tense standoff of several weeks and a bloody battle is the Saudi government able to regain control of the mosque complex. (The captured extremists are later beheaded.)

At the same time, Shiites in Saudi Arabia's Eastern Province riot and demonstrate against the government repeatedly, many of them holding posters of Ayatollah Khomeini. Several demonstrators are killed after 20,000 National Guard troops are called in to quell the disturbances. Both the occupation of the Grand Mosque and the Shiite riots are a major embarrassment for the Al Saud. They offer an early warning that religious extremism is very much alive and well in the kingdom.

The losers in these concessions were the advocates of secularism: writers, journalists, professors, and other Westernized intellectuals, who now lost the support of governments eager to placate the fundamentalists' anger. The concessions to the fundamentalists that I'm talking about covered a broad range. Commonly, a liberal journalist or professor might be fired for advocating secularism too loudly, for example, while fundamentalist rhetoric was tolerated or openly applauded. In addition, laws were passed in some countries conceding authority over sensitive areas like education to fundamentalists, and government funding could also be stepped up for fundamentalist groups. (All of these examples applied to Saudi Arabia, as you'll see amply demonstrated in the chapters ahead.) As a result of such measures, secularism became increasingly absent from public discourse in most Arab countries.

Nowhere was this more extreme than in Saudi Arabia, where the Al Saud and the Wahhabi clerics struck a deal. The clerics could attack the West to their heart's content, and counter Iranian fundamentalism by funding Wahhabi mosques and schools abroad. In exchange for being allowed to run roughshod over the West and export their own brand of fundamentalism, the Wahhabi clerics agreed not to attack the Al Saud at home. As you saw in the last chapter, both sides stuck to the deal—until the Gulf War changed the balance of power, and the more extreme Wahhabis began to openly denounce the Al Saud.

Cold War Flashback: Afghanistan in the 1980s

Only one thing kept the deal between the Wahhabis and Al Saud alive in the 1980s: Afghanistan. The Soviet invasion of Afghanistan in December 1979 turned out to be the answer to a lot of prayers. It had something for everyone—everyone except the Soviets and the Afghan people, that is.

For the Americans, the Soviet invasion of Afghanistan held out a hope that now the Communists would suffer their own Vietnam, the punishing "quagmire" of an unwinable war in a foreign land. America's humiliation in Vietnam was still an overpowering memory. If the Soviets could be trapped in a similar situation, it might mean the end of their "evil empire" and an American victory in the Cold War. Indeed, that's the way it turned out, but apparently it didn't occur to anyone that what might follow the Cold War could be even worse.

For the Al Saud, Afghanistan was a chance to distract the Wahhabis and other fundamentalists from the Saudis' alliance with the "Great Satan," the United States. For a decade, the Al Saud watched with a huge sigh of relief as the fundamentalists' rage was directed against the Soviets and their puppet Communist government in Kabul, the Afghan capital.

And for the fundamentalists themselves, Afghanistan offered a unifying cause, an outlet for their zeal and anger, and a focus for worldwide jihad. For the moment at least, even the Israeli-Palestinian conflict was overshadowed by the struggle in Afghanistan, a signal of how fundamentalism had replaced nationalism as the Muslim world's mass motivator. The conflict's religious overtones were sharpened by the Communists' official atheism, and in response to the threat devout young men from all around the Islamic world came to fight alongside the Afghan *mujahidin*, or holy warriors.

Sheik-Speak

The original **mujahidin** were the tough Afghan tribal warriors who fought the Soviets. Some experts still prefer to limit the definition to Afghans. Others include the "Afghan Arabs" and other foreign fighters among the mujahidin. Since the word itself simply means "those who fight a jihad" in Arabic, I'll use it in this book to include both the Afghan and the non-Afghan fighters.

Osama bin Laden and the "Afghan Arabs"

Among the tens of thousands of young Muslim men who came to join the jihad in Afghanistan in the 1980s were thousands of Arabs, many of them from Saudi Arabia. Their jumping-off point was the city of Peshawar in northern Pakistan, near the Afghan border. At first they were totally disorganized, much like the Afghan mujahidin they were going to help. But they had the support of the Saudi government, especially in the person of Prince Turki al Faisal, son of the late King Faisal and the head of Saudi intelligence. To help recruit and organize these "Afghan Arabs," Prince Turki chose Osama bin Laden, the idealistic young son of a well-known Saudi construction billionaire. Already a millionaire businessman in his own right, bin Laden added his own funds to the hundreds of millions of dollars that would eventually be made available to the cause by various Arab governments and by the CIA.

Bin Laden set up an office in Peshawar, which in those days teemed with agents of the KGB, the CIA, and various other intelligence agencies. At first he focused on creating support systems for the thousands of Afghan refugees in and around Peshawar, building schools, mosques, housing, and clinics. Soon, however, he was entering Afghanistan under cover, bringing arms and recruits over the border, setting up training camps, and helping dig a network of tunnels and forts that the fighters could use to attack the Soviet troops. Various reports also have him fighting in bloody hand-to-hand combat himself on several occasions in the mid 1980s.

Hostile Takeover

In 1984 bin Laden hooked up with a Palestinian named Abdullah Azzam, a former member of the Muslim Brotherhood who had studied in Eqypt and Saudi Arabia, and who also had an Afghan jihad operation running out of Peshawar. The two joined forces, with the younger bin Laden working as Azzam's deputy. Together they established the Afghan Service Bureau, which became the main organization under which they continued recruiting, training, and arming the young Arabs and other Muslim warriors. The Afghan Service Bureau, whose Arabic initials are MAK, is the group that eventually morphed into al Qaeda.

MAK played an enormous role in the mujahidin victory in Afghanistan. According to some sources, however, as that victory was drawing near in the late 1980s, a split developed between Azzam and bin Laden. Both agreed that the next step after victory over the Soviets should be to turn their attention worldwide, to other areas where Muslims were being oppressed. But Azzam wished to keep al Qaeda a guerrilla force, targeting enemy soldiers but avoiding civilian deaths. Bin Laden wanted instead to turn it into a global terrorist network, targeting the West, especially the United States, and including civilians among its victims.

Arabian Almanac

We've now come nearly full circle, having approached the watershed era of the Persian Gulf War from the perspective of the Islamic fundamentalist movement outside Saudi Arabia. At the same time, don't forget the other big conflict that was going on at the same time as the Afghan jihad: the Iran-Iraq War of 1980–1988 (discussed in Chapter 7).

How do these two big wars of the 1980s fit in with the Persian Gulf War and the 1990s? Taking all you've learned over the last few chapters, one way to think of it is as follows. The end of the Iran-Iraq War helped provoke the Persian Gulf War, by setting up Iraq's invasion of Kuwait. At the same time, the end of the Afghan jihad helped set up the fundamentalists' *reaction* to the Persian Gulf War, by offering up timely new targets for their jihadist rage. Those targets, of course, were the United States and the Al Saud. Thus did the events of the 1980s evolve into those of the 1990s.

Tattered and demoralized by the mujahidin, the Soviet Union withdrew its troops from Afghanistan in February 1989. Seven months later, in November, Azzam and his two sons were killed when their car exploded as they were driving to Friday prayers in Peshawar. Informed sources have claimed that bin Laden carried out the attack, though he's never publicly acknowledged it. But one thing is certain. Soon afterward, al Qaeda emerged as the world's first truly global terror network, with Osama bin Laden at its head. And as I described in the previous chapter, the Gulf War and the presence of U.S. troops in Saudi Arabia made the United States and the Al Saud into the new al Qaeda's primary targets.

The Saudis and Islamic Fundamentalism in the 1990s

I also described the way that the Gulf War shattered old alliances, both in the Arab world at large and within Saudi Arabia itself. By the early 1990s, you'll recall, the deal between the fundamentalists and the Al Saud had broken down, and by the mid 1990s Saudi extremists had turned to terrorism against the U.S. presence in the kingdom. Indeed, al Qaeda had extensive networks within Saudi Arabia, though the Al Saud continued to deny it, and though Osama bin Laden himself left Saudi Arabia for exile in the Islamic fundamentalist state of Sudan in 1991. Shortly afterward, he began calling for the overthrow of the Al Saud, and the explosions in Riyadh and Khobar have been credibly attributed to al Qaeda.

Yet despite being targeted by bin Laden and al Qaeda, the Al Saud continued to support fundamentalist movements abroad over the next decade, up to and beyond September 11, 2001. So, of course, did the Wahhabis, and so did al Qaeda. Here's a breakdown of where and how Saudis supported Islamic fundamentalist movements around the world in the 1990s:

- **Africa.** The Al Saud and the official Wahhabi ulema support Islamist movements in northern Nigeria and elsewhere. Meanwhile, the radical Islamist government of Sudan opposes the Al Saud. Sudan hosts bin Laden, al Qaeda, and other former fighters from Afghanistan. From their bases in Sudan, the former mujahidin take part in the massacre of 18 U.S. Marines in Mogadishu in October 1993. Sudan is forced by Western pressure to expel bin Laden in 1996.

- **The Balkans.** Official and unofficial Saudi aid to the Bosnian Muslims fails to create a fundamentalist groundswell there during their conflict with the Christian Serbs in the mid 1990s.

- **Western Europe.** Official and unofficial Saudi aid to mosques, schools, and other Islamic institutions radicalizes growing numbers of alienated young Muslim immigrants. By the late 1990s, Europe is proving a rich recruiting ground for al Qaeda (more on this in Chapter 17).

- **Chechnya.** Official and unofficial Saudi aid to Chechnya's Muslim rebels aids their ongoing effort to win independence from Russia. This bloody conflict in Central Asia becomes a new theatre of jihad for al Qaeda.

- **The Philippines.** Al Qaeda's assistance to Muslim rebels makes this Pacific island state a major new venue for jihad as well.

- **Pakistan and Afghanistan.** Here's where al Qaeda and Al Saud interests converge most closely. Official and unofficial Saudi aid goes to extremist mosques and schools throughout Pakistan in the 1990s. In addition, both Pakistan and Saudi Arabia are major supporters of the Taliban, the fundamentalists who come to power in Afghanistan in 1996. The Taliban welcome bin Laden and al Qaeda back to Afghanistan after bin Laden's expulsion from Sudan, also in 1996 (more on all this in Chapter 18).

The Last Word: "Modernization Without Secularization"?

Remember how I promised to come back to King Faisal's goal of "modernization without secularization," and to explain why I don't think it's truly possible?

It's not possible because, in a very real sense, modernization *is* secularization. Fundamentalism, the allergic religious reaction to modern values, is a reaction above all to the modern value of secularism. Thus, Sayyid Qutb identified the United States as the great enemy not because he thought it was decadent or corrupt, but because the

U.S. system is based on separation of church and state. Modern societies like America are modern because they're secular, and their prosperity and progress come directly from the tolerance, freedom, and democratic institutions that secularism helps promote. Not, I hasten to add, the harsh and aggressive secularism of the Arab nationalists. Allied with their police states, that false secularism attempted to crush religion, rather than to simply and amicably detach it from government and law. There's a crucial difference, but unfortunately the Arab nationalists gave secularism a bad name in the Arab world.

Put me down as a fan of secularism—and of religion. But not of fundamentalism. There are some critics who argue that Islam is by nature fundamentalist. They have a point: Islam does traditionally assume a bigger place in running society than other religions. Yet the millions of devout Muslims who are fine citizens of secular states (including the United States) prove these critics wrong. With some sadness, I predict that the Saudis' problems will worsen until they take at least some steps to limit Islam's role in their governmental and legal systems. I doubt they'll do that anytime soon, though. So my outlook for Saudi Arabia isn't rosy, but I'd sure love to be wrong.

The Least You Need to Know

- Fundamentalism occurs in every major world faith.

- In the 1970s, Islamic fundamentalism replaced Arab nationalism as the main rallying point for the Arab masses.

- The Soviet invasion of Afghanistan in 1979 gave the Islamic fundamentalists a "great cause" to fight for.

- After helping the Afghan jihad achieve victory, al Qaeda became a global terror network under Osama bin Laden.

- Al Qaeda's new enemy became the United States and the Al Saud.

Part 3

Who Are the Saudis? A Closer Look at Saudi Culture Today

Whew! Finally! All that history out of the way! Now for something a little lighter and a little more, well, "now." In this section of the book, I'll give you the "snapshot" of Saudi Arabia's land, people, and culture today that I've been promising. You'll soon find, however, that little of it would make any sense without the knowledge you've picked up about Saudi history. You'll also see that the past has a way of coming back to life for people in this highly conservative, traditional culture.

So in this section, as we look at Saudi Arabia in the present, you'll continue to feel strong traces of the past. Our "snapshot" is really more like a painting, one in which an old masterpiece has been thinly painted over with a new image by a lesser artist. The new layer of paint is too thin, and the previous picture clearly shows through the veneer, giving a ghostly image. When it comes to Saudi Arabia, the past always shows through—one way or another.

Chapter 11

Myths and Realities

In This Chapter

- ◆ Discover Saudi Arabia's unique landscape
- ◆ Sift fact from fiction in the lore of Arabia
- ◆ Explore the Arabian desert by camel
- ◆ Glimpse the vanishing life of the desert Bedouin

Cultural myths can be revealing, both the ones we create about ourselves, as well as the ones others create about us. They're a good place to start if you want to get a handle on what makes people tick. But myths are made up. They tell you more about wishes and perceptions than they do about hard facts. So to get a more complete picture, you need to balance the myths with a dose of reality.

In this chapter, I'll introduce you to Saudi culture by looking at the myths it holds dear, and asking how they relate to reality. We'll take a brief jaunt through the Arabian desert, and then examine how images of desert romance have been spread in the West. Finally, we'll ask how the Saudis see themselves and how they see others—as well as how others see them.

Geography 101: Saudi Arabia's Land and People

First, we'll take a moment for some basic geography. After all, the country's mostly arid, desert landscape lies at the heart of both the myths and the realities of life in Saudi Arabia.

Occupying 80 percent of the Arabian peninsula, Saudi Arabia is physically the biggest country in the Middle East, though many other Arab countries have larger populations. Saudi Arabia's total area is estimated to be some 900,000 square miles—about one quarter the size of the United States. I say "estimated," because there's no exact figure. The neutral zones the kingdom shared with Kuwait and Iraq were abolished by treaties in 1966 and 1975 respectively, and their lands divided both ways. But those neutral zones weren't the kingdom's only fuzzy borders. Apart from Saudi Arabia's northern borders with Jordan, Iraq, and Kuwait, only the very short border with Qatar and a small stretch of the border with Yemen have been precisely fixed. The rest of the kingdom's borders—that is, those along most of its southern stretches—are only approximate, as shown on the following map.

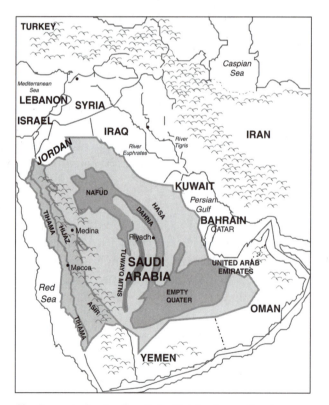

Here's a map showing Saudi Arabia's borders and major geographical features.

Arabian Almanac _____

With only about 15 to 20 million people (accurate figures aren't available), Saudi Arabia has a small population for its size—though that population is growing fast, at nearly 4 percent a year. This rapid growth rate is one of the world's highest, and it's given Saudi Arabia a very young population. It's thought that more than 60 percent of Saudis are under the age of 20. I'll remind you of this important fact in the next chapter, when we'll look at Saudi Arabia's demographics, government, and economy.

Traditional Arab tribal politics has always stressed ruling over groups of people more than on ruling over land, and the idea of fixed political boundaries was a modern, Western import. Still, plans are always underway to fix the boundaries more precisely, but it doesn't exactly seem to be a high priority. After all, these border areas are all uninhabited desert.

The map also shows Saudi Arabia's most important geographical regions. Each has its own history and distinct character—like the people who live there. From the historical material in Part 1 and Part 2, you already know about three of these regions: the Hijaz, the Najd, and the Hasa. Now I'll tell you about the others, as well.

The Hijaz and the Asir

The *Hijaz*, as you remember, is the narrow, mountainous strip that runs south from Jordan and the Gulf of Aqaba along the Red Sea. You'll also remember that it's crucial because it contains Mecca and Medina, Islam's two holiest sites. The *Asir*, another mountainous region to the south of the Hijaz, was considered part of Yemen in the past. You may recall from Chapter 4 that the future King Faisal conquered it on his father's behalf in 1924. Together, the Hijaz and the Asir make up Saudi Arabia's western edge.

Because of its importance in the Islamic world, the Hijaz has traditionally been better developed and more cosmopolitan than other parts of the Arabian peninsula. After it was conquered by Ibn Saud, he kept its smoothly functioning administrative institutions in place—indeed, he adopted and expanded many of them in running the rest of the country. In addition to Mecca and Medina, the Hijaz also contains the important port city of Jiddah, the traditional entry point for Muslim pilgrims journeying on the hajj. Along with Jiddah's port facilities, pilgrims now also land at the city's huge airport, which was built in the 1970s. Pilgrims have always been the key to the Hijaz's prosperity. The hajj is big enough to deserve a chapter of its own, and we'll return to this subject later, in Chapter 15.

Unlike the rest of the country, the Hijaz has population groups of non-Saudi origin that have put down roots in the kingdom. These are the descendants of pilgrims from earlier times who came and stayed. Most were originally from other Arab countries, but some are from further afield. In Medina, for example, you'll find families of Syrian, Turkish, Egyptian, and Central Asian descent, while Mecca is known for its Indian and Southeast Asian communities. Jiddah also adds to the Hijaz melting pot, with a large population of Yemeni descent, as well as ethnic Africans and Persians.

With its streams, trees, and mountain meadows, the Asir is less desert-like than the rest of the country. It more closely resembles the landscape of neighboring Yemen. Its people, too, carry on their Yemeni ways, with their distinct Arabic dialect and their own cultural traits.

The Central Plateau

The Central Plateau is Arabia's largest geographical feature, a huge desert upland that varies in elevation from 3,500 to 4,500 feet. It contains the following smaller, distinct regions.

- The *Nafud*, a red sand desert that merges into the Syrian desert as it approaches the Jordanian border, lies on the plateau's northern edge.

- The *Najd*, which you already know as the ancestral home of the Al Saud and of Wahhabism, occupies the heartland of the plateau. Isolated by desert on three sides, it contains the country's capital, Riyadh. Najdis are known for their conservative and somewhat stuck-up ways, and in the past they have been considered a bit backward by other Arabs.

  The stereotype Najdi is a Saudi version of the stereotype New England Yankee, right down to the parochial outlook, the patrician social traditions, and the dour, stiff-lipped religious values. Its old image as a backwater lingers on despite the facts that Najd is now the power center of the country, and that many of the most powerful Saudis are Najdis. Even the Prophet Muhammad scorned the Najd, reportedly saying that only earthquakes, strife, and the "horns of Satan" would ever come from its barren lands. Historically, the Najd has been dirt poor, though of course oil money has changed that.

- The Tuwayq Mountains, essentially a long, narrow ridgeline, run across the southern part of the plateau, south of the Najd.

- The Dahna, a long, narrow ribbon of sandy desert, curves around the eastern and southeastern edge of the plateau, below the Tuwayq Mountains.

The Hasa

Also called the Eastern Province, the *Hasa* (or Ahsa) region takes its name from the Hasa *oasis*, the world's largest, which sits inland from the Persian Gulf about 70 miles and contains the city of al Hufuf. The Hasa region holds nearly all of the country's oil reserves, but even before the discovery of oil it was a prosperous and well populated date-growing center. The province's capital city is Dammam, where oil was discovered in 1938 and which today is a massive industrial center for processing petroleum (see Chapter 5). South of Dammam is Dhahran, well known in the West as the headquarters of U.S. forces in the Gulf War. Northwards toward the Kuwaiti border are a number of other oil-processing centers, including Aramco's major terminal at Ras Tanura and the huge industrial plants of al Jubayl.

The Hasa is home to Saudi Arabia's significant Shiite minority, estimated at around a million people, or about 5 percent of the total population. These Saudi Shiites share the same Arab blood as other Saudis, but they follow a different version of Islam than the Sunni majority. (For background on the Sunni vs. Shiite split in Islam, see Chapter 3.) Because of their Shiite beliefs, they have cultural ties to Iran and Iraq, both of which have Shiite majorities. In the past a poor and excluded group, the Saudi Shiites have improved their lot as workers in the oil industry, although they still face discrimination from the rest of Saudi society. In the last chapter, I mentioned their protests in 1979, when their resentment—encouraged by the success of the Shiite revolution in Iran—boiled over into public violence. Since then, however, fears of further unrest have been largely unrealized.

Sheik-Speak

Most of Saudi Arabia's place names are simply descriptive terms in Arabic. Here's what some of the major regional names mean:

Hijaz: "Barrier" or "border."

Asir: "Rugged" or "dangerous."

Nafud: One of several Arabic words for "desert." The Nafud region is sometimes called "the Great Nafud" to distinguish it from the other deserts.

Najd: "Highlands" or "upland."

Hasa: "Sandy soil with water near the surface."

In addition to these Arabic place names, you should also know that an **oasis** is a fertile place in the desert where the presence of water has allowed vegetation to grow. Oases (the plural) are vital to life in the desert; most settlements in Saudi Arabia grew up around them.

The Empty Quarter

Finally, the southern fifth of the country is taken up by the world's largest sandy desert, the Rub al Khali or Empty Quarter, which merges on its northern edge with the Dahna. This is the setting that matches the classic Hollywood version of Arabia. Windswept, rippling sand dunes stretch as far as the eye can see, some so high—up to 1,000 feet—that they qualify as small mountains. Deep orange sunsets turn to startling blood-red, but the spectacle is over in just a few minutes because the horizon is so crisp and there's no water vapor to scatter the light.

There's a reason they call it the Empty Quarter. At 250,000 square miles, it's bigger than Arizona and Nevada put together. Yet nearly all of it is waterless and uninhabited, save for a handful of nomadic Bedouin tribes or the occasional sojourns of oil men. Their lonely figures leave tracks that are immediately swallowed up in the breathtaking vastness of the place. Not too long ago the tracks might have been made by camels, though now they're more likely to be made by a four-by-four, or maybe by the monster-truck tires of one of Aramco's exploration buggies.

Blowing Hot and Cold

Except for the Asir, Saudi Arabia generally has a basic desert climate of extreme hot during the day, extreme cold at night, and little or no rainfall. The biggest temperature swings come in the interior, where there's little humidity in the air to hold the heat. The temperature can drop by a staggering 70 degrees Fahrenheit in just a few hours after sunset. The major factor that determines how hot or cold it's going to get is altitude, with higher elevations being chillier. In coastal areas, the temperature extremes are less, since the air picks up some humidity from the sea. Summer highs of over 120 degrees Fahrenheit are common; winter lows can easily drop below freezing.

In the Hasa, on the Persian Gulf, winter breezes make the climate quite comfortable. Late spring and early summer, however, bring the strong northwesterly wind called the Shamal, which can blow for up to three months. The Shamal is worst in the east, where it kicks up vicious sandstorms that last for days and can bury homes and vehicles.

Saudi Arabia has no year-round rivers. In the high deserts of the Central Plateau and the north, seasonal rainstorms run off in sharply eroded ravines called wadis, which are like the arroyos of the American southwest. In the Empty Quarter, a decade may pass without rain.

Arabian Almanac _____

In a country as arid as Saudi Arabia, water is obviously a big issue. There are aquifers—deep underground reservoirs—but these are nonrenewable "fossil water" deposits left from ancient rainfall. They lie too deep to ever be replenished. Starting in the 1970s, a push for agricultural development resulted in these aquifers being used for highly subsidized and often wasteful irrigation of new wheat fields. The aquifers are now severely depleted and will soon be used up. The thought was good—to make the country more self-sufficient—but the execution was downright idiotic, since the water was nonrenewable while the wheat could have been cheaply imported.

The Saudis have also built a number of large desalinization plants that remove salt from seawater. These currently supply most of the kingdom's drinking water, but they are expensive. One exotic idea that surfaces on a regular basis is to tow giant icebergs from polar regions to use as a renewable source of fresh water.

Villagers and Nomads

Traditional life comes in two main forms, that of the settled villagers, *hadar*, and that of the nomadic *Bedouin*. But there's no clear cut division between them. It's more like a sliding scale. To today's city dweller, someone from a small oasis settlement may look like a Bedouin, while to the villager only the real nomad would be considered a Bedouin. At the other end of the scale, to a Bedouin camel herder—the real McCoy, so to speak—his goat or sheep herding Bedouin cousin is relatively citified. Goats and sheep need a lot more water than camels, so those who raise them tend to stick close to the oasis settlements. True camel nomads, by contrast, enjoy a much wider range of movement.

Sheik-Speak _____

The **hadar** and the **Bedouin** represent the two basic categories of traditional lifestyles in the Arabian peninsula. Hadar is the word for the settled farmers, merchants, and others who occupy villages and towns. The word "Bedouin" actually comes from the Arabic word for nomads (plural), *bawaadin*, and represents the French version of the Arabic word as it passed into English.

The Bedouin

I'm using the present tense to describe the Bedouin, but the sad fact is that true camel nomadism is fast disappearing in Saudi Arabia, as elsewhere in the Arab world. Bedouin once ranged from Iraq and Arabia in the east to Egypt, Libya, Algeria, and Morocco in the west. In the twentieth century, as these areas were formed into modern nation states, in one way or another they all undertook campaigns to settle their Bedouin down in one place. Bedouin and borders, it turns out, aren't a good match.

Mirage Ahead _____

In Saudi Arabia, society is traditionally divided into two main groups: Bedouins and villagers. In the rest of the Arab world, however, there's a third important category, the city dwellers. That's partly because high Islamic culture was essentially an urban phenomenon and helped give rise to great urban centers like Baghdad and Cairo. But great cities require food. With only about one tenth of 1 percent of its land suitable for farming, the Arabian peninsula never had the agricultural productivity to allow for much urban growth. Mecca and Medina, in the Hijaz, were as good as it got, and they relied on religion and trade.

Only in the late twentieth century did cities arise elsewhere in Saudi Arabia. Even as late as the 1950s, Riyadh—now the largest Saudi city—was little more than a small, dusty town. (For info on the growth of Saudi Arabia's cities, see the next chapter.) This is why traditional life in the Arabian peninsula comes in two flavors, not three as it does elsewhere in the Arab world. If you don't keep in mind how new cities are for the Saudis, it'll be hard to realize just how much of a shock the rapid urbanization of the last few decades has been for Saudi society.

Yet even as the life of the desert Bedouin disappears, its grip on the collective Arab imagination seems to gain in power. The Bedouin is to a Saudi what the cowboy is to an American—the model of the noble and independent loner, a tough and self-reliant hero who stands for all the best qualities of an idealized past.

When it comes to the Bedouin, the relationship between myth and reality is a complicated one—but it's an important one to get a grip on if you want to understand Saudi culture. And it's not just the Saudis, but the Arabs as a whole who look to the Bedouin for their core cultural values. The complexity can be seen in the attitudes that settled villagers or prosperous city folk display towards the Bedouin. On the surface, they may pretend to feel scorn or impatience for the Bedouin's poverty and cultural backwardness. Yet it doesn't take much to reveal that under the scorn lies a deeper layer of admiration and even envy—admiration for the way the Bedouin exemplifies an ancient, ancestral lifestyle, and envy for the freedom and purity of that unencumbered desert life. We'll explore some of these values more fully in Chapter 13.

In the meantime, what was Bedouin life really like? In a word, it was tough. On the most basic level, food and water are hard to come by in the desert, and so most

Bedouin have endured malnutrition or hunger at some point during their lives. Since modernization, the government has provided food, dug wells for water, and built homes for the Bedouin, as it also has for many villagers. The lure of such amenities has been one more factor pushing the Bedouin towards a settled life.

In the past, the Bedouin livelihood came from three main sources: camel raids on other Bedouin, tolls on camel caravans, and the sale of livestock to villagers. The camel raids were carried out according to strict rules of conduct, under which women and children were not to be touched, deaths were held to a minimum, and the target group was never left stranded with nothing in the desert. The goal was booty, not bloodshed. The raids thus amounted almost to sporting events, but were also the leading way that camels, the basis of the Bedouin economy, were exchanged between tribes.

In addition to raids, tolls were exacted on the camel caravans of merchants traveling through the desert territory of a Bedouin tribe. Finally, goats and sheep as well as camels were sold to villagers, or exchanged for food and goods needed by the Bedouin.

Arabian Almanac

First domesticated in southern Arabia, the camel has been the mainstay of Bedouin life since ancient times. Quicker, more enduring, and able to carry heavier loads over longer distances than the horse, the camel can travel for days on shrubs and bushes that even goats will turn down. It temporarily supplements such a meager diet by burning the fat stored in its hump.

The camel's importance went far beyond its role in carrying the Bedouin and their belongings from one grazing ground to the next, however. This versatile animal came in handy in just about every aspect of desert life. Its milk and flesh provided nourishment, its hair was woven into blankets, clothing, or saddlebags, and its skin supplied strong leather goods like containers and waterproof tents. A man's wealth was measured by the size and quality of his camel herd.

Marked with their owner's brand or *wasm*, camels were used to pay taxes, offered as settlements in blood feuds or dowries for marriage, and sold off to buy food or manufactured goods. With the arrival of cars and pickup trucks, the monetary value of camels has fallen—one more hardship that has led Bedouin to abandon their challenging life for the comforts of the city.

Their tough, Spartan life—along with constant raiding—made the Bedouin into fearsome desert warriors, and they were the backbone of the Muslim Arab armies that swept out of Arabia after the death of Muhammad in the seventh century. Their

Desert Dates

1953: The Saudi government abolishes tribal grazing rights, which the Bedouin tribes had jealously guarded in the past. Grazing rights—determined by conquest and constantly changing—had been the most important way that the Bedouin defined their tribe's territory. By legally abolishing these rights, the government deliberately struck at the heart of the Bedouin lifestyle, speeding the transformation from a nomadic to a sedentary existence.

mastery of the desert continued until the modern age. The European colonial powers' motorized armies, and especially their airplanes, finally limited the Bedouin's ability to attack without warning, and then fade with impunity back into the desert. With the end of the colonial age, Arab governments further suppressed Bedouin raids, and took steps to curtail the Bedouin's mobile way of life.

The Mystery of the Desert

Whatever the gritty and often poverty-stricken reality of Bedouin life, the Bedouin image contributed mightily to an air of mystique that arose around the desert, both in the West and among the Arabs themselves. Earlier I mentioned T. E. Lawrence, better known as Lawrence of Arabia, whose exploits against the Turks at the head of a Bedouin army made his name a household word in the West. For a modern audience, nothing better captures the romance of the desert than David Lean's 1962 movie *Lawrence of Arabia*, based on Lawrence's book about his adventures, *The Seven Pillars of Wisdom* (see Chapter 4).

For many Europeans, especially the British, the Bedouin represented the morally upright, Boy Scout-type "good" Arabs. This was in contrast to the perception that Arab cities were dens of corruption and iniquity. This idea is actually closer to the appeal that the desert holds for Arabs themselves, who view it in similar terms: pure, noble, clean. That holds true also for perceptions of Islam in both the West and Arab world, where Muhammad's religion is often portrayed as "born" in the spiritual "purity" of the desert. In fact, however, Islam was born in the urban, mercantile environment of Mecca and Medina.

Points of View

While we're on the subject of perceptions, it can be helpful to know how people see themselves, as well as how they're seen by others. Given human nature, probably none of these versions is ever completely accurate. But somewhere in between them all may lie the truth—if we can avoid the constant temptation to adopt simplistic, one-dimensional views, that is. Keeping that warning in mind, let's round out this chapter with a quick-and-easy breakdown of how the Saudis see, and are seen by, themselves and others.

How the Saudis See Themselves

First and foremost, their role as the protectors of Mecca and Medina is absolutely central to the Saudis' self-image. As I mentioned in Chapter 8, it's so important that since 1986 the Saudi monarch's official title has been "Custodian of the Two Holy Places." By extension, the Saudis also see themselves as the guardians of Islamic purity in a larger sense. Another important part of the Saudi self-image stems from the fact that their country is virtually the only part of the Middle East that never came under European colonial rule. Saudi pride dictates that in dealing with other countries—even superpowers like the United States—the Saudis participate as respected equals.

How does oil fit in? A common assumption is that God provided the oil as a reward for the country's piety. A further conclusion is that God intends the oil to make Saudi Arabia powerful, so that the Saudis can lead the Arabs and spread the message of Wahhabism throughout the world.

Yet all these outward signs of confidence are constantly being undercut by the reality of the country's decades-long reliance on outside help. I'll get to this in more detail in the next chapter, but keep in mind that the Gulf War heightened this sense of underlying anxiety. The Gulf War seemed to demonstrate that not only does Saudi Arabia require foreign help in modernizing, it also relies on the despised foreigners for its own defense—despite years of pumping oil money into its own military.

How Other Arabs See the Saudis

To other Arabs, the Saudis' dominant characteristic is their religious and cultural conservatism, which can come across as anything from noble to ridiculous, depending on the circumstances. Saudi Arabia is by far the most socially authoritarian society in the Arab world. When visiting the kingdom, other Arabs from more liberal, tolerant countries are sometimes shocked at seeing, for example, public dress codes or restrictions on women being enforced, often with violence, by the roving bands of "religious police." (More on such matters in Chapter 14.)

Yet for other Arabs, as for Muslims everywhere, Saudi Arabia retains its air of sanctity as the site of Mecca and Medina. So while more liberal Arabs might make fun of Saudi conservatism, on some level they also probably find it sort of appropriate.

How the West Sees the Saudis

Western perceptions of Saudi Arabia are dominated by oil. This is especially true of Americans, who generally ignore the country's complex history and culture. Many simply see the kingdom as nothing more than America's global gas station. Since September 11, however, this one-dimensional view is giving way to something a little more complex, if just as shallow. This new perception, alas, still casts Saudi Arabia in the role of America's global gas station—only now the gas station has fallen into the hands of religious hijackers. The problem is often portrayed as one of getting rid of the religious nuts so that America can resume filling its bottomless gas tank without worries.

How the Saudis See the Rest of the World

The Saudi view of the outside world can seem amazingly paranoid and conspiratorial, even by Arab standards. For example, in public sermons Wahhabi religious leaders insist over and over that Jews control both America's government and its major corporations, and for the most part the Saudis believe what they're told. Newspapers and government authorities repeat such claims uncritically. Many Saudis are honestly convinced that America is run by a Jewish conspiracy controlled from Israel.

In more general terms, Saudis see the outside world as an evil pit of impiety, corruption, and decadence. In the following chapters, as we delve further into Saudi culture, you'll discover some of the surprising consequences of this strange perception.

The Least You Need to Know

- The basic split in traditional Arabian culture is between villagers and Bedouin.

- Saudis look to the Bedouin for many of their core values, even though Bedouin life is fast disappearing.

- In the past, the romance of the desert has shaped Western perceptions of Arabia, but today those perceptions are dominated by oil and religious extremism.

- In general, Saudis and Westerners have equally simplistic and one-dimensional views of each other.

Chapter 12

Vital Statistics

In This Chapter

- Some demographic trends
- The constitution that wasn't
- The Saudi economy, including the oil industry
- The strange case of the foreign workforce

In this chapter, I'll add more detail to the introductory picture I sketched in the previous chapter. Where the last chapter focused largely on perceptions, this one puts the emphasis more on hard information. Consequently, if you want revealing facts and figures about the Saudis and the way they live, this is where you'll find them.

By the Numbers

In Chapter 11, I gave the estimate of 15 to 20 million for Saudi Arabia's total population, though I warned that accurate numbers aren't available. (Saudi government figures are notoriously unreliable.) I also mentioned that, since it's growing at the rapid rate of nearly 4 percent a year, the kingdom's population is a very young one, with more than 60 percent of Saudis thought to be under the age of 20.

Keep these basic numbers in mind as I give you a few figures to illustrate some key demographic trends. To put the Saudi numbers in context, I'll compare them, first, with those of other Arab countries, and second, with those of the world at large.

For example, there are about 280 million Arabs in the 22 countries of the Arab League. (Membership in the Arab League, which was founded in 1945, is generally accepted as the benchmark of what constitutes an "Arab" country.) Egypt, the largest, is home to nearly 70 million, while Qatar, the smallest, has fewer than 600,000. The total world population is roughly six billion, of which about one fifth, or just over one billion, are Muslims. Thus, Arabs make up about 25 percent of the world's Muslims, and about 5 percent of the overall world population.

Yet that last figure—the percentage of Arabs in the world population—has doubled in the last five decades. In other words, the Arab population is growing faster than the world population as a whole. Whereas the world population is increasing at an average of 1.4 percent a year, the overwhelming majority of Arab countries have annual growth rates of more than 2 percent. Six countries, including Saudi Arabia, have rates of more than 3 percent. Yemen caps them all, at 4.1 percent.

Arabian Almanac

The number of Arabs in the world, 280 million, is about equal to the population of the United States. The population of Saudi Arabia, between 15 and 20 million, is about equal to that of New York State. To get an idea of Saudi Arabia's low population density, imagine New York State's population spread out over an area one quarter the size of the United States.

One important result of these differences is that in most of the Arab countries, the rate of increase is still low enough that the proportion of children in the overall Arab population will fall in coming years, from about 40 percent to about 25 percent. But Saudi Arabia, Yemen, and the other fastest growers will be exceptions to this overall trend. In these high-birth-rate countries, the proportion of children to adults will continue to rise, making the average age of their populations younger and younger.

Give Me the City Life

In the last chapter, I also told you that many Bedouin have given up the hardships of nomadic life for the comforts of the city. But migration to the cities hasn't been limited to the Bedouin, by any means. Many village families have also opted for the modern amenities of city life, which became widely and cheaply available during King Faisal's modernization drive and the construction boom that came with it. From an overwhelmingly rural people just a few decades ago, the Saudis have become a nation of city-dwellers. About 80 percent of Saudis now live in the kingdom's urban centers.

Obviously, that means that the country's cities have experienced extraordinarily rapid growth in a very short time. For example, in the decade from the mid 1960s to the mid 1970s, Riyadh's population leaped from less than 160,000 to nearly 700,000. Jiddah's expansion in the same period was almost as rapid, from under 150,000 to over 550,000. Smaller cities such as Hufuf, Taif, and Medina also mushroomed.

That staggering rate of urbanization hasn't let up, either. By the end of the next decade, in 1985, Riyadh's population stood at over two million. By 2000, it was over three million, and today Riyadh is home to some four and a half million people. That's something like one quarter of the kingdom's entire population—in a city whose population was less than 20,000 in 1918.

A Monarchy? Absolutely!

In technical terms, Saudi Arabia's government has always been an absolute monarchy. That means there are no institutional limitations on the king's power. For example, Saudi Arabia does not have a written constitution as such, a legislature, or any popular elections. However, Arabic and Islamic traditions dictate that a ruler be subject to a number of informal checks, and that a certain degree of consensus be reached on important matters. More importantly, the ruler himself is not considered to be above the Sharia, or Islamic law. Citizens can bring lawsuits against the government, and a separate ministry exists to handle such suits. So the Saudi version of absolute monarchy differs considerably from the familiar European idea, as exemplified, say, by the Bourbon Kings of old France or the Romanov Tsars of old Russia.

Still a Monarchy? Basically...

In 1992, King Fahd issued a decree known as the Basic Law, which "basically" lays out the Saudi system of government. The Basic Law doesn't pretend to be a constitution, though it does fulfill part of a constitution's function. But among other things, the Basic Law asserts that the Koran and the Hadith are Saudi Arabia's constitution. (For discussion of these texts, Islam's holy scriptures, see Chapter 2.) Still, the Basic Law prohibits the government from arresting Saudi citizens without cause, or invading their privacy at home—domestic privacy being a sacrosanct cultural value to Saudis.

However, some things the Basic Law doesn't do is guarantee Saudi citizens freedom of religion, freedom of speech, or freedom of assembly, nor does it offer the people any degree of real political participation. The Saudi government maintains that such ideas are historically recent Western inventions, and that as such they are "unsuitable" for Saudi Arabia.

Desert Dates
March 1, 1992: King Fahd proclaims the Basic Law of Government, which amounts to the most recent update of the system that evolved under his father, Ibn Saud. The Basic Law declares Saudi Arabia to be a sovereign Islamic state with Riyadh as its capital, Arabic as its language, Islam as its only religion, and the Koran and the Hadith, Islam's holy texts, as its constitution.

As an example of what is suitable for Saudi Arabia, Fahd also established the long awaited Majlis as-Shura, or Consultative Council, which upgraded the traditional tribal majlis (council) to a place in national government. Some Western observers hailed this as a step towards democracy. Yet, this purely advisory body is appointed by the king, not elected. So it is not (as it is sometimes portrayed in the West) simply a Saudi version of a legislature or parliament. Though its limited duties include proposing some laws, those laws are still subject to the king's final approval. (Go to Chapter 9 to review the historical context of the Majlis as-Shura.) I'll get back to such issues in Chapter 14, when we'll look at the much-debated question of Islam and democracy.

How to Add Minister a Country

Much of the Basic Law is concerned with regional government, and confirms the kingdom's earlier division into 13 regional "emirates," each with its emir or governor. These emirs are given the rank of Minister, and they report to the Minister of the Interior. The document also defines the purviews of a bewildering array of other government ministries, most of which are headed up by princes of the Al Saud (from whose ranks most of the regional emirs are drawn as well).

All the ministers together make up the Council of Ministers, which is the main organ of the Saudi government (the Majlis as-Shura is far less influential and has no official authority). As you may have guessed, the Council of Ministers is dominated by Al Saud princes, who comprise the bulk of its membership. At the top, of course, is the king, who has the rank of Prime Minister. The Crown Prince, the king's designated successor, has the rank of Deputy Prime Minister.

Created by Ibn Saud in 1953, the Council of Ministers has gotten bigger and bigger over the years, as the government has expanded. In 1975, after the death of King Faisal, the number of ministries went from 14 to 20. Today it stands at some 23 plus. It includes a "Minister of Islamic Affairs" and a "Minister of Pilgrimage" as well as more conventional (in Western terms) government functions such as education, public works, communications, and foreign affairs. In addition to the ministers who have their own ministries, there's an unspecified number of "Ministers of State without portfolio" on the council, who are there to advise the king.

Arabian Almanac

In the throng that makes up the Council of Ministers, four positions have the most power. First, obviously, is the king, who holds the rank of Prime Minister. Second comes the Crown Prince, with the rank of Deputy Prime Minister, who is also (currently at least) head of the National Guard. The next prince in the line of succession holds the rank of Second Deputy Prime Minister, and he's in charge of the Ministry of Defense and Aviation. Between them, the Deputy Prime Minister and Second Deputy Prime Minister control the armed forces. The last of the big four is the Minister of the Interior, the powerful ministry that runs the police and internal security forces.

Here's who occupies these positions currently (they are all sons of Ibn Saud):

- ◆ Prime Minister: King Fahd
- ◆ Deputy Prime Minister: Crown Prince Abdullah
- ◆ Second Deputy Prime Minister: Prince Sultan
- ◆ Minister of the Interior: Prince Naif

The king's power center is the Royal Diwan, where he and his main advisors have their offices. This is where much of the government's daily work is carried out. Important agencies of the Royal Diwan include the Office of Bedouin Affairs; the Department of Religious Research, Missionary Activities, and Guidance; and the Committee for the Propagation of Virtue and the Prevention of Vice—better known in the West as the "religious police." I'll get back to them in Chapter 14, too.

A "Rentier" Economy

Before the discovery of oil in 1938, economic activity in the new state of Saudi Arabia was patchy at best. In the fertile oases of the Hasa (Eastern Province), a prosperous plantation economy produced dates and other cash crops. In the Hijaz, the main revenue generator was the web of service industries that grew up around the annual hajj, or Islamic pilgrimage to Mecca and Medina. Elsewhere, Bedouins herded goats, sheep, and camels, which they bartered for goods and food with the settled subsistence farmers of the villages.

Though Hasa farmers still grow some of the world's best dates, and Hijazis continue to rely on the hajj, oil has completely transformed the Saudi economy. (Well, for that matter—as should be abundantly clear by now—oil has completely transformed the entire country. But for the moment, let's stick to the economy.) Today, oil directly accounts for about 75 percent of Saudi economic productivity, and is indirectly responsible for much of the remaining 25 percent.

As a consequence of all the oil, Saudi Arabia has what economists call a "rentier" economy. That means the government controls the exploitation of a single resource that dominates the economy, and from which it derives "rents" or revenue. The government then goes into the business of sharing the rents with the population at large. This reverses the normal flow of revenue, which usually goes from the people to the government through taxes. In a rentier economy, the government supports the people rather than vice versa. Again, this will be familiar to you from earlier chapters in the historical parts of this book, but now you know the technical term for it.

The Oil Biz

The historical parts of the book will also have given you the background on the development of the oil industry, both in Saudi Arabia and in the rest of the world as well. In this brief section, I'll supplement that picture with some key insights into the Saudi oil industry today.

There are three main things you need to know:

♦ The Saudis still aspire to be the world's swing producer, though they've faltered in this often difficult role.

♦ The Saudi government pretty much leaves Saudi Aramco free to act independently.

♦ The people of Saudi Arabia have started to feel that the Al Saud are selling Saudi oil far too cheaply.

Let's look at each of these in turn, and I'll explain how they're connected by the Al Saud's desire to keep up their image in the rest of the world.

Saudi Arabia Tries to Be a Swing Producer

Saudi Arabia is the only oil producer with the excess production capacity to keep the price of oil relatively stable. In other words, if the oil flow from another producer is interrupted for some reason, Saudi Arabia can raise its own production to make up for it, thus preventing a price spike. Conversely, the Saudis can lower production in a glut to prevent *spot oil prices* from slumping. Obviously, this can be painful, since their own revenues then suffer.

Sheik-Speak

The **spot oil price** is the price that a barrel of oil will fetch on the open market, without any preexisting contract between buyer and seller. This is the standard way of expressing the market value of oil.

Experts estimate Saudi excess production capacity to be in the neighborhood of 2 million barrels a day, or about two thirds of the world's total excess capacity.

The kingdom currently produces about 8 million barrels a day, and took steps in the 1990s to raise their overall capacity to 10 or even 11 million barrels a day if needed. The Saudis have repeatedly led OPEC in keeping production high during market shortages, so that prices would stay down to between $25 and $30 per barrel. More recently, during the 2003 U.S. invasion of Iraq, the Saudis pledged to make up any shortfall caused by an interruption of the Iraqi oil flow. Iraq's oil production stood at around 1.5 to 2 million barrels a day, well within the Saudis' capacity to make up.

It's at the other end of the scale that the real crunch comes. In the depths of the oil glut in the late 1980s and early 1990s, the Saudis were temporarily forced to abandon their role as swing producer, by raising production to increase revenues.

Though Government-Owned, Saudi Aramco Generally Acts Like a Commercial Corporation

In keeping with their struggle to be a reliable swing producer, the Saudis want to be seen as a responsible force for stability in the world oil market. One way the Saudi government increases its credibility in this regard is by pursuing a "hands off" policy with its oil company, Saudi Aramco. For the most part, Saudi Aramco has been allowed to make its decisions with an eye to future profit, not political expediency. This is unusual in a state-owned company.

For example, in the past decade and a half, Saudi Aramco has sought to diversify its activities into *downstream* operations like marketing and refining. In 1988, the Saudi Arabian Marketing and Refining Company (Samarec) was created for this purpose. Among other ventures, Samarec bought a half share in Texaco's marketing and refining operations in the southern and eastern United States. In addition, Saudi Aramco has continued to spend money on developing *upstream* operations like new domestic oil fields. Both efforts have faced some obstacles, since they require large capital outlays, and the government has been cash-strapped during this time. Observers have praised the Saudi government for not milking Saudi Aramco more than it has.

However, all this "hands off" business only goes so far, as the Oil Embargo of 1973 illustrated only too well. Political considerations are bound to play a role when push comes to shove. For a state-owned company, political pressure will always trump commercial pressure, if the cause is urgent enough. But for many Saudis, the Al Saud haven't taken concerns like the Israeli-Palestinian conflict as seriously as they should in deciding oil policy towards the West.

Sheik-Speak

The oil industry thinks of its operations as being like a river of oil that flows from the ground into your gas tank. The flow originates **upstream** with oil fields and wells, and then moves **downstream** to refineries and gas stations.

The Saudi People Have Started to Believe That the Al Saud Are Selling Out Their Country's Resources to Cater to the West

In trying to uphold their role as swing producer, and in their "hands off" approach to Saudi Aramco, the Al Saud have been motivated in large part by a desire to be seen as reliable and responsible oil producers by the rest of the world. However, this has begun to backfire on them at home. The more responsive they are to the needs of the West, and to the United States in particular, the more the Al Saud come in for criticism by an increasingly anti-Western, anti-American public. It's left the Al Saud open to the charge that they are selling Saudi oil too cheaply and caving in to Western pressures too easily.

The Nonoil Sector

In the 1980s the Saudi government undertook a deliberate program to build up a whole array of domestic industries basically from scratch. Part of the idea was to use the nation's petroleum reserves as raw material or "feedstock" for producing petrochemicals, which can then be turned into plastics, solvents, synthetic fibers, and other essential commodities. A second aim, one that also took advantage of the Saudis' access to cheap energy, was to subsidize energy-intensive industries such as manufacturing.

Until the mid 1980s, manufacturing tended to cater to the construction business. With the end of the construction boom in the mid 1980s, Saudi businesses have looked more to light manufacturing, such as furniture, processed food products, and various other consumer items. From 1992 to 1999, the number of factories in the kingdom rose from about 2,000 to over 3,000.

One big story of the last decade or so is the rise of a private sector, from about a third of the overall gross domestic product in 1992 to about two-thirds of it by the end of the decade. At the same time, the government or public sector share in the economy has gone down just as sharply. That means that more and more Saudi businesses are in private hands, and fewer are run by the government. This goes against the usual situation in a rentier state, in which the economy typically relies heavily on the government. It's a sign that the Saudi economy may be struggling to break free of the rentier model.

Employment and Otherwise

But there's a catch to that bit of good news. While these new businesses may be owned by Saudis, not very many Saudis work in them. That's because Saudi Arabia's traditional culture lacks anything resembling a work ethic. Quite the opposite, in fact. Saudi culture has traditionally viewed work, and physical labor especially, as demeaning and undignified. The Saudis' cultural devaluation of work has had two important results.

A Foreign Workforce

The first result is that the vast majority of the Saudi labor force is made up of foreign nationals. The Saudi reliance on foreign labor began during the heady days of the oil boom and the modernization drive, but it's gotten worse since the boom ended in the mid 1980s. At that point, foreign labor comprised less than half of the work force. Now it's estimated to be about 70 percent. And for the private sector, that figure jumps to 90 percent. Those are staggering figures—and they keep going up, despite the official policy of "Saudization" (encouraging Saudis to get jobs, basically).

Remember that earlier I gave you the rough figure of 15 to 20 million for the total population of Saudi Arabia? Well, Saudi Arabia's foreign workforce is thought to be fully one quarter of the total population. So if you take the high number, 20 million, for the overall population, that makes 5 million of them expatriate workers. That's a lot of foreign workers—so many that you can't forget about them in thinking of the kingdom's population as a whole.

The foreign workforce in Saudi Arabia comes in two basic flavors: Westerners, who generally make up the highly skilled, white-collar workers, and so-called *Third Country Nationals* or TCNs, who mostly make up the blue-collar workers and manual laborers. Life is very different for the two groups, but they do have one thing in common. Both are kept as separate as possible from Saudi society, and both are viewed with suspicion and sometimes outright hostility by the Saudis. With the exceptions of TCNs who work as live-in domestics (more on them in a moment), both groups commonly live in separate housing compounds specially built for them.

But that's where the resemblance ends. The Westerners (and some educated TCNs) are generally very well paid, and their housing is clean, comfortable, and spacious. They're the country's doctors, technicians, engineers, and other affluent professionals. Often employed by large corporations or other companies under contract with the Saudi government, they have a whole network of support when things get tough. They usually bring their families with them, and they have Western friends and colleagues to socialize with. For most of them, Saudi Arabia isn't the peachiest of assignments, but they do okay. They know they won't be there forever, and most know how long they'll be staying.

Sheik-Speak

Third Country Nationals or **TCNs** is the term used for workers who have come to Saudi Arabia from Third World countries. In the 1970s and early 1980s, most TCNs were from other Arab countries, but by the late 1980s most were from Asia. Poor and poorly paid, most TCNs are heavily discriminated against both by their Saudi employers and by the Saudi government, and constitute a powerless, oppressed class inside the kingdom.

For the millions of less well-off TCNs, it's a much bleaker picture. They're herded around by big employment agencies, housed in barracks-style huts, and work 10 to 15 hours a day for maybe $200 or $300 a month. They're the kingdom's garbage men, janitors, street sweepers, maintenance workers, ditch diggers, crop pickers, cash register operators, construction workers, drivers, maids, and nannies.

They have practically no rights. They can't apply to become Saudi citizens, they can't own their own property, they don't enjoy the protection of Saudi law, and they can be deported instantly, or thrown in jail and lost in the system forever. They've come at various times from Yemen, Oman, Jordan, the West Bank or Gaza Strip, Afghanistan, Pakistan, Turkey, the Philippines, Korea, Thailand, Burma—wherever the labor is cheapest that year. The Saudi government mixes it up, so that no one country predominates.

> ⚠️ **CAUTION**
>
> ## Mirage Ahead
>
> The term "Third Country Nationals" was first used at the dawn of the oil boom, by Americans from the Army Corps of Engineers. But Americans have long since lost their early monopoly on helping modernize the kingdom, and the old economic dividing line between Westerners and TCNs has become less distinct. In recent years, developing countries have sent many educated workers to Saudi Arabia.

Arabian Almanac

Here's a joke that was popular among Westerners living and working in Saudi Arabia during the oil boom. Someone asks an American, a German, and a Saudi whether they think of sex as fun, or as work. The American doesn't hesitate. "Fun, definitely." The German is equally certain. "All I know is after a hard day at the office it feels like work to have to come home and make love to my wife." But the Saudi hesitates before answering. "Well, I guess it must be fun," he says finally. "If it were work, I'd get a foreigner to do it."

—Adapted from Sandra Mackey, *The Saudis*

While all of the TCNs have it bad, the female domestic servants have it the worst of all by far. Many are treated like slaves by their employers, for whom employment and slavery are almost interchangeable concepts anyway. Because they are foreign and do not enjoy the social protection of their own male family members, the female domestics are considered fair game for sexual predation by male members of the families that employ them. Meanwhile, the wife or wives of the Saudi household grind them into the ground on a daily basis, often out of jealousy or anger.

While we're on the subject of slavery, you should know that it was only abolished in Saudi Arabia in 1962, by the future King Faisal. Until then, it had been an integral part of the Saudi scene. So if it seems like the TCNs are treated like slaves, remember that there are plenty of Saudis still alive who would remember owning slaves. Along with non-Muslims and women, slaves are the third class of people who were not accorded full legal rights in traditional Islamic societies.

Saudi clerics, officials, and other commentators see the exploitation of female domestic servants as a major ill plaguing their society. Unfortunately, their concerns focus only on the threat the domestics pose to the traditional family structure—not at all on the welfare of the domestics themselves.

This perfectly sums up the attitude the Saudis take to the foreign workforce in general. It's a problem, sure—but the problem lies in the exposure of Saudis to dangerous foreign ways, not in the treatment of the foreign nationals themselves. Yet whatever the issue, the problem is there to stay. The Saudis built the infrastructure or paid others to build it and they know perfectly well it has to be maintained. If they aren't willing to do it themselves, they'll have to keep on paying others to do it for them.

Mirage Ahead

Many foreign workers in Saudi Arabia are Muslims, whether from African countries like Somalia and the Sudan or Asian ones like Pakistan and Indonesia. Saudi Arabia comes in for much criticism by other Muslim countries for the way it treats its foreign workers who are Muslims. For that matter, it also gets a lot of flack from other Arab countries for the way it treats its foreign Arab workers. In contrast, these countries don't seem too concerned with the non-Muslim or non-Arab workers. Such attitudes suggest that Muslim and Arab societies place the value of Muslim and Arab lives higher than the lives of non-Muslims and non-Arabs.

But if you think they're alone in that sort of behavior, listen to the news coverage next time there's a disaster somewhere in the world. If it's an American news source, you may notice that a few North American or European deaths seem to count for a lot more than the deaths of hundreds or even thousands of Africans, Asians, or South Americans. Maybe all cultures have a way of putting their own members first in such matters—and maybe it's something we should all watch out for, whatever culture we belong to.

The good news: In the past year or two, there are a few signs that more Saudis are taking jobs in some service industries that most would earlier have considered beneath their dignity. *New York Times* columnist Thomas Friedman, for example, reports encountering Saudi hotel clerks and retail personnel in his recent visits to the kingdom, where before such jobs would have been taken by TCNs.

Young, Jobless, and Frustrated

If a largely foreign workforce is the first result of the Saudis' cultural aversion to labor, the second result is that a lot of Saudis themselves end up with way too much time on their hands. No reliable figures exist for Saudi unemployment rates. But clearly they're high, and equally clearly they're getting higher.

Yet instead of aspiring to do the work that actually needs to be done, young Saudi men often prefer to try a line of work with greater social prestige. For many, that means becoming a religious leader, and a whole slew of shiny new universities now specialize in Wahhabi religious education. They turn out thousands of would-be Wahhabi clerics every year. Yet, on graduating these young men find that there are few actual job openings available for them at the mosques.

The employment situation thus ties in with education, which I'll cover in the next chapter. But in terms of the economy, here's the upshot: Each year, the system produces more and more young Saudi men who are unemployed and unemployable. Keep this in mind in the chapters ahead, as we explore some of the consequences of their mounting frustration.

The Least You Need to Know

- Saudi Arabia has one of the youngest and fastest-growing populations in the world.

- Foreign workers make up about 25 percent of the overall population, and an estimated 80 percent of the labor force, but they are kept away from contact with Saudis as much as possible.

- Most Saudis see the foreign workers as a necessary evil, viewing them as a serious and ongoing threat to Saudi cultural and religious values.

- There are lots of unemployed, angry young men (and women) in Saudi Arabia.

Chapter 13

Shame on You! Sex, Honor, and Family Values

In This Chapter

- ◆ Shame culture vs. guilt culture
- ◆ Family comes first
- ◆ Saudi women: protected, or oppressed?
- ◆ Saudi society: obsessed with sex?

So far in Part 3, I've introduced you to Saudi culture by examining some of the lore surrounding Arabia, and by giving you some key pieces of hard information about the Saudis themselves. Consider yourself introduced!

Now it's time to go into a little more depth about the cultural attitudes that help define this unusual people. In this chapter, we'll move in for our tightest focus yet on what it is that makes the Saudis tick. We'll start with their broadest cultural attitudes, then move in for close-ups on specific issues like family life and children. Finally, we'll tackle the most controversial question of all, Saudi attitudes toward women.

So stick around. This chapter is the place to look first if you really want to answer the question, "Who are the Saudis?"

Cultural Attitudes

Most of the information I've given you up to now is fairly comprehensible to anyone who grew up according to the familiar values shared by most of us in the West. However, a few things I've told you probably stand out as less understandable. For example, in the last chapter, I told you that Saudis don't have the sort of work ethic found in the West, and I showed you how that difference has had some important consequences for Saudi society. Western societies share a more or less recognizable form of work ethic, and the Saudi attitude to labor may not be immediately graspable to a Westerner steeped in the traditional work ethic found in the West.

Here's where I'll give you the information you need to make some of the Saudis' seemingly incomprehensible attitudes more readily understandable. It won't take as much as you might think. A few basic differences in hidden, underlying attitudes can lead to a whole array of easier-to-see cultural differences.

Shame, Shame, Shame

The first thing I want to explain is the difference between a guilt culture (like most Western countries) and a shame culture (like Saudi Arabia and other Arab countries). Once you understand this important difference, a lot of other things will fall into place.

The difference between guilt culture and shame culture comes down to how society judges and controls a person's behavior. In guilt cultures like those of most Western countries, what limits your behavior is usually how you judge yourself. Ideas of right and wrong are primarily internal, rather than external. Society still shapes these values, but they operate from inside you, so doing something "wrong" produces a feeling of guilt whether anyone sees it or not.

In shame cultures like Saudi Arabia, what limits your behavior is more commonly determined by what others, or society, will think of you. Ideas of right and wrong are primarily external, rather than internal. Hence, doing something "wrong" is risky because it will bring shame to you and your family if someone sees you.

In the context of the economic issues I discussed in the previous chapter, the kind of job you have reflects on your honor, and manual labor is perceived as dishonorable for a Saudi male. The native Saudi workforce is burdened with a lot of "generals," in other words, but no "soldiers," which is where the TCNs come in.

Shame culture explains a lot about the way Saudis behave. Just to take one more example, during the oil boom Western newspapers were full of stories about the escapades of Al Saud princes and other wealthy Saudis in Western cities like London and New York. The activities involved some heavy-duty partying, and included drinking, which is forbidden by Islam and illegal in Saudi Arabia. These were princes and others who considered themselves to be very pious Muslims. A Westerner might suspect that they were being hypocritical. Not so. It was all perfectly in keeping with their own social standards. The point is that if it's out of sight of Saudi society—the only society that matters—no shame can result from doing it. On a smaller scale, so-called "airport Muslims" are Saudis who act "Western" abroad and shift over to more proper "Islamic" behavior on landing back in Saudi Arabia, often changing clothes as well.

Mirage Ahead

Earlier I warned you about the dangers of trying to draw too clear a line between "moderates" and "fundamentalists" in talking about individual Saudis' approaches to Islam. Now I have a similar warning to make about guilt cultures and shame cultures. These are helpful terms, but don't make the mistake of thinking the difference between them is totally cut-and-dry. After all, you are most likely a product of a guilt culture (if you grew up in the West, at least). But you're also perfectly capable of feeling shame. Or of trying to get away with something when no one's looking, for that matter (if you're like me, anyway). By the same token, just because Saudis live in a shame culture doesn't mean they can't feel guilty, or that they have no "inner moral compass." What these terms refer to is not the behavior of all individuals at all times, but more like the average tendency of the culture as a whole.

Keep the idea of a shame culture in mind as you read the rest of this chapter, since it'll help explain some of the other cultural traits we'll be looking at. It doesn't stand alone, in other words, but comes in a package deal.

The Honor System

The most visible part of the shame culture package is the high value placed on honor, or—to use the familiar term from Japan, another shame culture—"face." The Japanese idea that you "lose face" if you're shamed in front of others is a concept that applies equally to the Saudis. The two cultures, in fact, have a whole lot in common. If you're familiar with Japanese culture, then you've got a head start in understanding the Saudis. More on honor—especially its sexual aspects—in a moment.

Arabian Almanac _____

Trivia quiz: In what Western European country has the idea of honor played a leading cultural role? Answer: Spain. From classical Spanish culture the idea spread to Latin America, where it also retains a strong influence. And how did the Spanish get their notion of honor? Hint: It's no coincidence that Spain was the only part of Western Europe to fall under Arab rule. From the Arab conquest of the late sixth and early seventh centuries until the Christian _reconquista_ before the discovery of the New World, much of Spain was part of the Arab Muslim empire. For a review of this history, go back to Chapter 3.

A lot of Spanish culture is Arabic in origin. One well-known example from music is the guitar, originally a stringed instrument known in Arabic as the _qitara_, and in Greek as the _kithara_. The Arabic name came into Spanish as _guitarra_, from which we get the English _guitar_.

How Westerners Think vs. How Saudis Think

Now that I've introduced the basic idea of a shame culture, together with the related concept of honor, I'll outline some of the other important beliefs and values held by the Saudis. The following table contrasts some common Western beliefs and values with their Saudi counterparts. Again, though, I need to warn you that these statements shouldn't be taken as applying to all individuals at all times. They are merely meant to give you an idea of an overall cultural tendency. As always, this sort of thing is a question of balance and emphasis, not absolutes.

How Westerners Think	How Saudis Think
The individual comes first.	The family comes first.
People are basically equal.	People are inherently unequal, with strong differences based on class, race, and gender.
Humans control their own destiny.	Human destiny is up to fate, which is ultimately determined by God. Everything that happens has God's approval.
Privacy is important, with moments of solitude needed as a break from social interaction.	Being alone is to be avoided.
Friends are for relaxing with.	Friends are expected to do constant favors for each other in their business and professional lives.
Business matters aren't personal.	All relationships are personal, including those in business.

How Westerners Think	How Saudis Think
Criticism can be constructive.	Criticism is insulting.
Skepticism and reason are healthy.	Skepticism and reason are impious, and therefore unhealthy.
Laws should govern society.	Rules and regulations are just guidelines that should give way to "the human element."

Many of these beliefs also hold true for Arab culture in general, not just the Saudis. Arab culture tends to be *fatalistic*, for example, accepting that whatever happens was meant to be. When an Arab suggests or proposes something, someone else will commonly say *Inshallah*, "If God wills it."

Westerners often express impatience with Arab fatalism, finding that it makes Arabs passive and too easily resigned to accepting obstacles rather than trying to overcome them. Arabs, for their part, find Westerners arrogant in their assumption that they can reverse an outcome that seems inevitable and divinely ordained.

Sheik-Speak

Fatalism is an important feature of the Arab worldview, and it's one that's generally shared by the Saudis. Fatalism says that whatever happens was meant to happen, and so everything that occurs is a direct result of God's will. The idea is exemplified in the common Arabic expression **Inshallah**, which means "If God wills it."

Arabs prize emotions and the warmth of human interaction over the cold reason and impersonal ways of the West. In the West, it's considered desirable to separate business from pleasure, and it's acceptable—even expected—to offer constructive criticism to a subordinate or a colleague. In the Arab world, by contrast, business meetings almost always begin with personal interaction—polite questions about each other's family, for example. Introductions can be accompanied by detailed accounts of one's family and social background. And as many a Western supervisor has found, criticizing an Arab's job performance will likely be taken as a mortal insult to his honor, so it has to handled very carefully.

It's also considered impolite to neglect a cordial greeting to a coworker, complete with an inquiry into the other person's welfare, even if you just saw the person yesterday. In general, manners and formality count for much more in the Arab world than in the West—and the Saudis are more formal and reserved than most other Arabs.

Family, Clan, and Tribe

Manners, upbringing, social background, honor—all of these things play a huge role in who you are if you're a Saudi, but in the end who you are comes down to one thing: family. What family you're born into, for example, determines your social status— upper class, part of the growing middle class, or lower class. Your manners are seen as a public reflection on your upbringing and your family. And, as I explained earlier, your personal honor is closely bound up with the honor of your family as a whole. If one is threatened or injured, so is the other. The extended family is the most important social institution in Saudi Arabia; in a moment I'll give you more details on how family life works.

After the family, the clan has the next-highest claim on a Saudi's loyalty and allegiance, and after the clan comes the tribe. There are no hard-and-fast rules about what divides the extended family from the clan, or the clan from the tribe. It's more like a sliding scale based on kinship. About four to six related families make up a clan, so that if you go back a few generations a clan's families will share a common ancestor somewhere. Similarly, a number of clans—say, seven to fifteen—make up a tribe, and again they'll all claim a common ancestor somewhere back in the mists of time.

Arabian Almanac

Traditionally, Saudis with prestigious family bloodlines traced those bloodlines back in their names. The individual's name is given first, followed by the father's, followed by *his* father's, and on like that until an arbitrary stopping point is reached, when finally a family name might be given. *Ibn*, you'll remember, means "son of," like the prefix "Mac-" in Scots.

To give Ibn Saud himself as an example, you might say his name as "Abdel Aziz ibn Abdel Rahman ibn Faisal ibn Turki ibn Abdullah ibn Muhammad Al Saud." But if you chose, you could go even further back than that in listing his ancestors. In the past, only the highest-ranking families had family names, although they've become more common as a feature of modernization.

Here are the basic building blocks of the Saudi social structure, in order of importance. All these groupings are patrilineal—that is, they descend through the male line (the fathers):

1. **The extended family:** Relatives descended from the same father or grandfather, along with their wives and children.

2. **The clan:** Four to six related families, who share a common ancestor a few more generations back.

3. **The tribe:** Perhaps seven to fifteen clans linked by a common ancestor even further back in time.

With the intense urbanization of recent years, tribal and clan affiliations have become weak and blurred. Fewer and fewer Saudis can recount their tribe's history, and growing numbers claim no tribal affiliation at all. One of the main complaints of the conservatives who oppose modernization is that the family, too, is being weakened in its role as the central pillar of Saudi life.

All in the Family

Having summarized the three-part social structure of family, clan, and tribe, now I'll tell you more about the most important unit in that structure, the family.

Marriage

Saudis have a very different way of thinking about marriage from most Westerners. In the West, the "romantic" idea prevails, with two people meeting, falling in love, starting a family, and living happily ever after. Or not, as the case may be, in this age of socially acceptable divorce.

Most Saudis uphold a much older and more traditional idea of marriage. Here are the two most important things to know about the way Saudis get married.

◆ Nearly all Saudi marriages are arranged by the two families, although the bride and groom usually have an informal "veto." Even if choosing a spouse for themselves, a "modern" or Westernized bride and groom will always seek family approval.

◆ It's preferable to marry a relative, and marriage to cousins is actually on the rise throughout the Arab world. Saudi Arabia has the second-highest rate of marriage between first cousins: 55 percent (only Iraq is higher, with 58 percent).

The goal of a Saudi marriage is a happy and stable family life, as contrasted with the exaggerated expectations of endless romantic fulfillment that marriages have to struggle under in the West. Romance is only one of a number of goals for young Saudi newlyweds. Financial security and social standing are equally important. That's why so many marriages are arranged, and why marriage between cousins is so common—the families already know each other's backgrounds, so there's less risk of an unpleasant surprise.

In addition, the bride comes with a dowry (a sum of money from her family), and under Islamic law she will also inherit part of her father's estate. Marriage between cousins is a way of keeping these financial resources within the family.

Arabian Almanac

Owing to Saudi society's strict segregation of the sexes, the groom is the only man who attends traditional Saudi wedding festivities. All the other guests are women. If the families are wealthy, the wedding celebration becomes a fashion frenzy, with the women competing for attention among each other in their splendid dresses and jewelry. As in the West, the bride's father is supposed to pay for the wedding, and the celebration's extravagance is a measure of his wealth and generosity. Meanwhile, the men gather somewhere else and sip coffee or tea.

Saudis marry much younger than Westerners, and the lower classes marry youngest of all. It's not unheard of for a girl of 10 to be married, though in most cases the bride's age is from about 16 to 18 years, and the groom's age is from about 16 to 20. Islamic tradition lets a man marry up to four wives, but he must provide for them equally. In polygamous households, often a very young bride will end up as a "junior" wife to a much older man. Polygamy is becoming rarer, though, especially among the upper classes. One wife or many, the traditional view holds that a wife's only purpose is to produce children and satisfy her husband's sexual needs.

Divorce

Instant, hassle-free divorce is as easy as pie in Saudi Arabia—as long as you're a man. All you need is the ability to say, "I divorce you," and it's done. It's relatively common, and society considers it no big deal. Traditional Saudi men can go through as many as 30 wives or more in a lifetime.

If you're a woman, you can basically forget about obtaining a divorce, unless you're willing to go to a religious judge and try to prove adultery, physical abuse, or something along those lines. Options include claiming that your husband is impotent, which is viewed as being in the same ballpark as adultery or abuse.

Children

Saudis love children, and the arrival of a child brings great joy to a couple and to their families—if the child is a boy, that is. The mother of a girl is viewed as having failed, so far, in her most important duty. Only when the mother produces a boy is she considered to have fulfilled her greatest destiny. Say her name is Fatima, and the boy's name is Muhammad. After his birth, those who wish to compliment her might call her *Fatima umm Muhammad*, "Fatima, Mother of Muhammad," or simply *umm Muhammad*, "Mother of Muhammad."

Until the age of about seven, children of both sexes are generally reared together in the harem, the household's female precincts. Boys, being highly favored over girls, are breast-fed until three or four years of age, while girls are weaned relatively early. The boys, moreover, are fed on demand, whenever they feel like it. When discipline is called for, adults tend to shame children rather than reasoning with them. Instead of trying to explain why the child's behavior is inappropriate or wrong, parents simply inform children that their behavior threatens to bring shame on the family. "You can't do that—what will people think?" is a common way of bringing a child's behavior into line. Physical punishment is rare. Saudis usually treat children very gently.

Saudi boys are raised, essentially, to believe that they are the center of the universe. They're fussed over not just by their own mothers, but by all of their father's wives in the harem. As with the breast feeding, much of this intensive communal care can leave a strongly erotic aftertaste in the boy's memory. For example, a common way for the women to stop a baby boy from crying is by caressing and stroking his genitals. Such practices have been credited with contributing to the way that Saudi men tend to view women as mere sex objects, placed on this earth solely to gratify the men's physical appetites.

Meanwhile, girls are taught to understand and accept that their existence has no meaning whatsoever, except as it relates to the men in their family. When a girl is young, her parents are merely ashamed that she wasn't a boy. Her main role is to help care for her brothers. Later, however, the parents will be anxiety-ridden over the possibility that she might bring shame upon her family. Just as a mother will later be called after her son, so are girls called after their father. If Fatima's father is named Abdullah, she will be known as *Fatima bint Abdullah*, "Fatima, Daughter of Abdullah," until the day she has a son.

Men and Women

Men and women each have their honor to uphold: for men it's called *sharaf*, and for women it's called *ird*. A man's sharaf, however, is in large part dependent on the ird of the women in his family. And the women's ird is sexual and highly fragile—it can be lost not just if she sleeps with someone other than her husband, but if she so much as smiles or even talks to the wrong man. Saudi men live in constant fear that their honor will be injured by the misbehavior of "their" women. Their fear is reinforced by the belief that women are by nature sexually voracious and provocative, and by the fact that society doesn't blame men for responding to them. Indeed, virility is among the highest of values for a Saudi male.

Obviously, Western values say this is a heinous double standard. True enough. The point I want to make, though, is that both men and women are thought of as *constantly prey to uncontrollable sexual urges.*

Hence, nearly every social institution in Saudi life is dedicated to keeping unrelated men and women apart from each other. Should a man and woman end up alone together, it's thought, they'd be tearing each other's clothes off and fornicating madly in about five seconds flat.

Sheik-Speak

Honor comes in two forms: **sharaf**, a man's honor, and **ird**, a woman's honor. The man's concept of honor is broad, but a large part of it relies on upholding the ird of the women in his family. The concept of a woman's ird, by contrast, is narrow—it's totally defined by her chastity.

The penalty for fornication, as for adultery, is death. If a wife commits adultery, it's not her husband's sharaf that is injured, but her father's and brothers'. In terms of her honor, a wife continues to be considered part of her original family, not the family she married into. In cases where a young unmarried woman has a child out of wedlock, her father or brothers have been known to kill her. In such cases, courts are reluctant to convict, and any punishment is light.

In Saudi Arabia, in other words, the slightest contact with the opposite sex is charged with erotic danger. And it's not just the men, but the women, too. This is a seriously sex-obsessed society.

In Public

In public what this means, basically, is that no part of a woman's body is allowed to be seen. A Saudi woman is expected to wear the *hijab* or veil, a piece of black gauze that covers her face, whenever she goes out. She can see out, barely, but no one can see in. In addition, she covers her entire body with clothing, and then—just to be on the safe side—covers the clothing with another protective layer of drapery called the *abaya*.

All of this is to prevent any man who looks at her from being inflamed with uncontrollable lust. She then walks a respectful and subservient distance behind her husband and sons. Her husband or male relatives are the only men she's allowed to speak to. At mixed social gatherings, Saudis usually separate naturally into men's and women's groups.

Western women are cut a little slack in the dress department. They don't need to wear veils, but they are expected to cover their arms and hair. Long dresses are pretty much obligatory—no pants, and above all, no shorts. Saudi men assume that all Western women are promiscuous, and the men don't hesitate to make blunt advances to any Western woman they can get alone.

Sheik-Speak

The **hijab** or black gauze veil is the best-known symbol of the subordinate role of women in the Islamic world.

The **abaya** is a cloak-like garment, usually black, wrapped loosely over a woman's outer clothing.

Mirage Ahead

The hijab's origins are themselves veiled in mystery. Some authorities believe Islamic culture adopted the veil from Byzantium, where women are known to have veiled themselves in public. Byzantine society, too, generally kept women sequestered in the home. (For background on Byzantium, see Chapters 1 and 2.) One thing is certain, however: There's no commandment for women to wear veils in the Koran or in the Hadith, Islam's sacred texts. Some Saudis and many Islamists try to argue that the veil is part of the Islamic religious tradition. Not so. While Islamic (like Judaic) scripture says that a woman's hair should not be shown, it says nothing about her face. The veil has nothing to do with Islam. It's a purely cultural tradition that happens to have been picked up by many Islamic societies over the centuries. So don't be fooled by those who want to persuade others that women have to wear the veil in order to be "good" Muslims. It's a cultural thing, not a religious thing.

As well as covering herself completely, when a woman does leave the house she's supposed to be accompanied by an adult male relative—her husband, brother, or father. Only the most Westernized Saudi families ignore this custom, and if a woman does go out unaccompanied, it's only because her liberal husband or father decided to let her. Even then, she faces a scolding or worse if she's caught by the religious police. Shops, banks, schools, waiting rooms, restaurants, buses—everything either has separate facilities for men and woman, or is open only for single-sex use. There are special women's banks, for example, that opened during the 1980s, as women came into control of larger sums of money in the oil boom. Only about 10 percent of Saudi women work, since they can only work in such all-women institutions.

The two areas of life in which Saudi women have some degree of authority are their own finances and the home. Sharia or Islamic law stipulates that women retain control of their dowries and inheritances (more on Sharia in the next chapter). Arab custom also dictates that the women control the household. The home is usually run by an older woman, a matriarch who may be the husband's mother or his senior wife.

With modernization, there is increasing evidence that many Saudi women are becoming impatient with their constant "protection," but it's hard to get a read on exactly how high the level of impatience is. Most women, for now, seem willing to remain in their position of subservience. The question is, for how long? Many wealthy Saudi women, for example, constantly travel abroad to escape the restrictions they face at home. They spend large blocks of time in Europe or America, enjoying the ability to simply walk around in public alone, unveiled. How long will they remain willing to conform to traditional ways when they return home?

There's no way to tell, but it's an absolutely central issue to watch, since upholding the traditional role of women is at the core of the conservative, anti-Western forces in Saudi society. Indeed, when religious conservatives talk about preserving "the family," they're really talking about preserving the traditional oppression of women.

At Home

Sexual segregation continues in the home, with men and women having separate living quarters. It's the women's communal space, the harem, that is so famous in the West. There the women gather and relax, at least in wealthy homes, where there are abundant servants to do the work and therefore also abundant time. In fact, the biggest problem for wealthy Saudi women is total, complete, mind-numbing boredom. Even shopping is limited, since they can't go out without their husbands. (That gives you an idea of the burden of inconvenience placed on the men by all this "protection.") If a woman is home alone, she cannot let a male visitor into the house.

Wealthy Saudi women mostly sleep late, shop, read cheesy romances, and watch American videos. The last two pursuits, of course, make them focus all the more on sex, sex, sex. When Saudi women get together, therefore, sex is the main topic of conversation, and by all accounts things can get pretty risqué. And there are always a few stories circulating about wealthy Saudi women seducing foreign workers—at least enough to keep the gossips in the large expatriate community busy.

One problem that has been receiving public attention is that of widespread physical abuse of wives by their husbands. In the past, this has been one of those things that everyone knew went on, but no one talked about. In recent years, Saudi newspapers have been speaking out strongly against spousal abuse.

The Least You Need to Know

- Saudis live in a "shame culture," not a "guilt culture."

- A Saudi man's honor depends in large part on the women in his family preserving their sexual honor.

- Saudi social institutions are geared toward keeping men and women apart so they won't have illicit sexual relations.

- Underneath all the repression, Saudi society is obsessed with sex.

Policing the Faithful: Islam in Saudi Arabia

In This Chapter

- ◆ Fear is the key
- ◆ The religious police get busted
- ◆ Law and education in the land of the believers
- ◆ Hating in the name of God

Earlier I told you that Saudis see the outside world as a seething pit of immorality that's constantly threatening their own moral purity. At this point, it won't surprise you to hear that the engine behind this rather paranoid take on things is Wahhabism, the Saudis' version of Islam.

You already know a lot about the historical background of Wahhabism. For example, in Chapter 4, you learned how Wahhabism's founder, Muhammad ibn Abdel Wahhab, allied himself with the Saudi royal family in the eighteenth century. In that same chapter, you saw the founder of modern Saudi Arabia, Ibn Saud, use the Wahhabi fighters called the Ikhwan, or Brotherhood, to help consolidate his own rule. Later, when these fierce desert warriors turned against him, Ibn Saud was forced to break up the Ikhwan.

Then, in subsequent chapters, you saw Wahhabism at work in further shaping Saudi politics, history, and current events, right up to the current wave of al Qaeda terrorism.

In this chapter, we'll look at how Wahhabi religious beliefs play out in Saudi public life. I'll start with an overview of the Saudi religious outlook, then move on to specifics like Saudi Arabia's notorious religious police, its ultra-harsh version of Islamic law, and its highly religious educational system. Finally, I'll ask and answer a few questions about Wahhabism, Islam as a whole, and "Western" ideas like democracy, tolerance, and pluralism.

State of Siege

A good way to sum up Saudi society's general religious outlook is to say that it reflects a siege mentality. In other words, the Wahhabi attitude resembles that of defenders in an isolated castle, who have long been under siege by a wicked and tireless enemy force. That enemy force includes not just the West and its modernizing influences, but also nearly every other major version of Islam, since most fail to measure up to the Wahhabis' stripped-down, no-frills approach to God.

Sheik-Speak

Xenophobia comes from the Greek words *xenos*, "stranger" or "foreigner," and *phobia*, "fear." From its primary meaning, "fear of foreigners," xenophobia is often extended to mean contempt, dislike, or hatred of anything foreign. This meaning also applies to the Saudis. See the connection between fear and hatred?

As so much of the Saudi outlook as a whole is shaped by their religious outlook, the siege mentality goes for the people as a whole, too. Its main symptom is the rabid *xenophobia*, or fear of foreigners, that characterizes Saudi culture. Saudis see themselves as isolated and vulnerable—both spiritually and geographically—in a hostile world. Thus, Saudi Arabia itself might appropriately be termed a "state of siege."

Desert Roots?

The Saudis' sense of geographical isolation, of course, has a basis in reality, since another way to think of Saudi Arabia is as an "island" surrounded by a protective sea of sand. This is an image that the Saudis often use to describe themselves, and it ties in with the whole desert mystique thing I described earlier, in Chapter 11. Part of that mystique is the idea that the desert is clean and pure, and that this purity has somehow transferred itself to Islam, which is often thought of as being born in the desert. I mentioned that Islam was, in fact, born in the urban environment of Medina—yet at the same time it's also true that the desert traditions of the tribal Bedouin did play a huge role in shaping the new religion.

Regardless of Islam's actual origins, the Saudis see the core of their own religious values as coming out of their "pure" desert environment. In other words, there's a definite tie-in between the stark, unforgiving nature of the desert, and the stark, unforgiving nature of Wahhabism. At least, such a tie-in exists in the Saudis' minds, and that's what counts, after all. This sense of purity is seen as being endangered by the alien, threatening values of the world beyond the protective desert.

Lustbusters

There's another way that Saudis see themselves as vulnerable, and its origins are harder to pin down, even speculatively. In the last chapter, I described the obsessive concern with sex and female chastity that lies at the heart of Saudi social values. I also said that this concern arises from the belief that men and women, if allowed to mix freely, would be jumping each other's bones every time they're alone together for a few minutes. Though it sounds like a joke, it's really not. That's what most Saudis believe. Men and women, in the traditional Saudi view, are always vulnerable to the flames of uncontrollable lust, which they believe will erupt without fail if given the slightest opportunity.

Arabian Almanac

There are three main ways the Saudis see themselves as vulnerable.

- **Spiritual vulnerability.** Without constant vigilance, the purity of Wahhabi Islam will be corrupted by outside influences.
- **Geographical vulnerability.** Physical isolation has bred extreme xenophobia, a deep fear of the outside world and its alien ways.
- **Sexual vulnerability.** All adults are constantly prey to uncontrollable lust.

Each of these vulnerabilities creates its own brand of exaggerated fear. If there's a single key to understanding the Saudis, it's grasping the exaggerated fears that dominate their outlook.

This is a cultural trait, but it's also the official Wahhabi party line. It's a big reason the Wahhabis are so virulently anti-Western. And hey, with boobs, butts, and buff bodies among the most visible aspects of Western culture, is it any wonder the Wahhabis see the West as a den of sin? Inflaming people's lust, after all, is the main objective of nearly all Western advertising and entertainment. (What's the Madison Avenue mantra? "Sex sells," right?) Political considerations aside, by calling for the rejection of Western values, Wahhabi clerics in part are simply fulfilling their self-appointed role as society's lustbusters.

The Religious Police

At the front line of the lustbuster brigade—the "early responders" of Wahhabi puritanism—are the notorious *Mutawain*, or the Committee for the Propagation of Virtue and the Prevention of Vice, better known in the West as the Religious Police. Numbering more than 3,500 male religious zealots, this independent arm of the government has broad powers to arrest or punish on the spot those deemed to be violating Wahhabi norms of dress and behavior.

Sheik-Speak

The word **Mutawain** (*moo tah wah EEN;* singular *mutawa*) means "volunteers," and it's the informal name for the government agency whose official title is the Committee for the Propagation of Virtue and the Prevention of Vice. Most often described in the Western press as the Religious Police, it's also sometimes called the Committee for Public Morality or some similar name.

Arabian Almanac

Each year, Saudi religious universities turn out thousands of young men who are burning with zeal to become Wahhabi clerics. But there aren't enough job openings. Some of these angry young men become Mutawain or Religious Police, but many remain unemployable. For background on Saudi unemployment, see Chapter 12.

There's a separate civil police force in charge of what Westerners would think of as regular law enforcement, but in Saudi Arabia the religious and civil realms constantly overlap. Sometimes there's a potential conflict, and in such cases the civil police are usually afraid to mess with the Mutawain.

A quintessential Wahhabi institution, the Mutawain have been around in the Najd since the rise of Wahhabism there in the eighteenth century. In 1806, a Western observer in the Najd wrote that these "constables for the punctuality of prayers … with an enormous staff in their hand, were ordered to shout, to scold, and to drag people by the shoulders to force them to take part in public prayers, five times a day." With the foundation of the modern Saudi state in the twentieth century, the "constables for public prayer" became part of the official state apparatus.

Today, the responsibilities of the Mutawain include …

◆ Enforcing attendance at prayer five times daily.

◆ Making sure that shops close at prayer time.

◆ Being on the lookout for violations of "public morality" like playing music, smoking, drinking alcoholic beverages, men and women holding hands, unmarried couples out in public together, long hair for men or uncovered hair for women, and, above all, "immodest" dress by women.

Angry Young Men with Canes

Instead of the "enormous staff" reported by the nineteenth-century observer I just quoted, today's Mutawain carry thin canes or camel whips, which they use to beat the unfortunate "offenders" they've singled out for their wrath. They roam the streets and shopping malls at will, and no one is exempt from their attentions. The expatriate community is rife with stories about Westerners who've been accosted, shouted at, bullied, beaten, or hauled off to jail for some real or imagined infraction.

Despite official instructions to the Mutawain to back off from harassing Westerners, in effect they remained unchecked into the twenty-first century. In May 2001, for example, three Western nurses were arrested, strip searched, and jailed for several days because two of them were wearing short sleeves.

Tragedy and Outrage

However, the Religious Police may finally have gone too far.

On a March morning in 2002, a fire broke out in a stairwell at the 31st Girls' Middle School in suburban Mecca. The shoddily built four-story building held over 800 students and some 55 teachers. When the girls rushed to the building's single exit, they found it locked. The school's male guard—the only person with the key—was away. Onlookers rushed to the scene, followed by civil police officers and firemen, who attempted to open the door.

But the Religious Police had also arrived. Reports vary about exactly what happened next. Some witnesses said the Religious Police stopped the firemen and civil police from opening the door. Others claimed that the Religious Police actually forced fleeing girls back into the burning building. What seems certain is that the door was locked, that it stayed locked for some time, and that the Religious Police blocked attempts to open it. According to some later reports, one member of the Religious Police fought openly with an officer of the civil police, declaring that the girls—who had neglected to don their robe-like abayas before fleeing—could have no contact whatsoever with the male rescuers until they were modestly dressed. One government official said he saw Religious Police "beating young girls to prevent them from leaving the school."

Fourteen girls perished in the fire, and another died later in the hospital. A number of others were badly injured when they were trampled inside the chaotic building by panicked schoolmates.

Emboldened by shock and anger, the usually tame Saudi press reacted with indignation. Reporters sought out eyewitnesses and questioned them fully, and the eyewitness accounts of the fire ran in newspapers across the country. Editorials condemned the Religious Police and publicly questioned a social system that required a locked front door in a girls' school in the first place. All of this was a first in a land where censorship is largely self-imposed, and where bland evasion normally triumphs over substantive inquiry.

Stirrings of Reform?

The deaths of the 15 girls in the Mecca school fire sent out shock waves that are still rumbling through the rigid, hidebound Saudi system. Soon after the fire, Crown Prince Abdullah, who rules in place of the ailing King Fahd, appointed a high-level commission to investigate the disaster. Abdullah is widely regarded as a reformist who (like his older brother King Faisal) also has strong religious credentials.

Remember how I mentioned in Chapter 6 that King Faisal's wife, Iffat al Thunayan, had been instrumental in pushing to include girls' education in the modernization drive? As part of the deal to placate the conservative Wahhabi opposition to education for girls, the girls' schools had been put under their management. Since then, girls' schools had been run by the Presidency for Girls' Education, which was always under the control of the religious conservatives. Now, however, Abdullah took the responsibility for girls' education away from the Wahhabi clerics, and gave it to the Ministry of Education, which had previously been in charge only of the boys' schools. (In accordance with Wahhabi dictates, of course, there are no mixed gender schools in the kingdom.)

Arabian Almanac

Though it's still too early to predict the outcome, it's thought that Crown Prince Abdullah took the opportunity presented by the girls' school fire to open a campaign for reforms against the extreme conservative wing of the religious leadership. Whatever the ultimate result, Abdullah made a very important reform in the weeks immediately after the fire: he took girls' education away from the Wahhabis, and placed it under the authority of the Education Ministry, whose head is a secularist reformer.

This put girls' education under the direction of the education minister, Qaidir ibn Olayan al Quraishi, reportedly a secularist reformer who enjoys Crown Prince Abdullah's full support. Qaidir already had plans to reduce the heavily religious content of boys' education, and in the summer of 2002 he began moving to bring girls' schooling more into line with that offered to boys. And girls, after all, become women. What they are taught now is what tomorrow's women will believe. So girls' education is crucially important, because it touches on the whole issue of women and their role in Saudi society. That issue, as I suggested in the previous chapter, may be the biggest one of all for Saudi society.

Education

So, although only time will tell, it seems that the girls' school tragedy in Mecca may have helped push the Saudi educational system toward a decisive crossroads. It would be high time. So far, when Saudis talk about "education," what they really mean is more like "indoctrination." Unless they're talking about going to school in another country, like the United States or Great Britain, that is. And with the expansion of the university system in the past two decades, fewer Saudis are now going abroad to study.

Most primary and secondary education in Saudi Arabia has one purpose: to raise good Wahhabis. For girls, this means cooking, sewing, and memorizing the Koran (at least so far). For boys, it means a curriculum dominated by religious studies and Arabic studies (Arabic language, history, and literature), along with geography, math, and science.

At the university level, men have a choice between the religious universities (where only Islamic subjects are taught) or the "non-religious" universities, which teach other subjects along with religion. Women in the universities theoretically have nearly the same options, but in practice their choices are limited by segregation. Women students have separate classes, which are taught only by women. They can't mix with the male students at all, and the men have first crack at facilities. Women students at King Saud University (formerly Riyadh University) can't use the library, for example, but must write out request forms for the books they need, which are then delivered to the women's section of the university.

 **Arabian Almanac**

Saudi Arabia has eight major universities, six of which admit women. The 10 percent (or less) of women who do work mostly go into health or teaching, so women students concentrate on these areas.

The Saudis have certainly made progress in education, much of it due to King Fahd, who was Minister of Education during the modernization drive. Literacy has gone from close to zero in the 1950s to around 75 percent for adults, a considerable achievement in a half-century. The kingdom's schools and universities had a total enrollment of nearly 250,000 in 2000, with male and female students equally represented. Equal numbers of women and men (about 10,000 each) now graduate from Saudi universities every year. Yet two out of three doctorates given to Saudi students are for "Islamic studies," which leaves them totally unsuited for the job market.

Yet Saudi education remains geared towards rote memorization and religious indoctrination rather than independent thinking. There's little or no exposure to other cultural traditions, unlike in Western schools and universities. Though many Saudis learn English, they can't take a class in Italian literature or Chinese history. Political science is unheard of (danger, Will Robinson!). Science and math content is kept strictly in line with Wahhabi doctrine. And the religious universities teach courses in nothing other than hatred, instructing their students to despise Jews, Christians, Shiites—anyone who doesn't conform to Wahhabi doctrine. All in the name of God, of course.

Sharia Law

Saudi Arabia adheres almost exclusively to Sharia law, the Islamic legal system based on the Koran and the Hadith, Islam's two sacred texts. Much of Sharia law is concerned with religious practices, marriage and divorce, inheritance, and similar matters. Although the king sets up special courts from time to time to handle special cases not covered by the Sharia, for the most part Saudi Arabia's courts are religious courts, and the *qadis*, or judges, are generally conservative Wahhabis.

Like other Muslims who call for the "application" of Sharia law, the Saudis view Sharia law as divinely inspired, rather than created by human beings, and they see it as unchanged since its original formulation. However, since the Koran and the Hadith have limited material that can be used to guide lawmakers, there has always been a significant need for scholarly interpretation. Much of that interpretation also relied on pre-Islamic laws and customs. Sharia law was first set down in various forms by Islamic jurists and legal scholars in the centuries after Muhammad's death—and more changes have occurred since then than the fundamentalists would like to admit.

Sheik-Speak

The **qadi** is the judge who traditionally hands down legal decisions under Sharia law.

There are four branches of Sharia law spread across the Sunni Islamic world, each founded by a scholar from the eighth or ninth century, and they vary widely in strictness. (Shiites have their own branches, which also vary widely.)

CAUTION

Mirage Ahead

Hold on a minute! Before you go any further in reading about Sharia law, you may need to adjust your approach to the law a little—especially if you happen to be a lawyer. There are some fundamental differences that you should know about between Western and Islamic approaches to the law.

In Western law, an act is either legal or illegal, period. There are lots of various classes of crimes, but only two kinds of acts: legal and illegal. In Islamic law, by contrast, there are *five* categories of acts: those you are obliged to do, those you are advised to do, those you are advised not to do, those you are prohibited from doing, and those that are "neutral," i.e., that Islamic law doesn't care about.

Here are the four main branches of Sunni Sharia law, along with their founders and the areas where each branch is followed.

- **The Hanafi branch** (followers of Abu Hanifa, d. 767): Turkey, Syria, Iraq, Central Asia, India.

- **The Maliki branch** (followers of Malik ibn Anas, d. 795): North Africa, Central Africa, West Africa.

- **The Shafii branch** (followers of Muhammad ibn Idris Al Shafii, d. 820): Egypt, the southern Arabian peninsula, East Africa, South East Asia.

- **The Hanbali branch** (followers of Ahmad ibn Hanbal, d. 855): Saudi Arabia.

Saudi Arabia's laws are based on the Hanbali school, which is the strictest of the four Sunni branches. The strictness is most evident in religious and social matters, though. When it comes to business, the Hanbali branch is widely seen as the most permissive, to the point where normal Saudi business practices can be perceived as unethical or corrupt by outsiders. (More on Saudi business practices in Chapter 16.)

As followed by the Saudis, the Hanbali branch of Sharia law embodies your classic "eye-for-an-eye, tooth-for-a-tooth" approach to crime and punishment. From ancient times, Arabian customs have dictated that offenders be punished by suffering whatever wrong they inflicted on another. Lashing with a whip is one traditional punishment still routinely imposed by the Saudi penal system. For more serious crimes, harsher vengeance can be exacted in order to preserve social order. It's not unusual for repeatedly convicted thieves to have their hands amputated at the wrist, for example. The severed hands are then tied to a line by the middle finger and dangled in public as a lesson to others. Saudi Arabia's very low crime rate is often credited to such deterrents.

Four offenses are officially punishable by death: murder, apostasy (a fancy word for leaving the faith, in this case Islam), rape, and adultery. Unofficially, as I mentioned in the last chapter, Saudi courts generally go easy on male family members who murder a girl or woman for having sex before marriage.

In murder cases, the death penalty can be avoided if the victim's family agrees to accept restitution—usually a sum of money—from the offender. Like fornication, rape and adultery are viewed as terrible crimes against society, because they threaten the stability of the family. A woman convicted of adultery may be publicly stoned to death, while a man may be publicly beheaded. Because the penalty is so severe, adultery requires a high level of proof: four male witnesses or eight female ones must be produced to attest to the deed. (A woman's testimony is seen as being worth half as much as a man's.) Consequently, executions for adultery are very rare.

Islam and Democracy

In recent years, one of the most widely discussed aspects of Islam—both in the West and in the Islamic world itself—is the question of whether or not Islam is compatible with democracy. The surprising part is that Islamic fundamentalists and the Western media seem to agree: The answer they give to that question is "no." Islam, we're repeatedly told by Islamic militants and Western pundits alike, is by its very nature incompatible with democracy. Especially after the September 11, 2001, terrorist attacks, the Western press seems to have concluded that there's something different about Islam, something that sets it apart from the world's other religions. And that something, whatever it is, has put Islam on an inevitable collision course with the democratic nations of the West. Furthermore, we're told, this is part of a global "clash of civilizations" that's unavoidably going to unfold in a welter of terrorism and violence.

You know what I say to that? Phooey! But before I tell you why I think the militants and the pundits are equally full of horse-puckey, let me tell you why the question of Islam and democracy matters so much when it comes to the subject of Saudi Arabia.

The Official Saudi View

First of all, it matters because Saudi Arabia is easily the oldest and most conservative Islamic state currently around. Moreover, it's home to Islam's holiest sites, Mecca and Medina. Islamic credentials lie at the heart of the Saudi identity. And at the same time, Saudi Arabia is the least democratic of Islamic states, and one of the least democratic of Arab states as well. So, of all the world's nations, Saudi Arabia best combines Islamic legitimacy with anti-democratic politics. In Saudi Arabia, in other words, you've got what appears to be iron-clad confirmation of the idea that Islam and democracy just aren't meant for each other.

The official Saudi view wholeheartedly endorses this conclusion. Democracy may be okay for other people, King Fahd said in 1992 when he announced the formation of the Majlis as-Shura, the kingdom's non-elected Consultative Council (see Chapter 10). But given the Islamic character of his nation, Fahd asserted, "the democratic system prevailing in the world doesn't suit us." Instead, he went on, "Islam is our social and political law. It is a complete constitution of social and economic laws and a system of government and justice."

Well, that sounds great, and it's also the line echoed by the Islamic fundamentalists and by many Western pundits. There's only one small problem: It's almost completely untrue. And the part that is true is completely irrelevant.

Let me explain what I mean by introducing some other views on Islam and democracy.

Other Views

Let's begin with the part of King Fahd's statement that *is* true: Islam aspires to be a complete social system. Indeed, this is pretty much what I told you when I introduced you to Islam way back in Chapter 1. But—and here's the point—that has absolutely nothing whatsoever to do with democracy. Democracy is not about society as such—it's about *politics*. It does have social consequences (which is why we talk about "democratic societies"), but that's a different matter. Democracy is a kind of political system, not a kind of social system.

Now for the parts of King Fahd's statement that are untrue: Islam offers a complete "constitution" of economic, governmental, and political laws. Where exactly? Not in the Koran. Not in the Hadith. Not anywhere, in fact. You can comb through Islam's most revered texts and you won't find anything that clearly favors monarchy over democracy, for example, or free-market capitalism over socialism.

In fact, as numerous Muslim writers have pointed out, much in the Islamic tradition has a distinctly democratic, egalitarian flavor. These writers point to well-known passages in the Koran that seem to encourage tolerance and pluralism. One commonly cited example is in Sura 2, Verse 256: "There shall be no compulsion in religion."

Yet I also reluctantly disagree with those who quote such passages to argue that Islam is inherently democratic. For every "tolerant" verse, you can find one like Sura 3, Verse 28: "Let not believers make friends with infidels." This sounds much closer to Wahhabi unfriendliness—but (like the other quote) it doesn't have much to do with politics, democratic or otherwise. The bottom line is that Islam's sacred texts don't endorse or propose any kind of political, governmental, or economic system at all.

Desert Dates

May 12, 2003: Suicide bombers in Riyadh kill 25, including 8 Americans and 7 Saudis (see Chapter 20). Like the girls' school fire, this incident encourages more Saudis to think twice about Wahhabi doctrines of hate and intolerance. On May 25, 2003, for example, a *New York Times* article describes Mansour al-Nogaidan, an ex-Wahhabi cleric whose views have been reversed by the bombing. Shortly after it happens, Nogaidan goes on record as publicly blaming Wahhabism for fomenting violence in Saudi Arabia and around the world. The article also features Abdel Aziz Qasim, a young Saudi Islamic scholar and a former qadi, who plans to publish a collection of Muhammad's most tolerant sayings in Saudi Arabia. "The challenge," Qasim observes, "is whether the government is willing to disregard the Wahhabi teachings or not."

Of Muhammad and Madison

Which brings us back to our old friend, secularism. As I suggested earlier in this chapter, the Saudi approach to religion springs from fear. The Saudis seem to believe that Islam is so weak and insecure that it needs the full support of the state in order to survive. This sort of faith, it seems to me, doesn't have much to brag about. If Islam enjoys God's favor, surely the Saudis and others can trust it to stand on its own, without the fearful support of an autocratic, paranoid state apparatus.

James Madison, the father of the U.S. Constitution, wrote that religion actually benefits if it's not part of the state. State support, Madison argued, hinders religion rather than helping it. Look at the United States, which is strongly secular and vibrantly religious at the same time. Then look at Saudi Arabia, where both state and religion seem paralyzed by being so closely intertwined.

Two Faces?

Also way back in Chapter 2, I promised to tell you what I thought about other controversial issues, like whether Islam is inherently anti-Jewish and anti-Christian. So here's my opinion, for what it's worth. There are parts of the Koran you can quote that seem unfriendly to Jews and Christians. But there are also parts that seem friendly. Indeed, traditions of both tolerance and intolerance run right through the whole of Islamic history. One recent writer on the Wahhabis calls this "the two faces of Islam," with Wahhabism representing the intolerant face.

Personally, I don't think Islam is alone in having "two faces." You can find similar opposing traditions in every major world faith, including Judaism and Christianity, and for good reason. In every society and every age, there are always people who want to kill their neighbors, and there are always people who want to love them. And world religions get to be world religions only by appealing to everyone. Otherwise, they remain small or disappear entirely.

When it comes to religion and politics, therefore, you can always find "religious" justification for just about anything. The important thing is not what the religions say (since you can make them say anything), but how people use religious justifications to get and keep power for themselves. After all, who is it telling you how Islam and democracy aren't compatible? Kings, other autocratic rulers, and terrorists who want to fulfill their own lust for power or glory. Oh yes, and TV pundits who promote themselves by simplifying things and playing on your fear of a "clash of civilizations." It's people with agendas who clash, not religions and not civilizations.

The Least You Need to Know

- The intolerant Saudi religious outlook is shaped by fear, which comes from a sense of vulnerability.

- Recent events like the 2002 girls' school fire and the May 2003 Riyadh bombing have increasingly led Saudis to publicly question Wahhabi intolerance and hatred.

- Islam is no more or less incompatible with democracy than any other religion.

Pilgrims' Progress

In This Chapter

◆ How Saudis worship in their daily lives

◆ Some famous pilgrims who never heard of the *Mayflower*

◆ The hajj—up close and personal

◆ How the Saudis handle millions of people arriving from around the world, all at the same time and place, every year

The previous chapter gave you the big picture on the part that Islam plays in Saudi public life. In this chapter, we'll stay on the subject of Islam, but we'll shift from its role in public life over to the realm of private worship. And for a Saudi, as for any Muslim, the climax of private worship is the hajj—the annual pilgrimage to the holy city of Mecca, which all Muslims who can are supposed to make at least once in their lives. The hajj, therefore, will be the main focus of this chapter.

Each year at the appointed time, some 2.5 million Muslims (including about 1 million Saudis) arrive in Mecca to undertake a sacred procession to Islam's holiest sites in and around the Saudi city. During that time, which lasts about a week, they go through a complex series of time-honored rituals. It's a deeply spiritual occasion that represents the high point of a Muslim's life and the fulfillment of his or her religious duty.

After meeting some famous pilgrims from the past, you'll learn how the Saudis have brought the hajj up to date for the jet age, while still preserving its spiritual significance. You'll then step into a pilgrim's sandals yourself (shoes are prohibited). Finally, you'll learn how the Saudis manage this huge yearly influx of people into the kingdom.

Personal Devotions

Before focusing on the hajj, however, I want to make sure that you have a clear idea of Islam's pervasive presence in the daily lives of all Saudis. You might even say that Saudis practice their faith all day, every day, so completely have religious reminders and rituals been woven into the fabric of day-to-day life. In general, Arabs are highly religious, but the Saudis take personal devotion to an extreme that is unusual even among Arabs.

Arabian Almanac

Saudi speech is laced with religious expressions, which also appear on business and private letterheads, retail receipts, personal jewelry, home decorations, and plaques on automobiles. Most are brief quotations from the Koran, or formulas that reappear in it, a popular example being the verse that opens all but one chapter of the Koran: "In the name of God, the Merciful, the Compassionate."

In Chapter 2 I gave you a brief summary of Muslims' main beliefs and practices. I also listed the "Five Pillars of Islam": making the declaration of belief, praying five times daily, giving to charity, fasting from dawn to dusk during the holy month of Ramadan, and undertaking the hajj. These are the main religious obligations of all Muslims, and Saudis take them very seriously.

The first of these, the shahada or declaration of belief, is pretty much self-explanatory: you simply say "There is no God but God, and Muhammad is His Prophet." As I pointed out, if you say this sincerely, you're considered to be a Muslim. The last obligation, the hajj, we'll get to in a moment. That leaves the middle three: prayer, charity, and fasting.

Mirage Ahead

Piety is among the highest of Saudi social values, and though Wahhabi clerics frequently rail against Jews and Christians, most Saudis are ready to respect the sincere religious beliefs of others. Conversely, the quickest way to turn off a Saudi acquaintance is to tell him or her that you're either an agnostic or an atheist. People are thought to be naturally religious, so a lack of religious belief is viewed as unnatural and depraved. If you're a devout person, you'll win respect from Saudis you meet. On the other hand, if you openly express religious doubts or atheistic opinions in Saudi company, be ready for unfavorable reactions.

Prayer

Muslims are required to pray five times a day: at dawn, noon, afternoon, sunset, and evening. The times vary slightly from day to day and place to place, depending on the time of sunrise and sunset. So at each mosque, it's the job of the *muezzin* to give the "call to prayer," which summons the faithful at the proper time. While prayers are commonly done in the mosque, they don't have to be. Muslims may pray at home, in public, or at work. The important thing is to pray at the right time, wherever you happen to be, and to pray while bowing down in the direction of Mecca. It's also important to perform ritual ablution or washing before praying. (Ritual washing plays a big role in many Islamic religious ceremonies, which reflects the symbolic value of cleanliness for a people historically short of water.) After spreading out a clean prayer rug, worshippers bend down on their knees, towards Mecca, and touch their foreheads to the floor while praying. Shoes are considered unclean and must be removed before entering a mosque; many Muslims also wash their feet before praying.

In Saudi Arabia, prayer times are published in the newspapers, and everything grinds to a halt during the designated hours. The Religious Police make the rounds at the start of each prayer period, rapping on windows to ensure that shops close, and hustling people off to the mosques. Shoppers in Saudi Arabia, therefore, are limited to a series of two-to-three hour windows between prayer times.

Sheik-Speak

The **muezzin** is the religious official who traditionally chants the summons to prayer five times a day from the minarets (slender towers) that adorn most mosques. Nowadays nearly all mosques use blaring public address systems with powerful speakers, and the call itself is usually recorded.

Friday is the Muslim holy day, and a weekly sermon is offered at most mosques on Friday after the noon prayer. The Friday sermon has traditionally been a time for Muslim clerics to voice social or political protest. In Saudi Arabia, it routinely includes Wahhabi verbal attacks on Western culture, American foreign policy, Jews and Christians everywhere, and, in recent years, on the Al Saud as well.

Charity

Giving alms or charity to the poor is a serious obligation for Muslims that Muhammad repeatedly mentions in the Koran. In fact, almsgiving—called zakat—is important enough to be fixed by Sharia law: Muslims are obliged to give 2.5 percent of their net yearly income, minus basic expenses, to charities for the poor. Keep this obligation in mind, since we'll need to take it into consideration later, when we get to the charity money that found its way into the coffers of al Qaeda.

Fasting

During the holy month of Ramadan (the ninth month of the Muslim lunar calendar), Muslims are not allowed to eat, drink, smoke, or have sexual relations between sunrise and sunset. Ramadan is the biggest holiday period in the Muslim world. During the day, the devout practice spiritual development through self-denial. And at sunset— traditionally determined as the moment it becomes impossible to tell a black thread from a white one— families gather to break the fast together with a festive meal. As at prayer times during normal months, shops and restaurants close up during Ramadan and life slows down or comes to a halt completely.

Arabian Almanac

Because the Muslim calendar is a lunar one, Ramadan falls at a slightly different time each year. The beginning of Ramadan is signaled by the appearance of the ninth new moon, and the first sighting of the moon is eagerly awaited. Whoever spots the new moon first and reports it to the authorities is given a cash reward. Competing claims for the reward are decided by the courts.

In Saudi Arabia, fasting during daylight hours is compulsory under law for both Muslims and non-Muslims alike in the month of Ramadan. Arrests for eating are common. Even taking a drink of water in the heat of the desert sun can bring on an attack by the cane-wielding Religious Police. Not surprisingly, many wealthy Saudis and foreigners alike take the opportunity to travel abroad during Ramadan.

A Brief History of the Hajj

Most religions have pilgrimage traditions, whereby believers undertake a journey to a sacred place in order to affirm and celebrate their faith. Jerusalem, a holy city to Jews, Christians, and Muslims, has historically seen the highest numbers of pilgrims overall. The first recorded Christian pilgrim is said to have journeyed there in the year 217 C.E., and Christians made regular pilgrimages to Jerusalem throughout the Middle Ages. Christian pilgrimage played a big role in history starting in the eleventh century, when Pope Urban II launched the Crusades after pilgrim routes from Western Europe to Jerusalem were blocked by the Seljuk Turks. (To review the historical background on the Middle Ages, go back to Chapters 2 and 3.)

But Islam is the only religion that actually requires its followers to go on a pilgrimage. "Pilgrimage to the House is a duty to God for all those who can make the journey," says the Koran in Sura 3, verse 98. "The House" is another name for the Great Mosque in Mecca. It's the site of the Kaaba, the cube-shaped shrine built around the ancient Black Stone (thought to be a meteorite) that pagan Arabs had worshipped in Mecca since time immemorial. Because of the Kaaba, Mecca was already a major religious center and pilgrim destination for the pagan Arabs before the rise of Islam.

Muhammad adopted Mecca as the destination for Muslim pilgrims as well, and many of the rites that Muslims perform during the hajj came from the earlier pagan rituals.

Desert Dates

January, 624: Muhammad commands Muslims to face Mecca when they pray. Previously, Muslims were supposed to pray in the direction of Jerusalem, which to this day remains the third-holiest city for Muslims (after Mecca and Medina). Changing the direction of prayer (the *qiblah*) is often seen as Muhammad's "declaration of independence" for the new faith, as Islam breaks away from its Judeo-Christian roots and orients itself firmly toward the Arab world.

When Muhammad changed the orientation of prayer away from Jerusalem and toward Mecca in 624, he changed the orientation of Islam itself—away from the monotheism's old home and toward its new, Arab, dwelling place. At the same time, he claimed for Mecca a founding role in the Judaic tradition: According to the Koran, Mecca is where Abraham, the founder of Judaism, first experienced his revelation from God. Other Koranic verses say that the Kaaba was built by Adam, then rebuilt by Abraham and Ishmael. The old pagan shrine thus became the focal point for Muslim prayers, and around it was built a unique mosque—the Haram, as it's called, or the Great Mosque. It's toward the Kaaba in particular that Muslims are praying when they bow in the direction of Mecca.

Classic Accounts

Muslims began making pilgrimages to Mecca during Muhammad's lifetime, with the Prophet himself leading the first ones. Since then the hajj has been a central element not only of the Islamic religious experience, but also of Arab and Islamic culture in general. For centuries, the pilgrims' travel network was the main way that Muslims moved around within the vast region that made up the Islamic world. The pilgrims, called hajis, would arrive in Cairo, Damascus, or Baghdad from as far afield as Spain and India. They would band together, paying a fee to join caravans organized specially for the pilgrim trade. The caravans would then proceed overland to Mecca, paying protection money to the various Bedouin tribes whose territories they crossed on the way.

Desert Dates

632: Leading some 90,000 followers, the Prophet Muhammad undertakes what he seems to know will be his final pilgrimage to Mecca, which Muslims call the Farewell Hajj. During it, Muhammad establishes many of the hajj rituals that Muslims still perform. Muhammad dies in June 632, less than three months after returning from the Farewell Hajj.

Islamic culture is highly literary, and a number of hajis wrote colorful and exciting accounts of their adventures that became classics of Islamic literature. Here's a brief sampler with the three "greatest hits" of hajj writing from Islam's Golden Age:

♦ **Naser-e Khosraw** (eleventh century). A Persian Shiite, Naser-e Khosraw was a civil servant and an advisor of Seljuk princes in Persia who performed the hajj in the year 1047. He recorded his experiences in *The Book of Travels*, which established a long tradition of Persian travel writing.

♦ **Ibn Jubayr** (twelfth century). A sophisticated courtier from the vibrant culture of Arab-ruled Spain, Ibn Jubayr voyaged from Spain to Mecca and back again from 1183 to1185, staying in Mecca for eight months. Like Khosraw's book but fuller and more detailed, the *Travels of Ibn Jubayr* founded its own genre, the Arabic *rihla*, or traveler's diary.

♦ **Ibn Battuta** (fourteenth century). One of history's greatest travelers, this Morrocan Arab—unlike his predecessors—made the hajj the starting point of his travels, rather than the endpoint. Setting out from North Africa for Mecca in 1325, he performed the hajj in 1326. His appetite for travel, however, was merely whetted. Ibn Battuta went on to journey throughout the Middle East and Central Asia, reaching Nepal, Burma, Sumatra, and probably China before finally returning home in 1350—some 75,000 miles and 25 years later. His *Travels of Ibn Battuta* runs to over a thousand pages, and is full of suspenseful adventure, shrewd observation, and lively description.

Arabian Almanac

A number of Westerners have offered their own descriptions of the hajj. Some of the most vivid accounts were written by European scholar-adventurers who defied the ban on non-Muslims (who are prohibited from entering Mecca) to sneak in and perform the hajj undercover. These intrepid interlopers included the groundbreaking Swiss scholar John Lewis Burkhardt (1784–1817) and the dashing British explorer Sir Richard Burton (1821–1890). One British haji who did convert to Islam was the twentieth-century adventurer Harry St. John Philby, a colorful eccentric who lived in Saudi Arabia for years and was a close crony of Ibn Saud's. (He was also the father of the infamous spy Kim Philby.) Finally, no summary of famous hajj accounts would be complete without mentioning the best-known American haji, the black activist Malcolm X, who converted to Islam (1925–1965). His remarkable story is told in *The Autobiography of Malcolm X.*

The Jet Age

With the advent of relatively inexpensive air travel, the numbers of Muslims making the hajj jumped sharply, and the old overland routes—used by camel caravans and for a few decades by cars—fell into disuse. The journey itself, obviously, also became far briefer and less arduous. Today, nearly all hajis fly into Jiddah's massive airport, built during the modernization drive of the 1970s. Even for those from nearby countries like Iraq and Syria, the Saudi government insists on air travel rather than overland auto trips, for security reasons. When the hajj is in high gear, there's a plane landing at Jiddah once a minute.

The hajis are funneled off the planes and into the huge, specially built hajj terminal, which looms beyond the airport's main terminal. After waiting patiently in line to have their special hajj visas carefully checked by Saudi immigration officials, they jam into buses for the short trip to the area called the Holy Haram, a twenty-mile by five-mile rectangle of desert in the outskirts of Mecca, not far from the Great Mosque. There the masses are accommodated in what amounts to a vast, temporary city of white tents. (A lucky handful of wealthy or VIP hajis get to be put up in luxury hotels.) Uniformed guards with walkie-talkies patrol everywhere, and the authorities provide food, water, sanitation, emergency medical service, transportation, and traffic control.

A Pilgrim's Tale

Now that you've got the general picture, how would you like to experience the hajj itself firsthand, through the eyes of a participant? Here's where you get to find out what the hajj is really all about. In other words, it's time for *you* to become a haji.

Arrival and Purification

Your experience of the hajj begins well before your plane lands in Jiddah, as you begin to prepare yourself for the hajj rites. First off, you have to be an adult (over the age of puberty), of sound mind, and you have put your affairs in order before you go. You must settle your debts and provide for any dependents you'll be leaving behind. (This is a hold-over from the days when the hajj might take months or even years.) You also have to arrange for the hajj visa, and acquaint yourself ahead of time with the rites you'll be performing.

In addition, if you're like many of your fellow hajis, you'll take the opportunity on the plane to enter the state known as *ihram* or purification. If you don't, there are a number of stations called *miqats* outside of Mecca where the ihram preparations may be made. You'll perform ritual cleansing, washing, and if possible, cutting your nails and hair. Many men shave their heads completely, whereas women traditionally cut three locks of hair.

Arabian Almanac

The hajj begins two months after Ramadan, and officially takes place in and around Mecca between the eighth and thirteenth days of the Islamic calendar's last month, Dhu al Hijjah. After the thirteenth day, however, many hajis go on to visit Medina, where they pray at the Prophet's Mosque—the very first mosque, and the inspiration for those built later.

Muslims entering Mecca at any other time of year must perform the "little pilgrimage" called the *umrah*, which contains some (not all) of the same rites as the hajj.

Sheik-Speak

Ihram is the state of ritual purification that Muslims must enter before beginning the rites of the hajj. The word also applies to the simple clothes worn by hajis in the state of ihram. **Miqats** are the stations outside of Mecca where hajis may go through the ritual steps required to assume ihram. Nowadays, however, many hajis enter ihram before landing at the Jiddah airport.

Afterward, you'll don the simple clothes (also called ihram) that signify your purified state. Shoes are forbidden, but you can wear simple sandals. For men, ihram dress consists of two seamless strips of white cloth, one wrapped around the waist and the other draped over the shoulder. Women are allowed more leeway, but usually wear simple white or cream-colored dresses and robes. Women don't have to wear veils. Indeed, the hajj is one of the few occasions in Saudi Arabia where men and women are treated equally and permitted to mix. You'll remain in ihram for the duration of the rites, and you can't cut your hair or nails again, or have sexual intercourse, until you leave ihram (I'll tell you when).

The Rites in Mecca

You're now ready to enter Mecca, where you join the huge crowds in performing two important rites:

1. The turning, or *tawaf*. In this dramatic ritual, you and hundreds of thousands of others jam into the courtyard of the Great Mosque, where you all walk seven times around the Kaaba. You'll also do this later on in the hajj. This first time is called the arrival turning (*tawaf al qudum*). If you feel especially strong, you may attempt to kiss the famous Black Stone, built into a corner of the Kaaba, as you pass by. It's next to impossible to get close, though, because of the crowds.

2. The running, or *say*. After the turning, you might step aside to the nearby Zamzam Well, which Muslims believe God created by striking a rock to bring forth water for Hagar, Abraham's second wife, and the mother of Ishmael. (It's believed that Arabs are descended from Ishmael, or Ismail in Arabic, while Jews are descended from Isaac, Abraham's son by his first wife, Sarah.) Two small

hills, al Safa and al Marwa, lie nearby, and you now perform the *say*, which consists of running between the hills seven times. This ritual commemorates Hagar's desperate search for water as she and Ishmael were about to die of thirst.

These rites can performed in advance if you want; there's no set time for them, though many perform them early on the eighth day of the month Dhu al Hijjah. The only requirement is to be in the purified state of ihram. The following rites, however, have set times, and start on the eighth day of Dhu al Hijjah.

Desert Vigils and Processions

Late on the eighth day, after the ceremonial washing of the Kaaba and a special sermon in the courtyard of the Great Mosque, the crowds leave Mecca for the desert to the east. Some hajis spend the night at a tent city in the town of Mina, about five miles outside of Mecca. Others push on to the Plain of Arafat, about 12 miles east of Mecca, where there are also tents. (Both Mina and Arafat lie within the area of the Holy Haram, which, as I mentioned earlier, basically fills up with tents during the hajj.)

Either way, you and 2.5 million others end up at the Plain of Arafat the next morning, which brings the climax of the hajj: the day of standing, or *yawm al wuquf*. From noon to sunset on the ninth day of Dhu al Hijjah, all hajis stand in prayer on the broad plain. A preferred spot is on the hill called Jabal al Rahma, or Mount Mercy, that protrudes from the otherwise level region. This is where the angel Gabriel is said to have taught Adam and Eve to pray, and here the pilgrims stand humbly before God's majesty. To miss the wuquf negates the entire hajj. It's the essential rite of the whole pilgrimage—but be sure you have plenty of water, since heat stroke is a constant danger.

After the serenity of the wuquf, you're plunged into the hajj's most chaotic event, the rushing, or *nafra* (also called the pouring forth, or *ifada*). From Arafat, you and all the others walk, run, drive, ride, or get whatever transportation you can to Muzdalifa, a small town about three miles back in the direction of Mecca. Ranks of superhighways, all running parallel to each other, have been built just for this ritual, which resembles a race. In the past, lives were lost in the competition between rival caravans during the scramble for Muzdalifa. Once there, you'll stand another vigil and perhaps hear the sermon given that night, but mainly you'll probably be collecting stones for the next day's rites.

The Days of Stoning and Feasting

On the tenth day of Dhu al Hijja, you'll continue with everyone else back toward Mecca, stopping in the town of Mina. There, over the next three days, you'll throw

41 stones at three pillars or *jamaras* that lie on the edge of town. The pillars represent Satan, and the stoning of the pillars recalls a tradition that tells how Abraham hurled stones at Satan, after Satan tempted Abraham to disobey God's commandment that he sacrifice his son Isaac.

During this time (the tenth through the twelfth days of Dhu al Hijjah), you'll also celebrate the *id al adha*, the feast of sacrifice, which commemorates Abraham's ultimate willingness to obey God's command. This celebration is observed by the rest of the Muslim world as well, with feasting and socializing with friends and family. Each family sacrifices an unblemished animal to eat—which can be as fancy as a goat or sheep, or as modest as a pigeon. In Mina, the Saudis provide more than 1 million animals for sacrifice, and the leftover meat is carefully distributed to the poor throughout the Muslim world.

Sheik-Speak

Here are the most important rituals of the hajj.

- The **tawaf** or "turning": Hajis walk in a circle seven times around the Kaaba. There are three tawafs in the hajj, beginning with the **tawaf al qudum,** or arrival tawaf.

- The **say** or "running": Hajis run seven times between two hills near the Zamzam Well.

- The **yawm al wuquf** or "day of standing": Hajis stand a prayer vigil from noon to sunset on the Plain of Arafat.

- The **nafra** or "rushing": Hajis rush en masse from Arafat to Muzdalifa. Also called the **ifada** or "pouring forth."

- The stoning of the **jamaras,** the three pillars in the town of Mina that represent Satan.

- The **id al adha** or feast of sacrifice, celebrating Abraham's willingness to obey God and sacrifice his son Isaac.

Mecca and Medina

The stoning of the pillars in Mina begins the process of leaving the purified state of ihram, and other rites mark further stages in the progression (like a ritual haircut, for example). The process is only completed by returning to Mecca on the thirteenth day of Dhu al Hijjah. Once back in Mecca, you perform a second turning, which is called the return tawaf. After that, you're free from all ihram restrictions. A third turning, the farewell tawaf, completes your hajj. Congratulations—you're now officially entitled to call yourself haji. (Although for convenience I've been using the word haji to describe those performing the rituals, technically the hajj needs to be completed first.)

The hajj is now over, but most hajis go on to spend some time in Medina if they haven't already. Medina's main attraction is the Prophet's Mosque, which I mentioned earlier.

Looking After the Pilgrims

It's impossible to really grasp the hajj unless you've experienced it yourself, and for that, obviously, you have to be a Muslim. In addition to the sheer mass of people, however, don't forget that nearly two million of the hajis come from abroad, and that they speak some 70 languages among them. Furthermore, many of them are illiterate, so written signs aren't always effective, and on top of that many are also elderly and infirm. Inevitably, there are deaths during the hajj, but for a devout Muslim to die during the hajj is considered a blessing and an honor that many would welcome.

Arabian Almanac

There are four types of guides that the hajis rely on. Each has its own guild, with duties that are strictly regulated by the government. Often, a family has a tradition of membership in one of the guilds:

- The *mutawaffin* have the biggest job: to assist hajis in getting to Saudi Arabia, and then to look after them while they're in Mecca. (The name comes from the word tawaf, "turning.")
- The *zamzamia* (named after the Zamzam Well) help the mutawaffin.
- The *adilla* or "agents" take care of the hajis who go to Medina.
- The *wukala* or "deputies" are on hand to greet arriving hajis at the Jiddah airport and get them through customs. They also assist the hajis in leaving Jiddah to return home.

A whole service industry has arisen around the hajj, with much of the framework already in place even before Ibn Saud incorporated the Hijaz into his growing kingdom early in the twentieth century. Many families in the Hijaz are descended from past hajis who stayed on, and a large number of those families have long traditions of guiding pilgrims who come from their original countries.

Guardians of the Holy Places

If Ramadan is the biggest holiday period, the hajj is the biggest single event in Saudi Arabia's yearly calendar. All eyes are focused on it, not just in Saudi Arabia but throughout the Muslim world. In the past, the Wahhabis have attempted to bring all hajj rites into line with Wahhabi practice, banning activities like singing or dancing that were important parts of traditional rites observed by other Muslims. When Ibn Saud conquered the Hijaz, however, he agreed that all hajis would be able to worship according to their own religious customs.

That attitude has done much to uphold the precious claim of the Al Saud to be the "Guardians of the Holy Places." The Al Saud have also bolstered this claim by pouring millions of dollars into repeatedly renovating and expanding hajj facilities, including major work in rebuilding the Great Mosque in Mecca and the Prophet's Mosque in Medina. One big renovation campaign came in the 1950s, while another was undertaken by King Fahd in the 1980s. As King Fahd himself put it, "Spending on the Holy Places will be unlimited in accordance with their status in our hearts as Saudis and in the hearts of Muslims throughout the world."

The Least You Need to Know

- ◆ The "Five Pillars of Islam" are the declaration of belief, prayer five times a day, fasting at Ramadan, giving to charity, and performing the hajj.

- ◆ The hajj is the culmination of a Muslim's spiritual life.

- ◆ The main focus of the hajj—as for Islamic prayer—is the Great Mosque in Mecca, and within it the Kaaba.

- ◆ Much of the Al Saud's credibility as rulers comes from their competence in administering the hajj every year.

Connections

In This Chapter

- ◆ The Saudi business world
- ◆ The strange realm of politics without voting
- ◆ Saudi TV and the web from Riyadh
- ◆ Saudi thinking revisited

In this chapter, I'll round off your journey into contemporary Saudi culture with an excursion into the arenas of business, politics, and the media. The first two, business and politics, are closely connected—indeed, "connections" are what both are all about in Saudi Arabia. But as you'll see, the idea of politics has a very different meaning in a country where there are no elections.

Next, we'll investigate some other sorts of connections, as we examine the heavily censored Saudi media: newspapers, books, TV, and radio, plus look at how the ever-sensitive Saudi authorities are handling the Internet. Despite continuing censorship, as you've seen already there are signs that many Saudis are beginning to rebel against the tyranny of blandness that plagues most public dialogue in the kingdom.

We'll also revisit the always-fascinating subject of how Saudis think, and how they differ in their thinking from Westerners. Last time I brought this up (in Chapter 13), I focused on the cultural assumptions behind such differences. This time, we'll look at decision-making itself, examining how Saudi leaders and others arrive at their conclusions. I think you'll find some surprises in store. Finally, we'll briefly revisit another familiar subject, but one that always seems to have the final word when it comes to anything to do with Saudi Arabia: religion.

Doing Business in Saudi Arabia

In Chapter 14, I told you that Saudi Arabia's Hanbali branch of Sharia law is the most permissive of all the branches when it comes to the regulation of business practices. (As you've seen, however, it's the strictest branch of Sharia law in other matters.) Because of this permissiveness, doing business in the kingdom can feel like a free-for-all to Westerners who aren't used to Saudi business practices. Westerners have long complained that corruption, bribery, and influence peddling are rife in the Saudi business world. While there's certainly some foundation to the complaints, it's also true that the Saudis have a very different way of doing business, and that has also contributed to the Western perceptions.

Arabian Almanac

Western complaints of Saudi corruption and waste were widespread in the hectic, cash-gorged days of the oil boom and modernization drive. In those days, American or European corporations paid huge bribes to well-connected Saudi agents, who helped them close lucrative deals in the kingdom. Massive construction projects were undertaken with little or no planning, then torn down and rebuilt all over again. The complaints have become less common as Westerners have grown more familiar with Saudi ways, and as the frontier, boomtown atmosphere has given way to a calmer business environment. Plus, the oceans of free-floating cash have dried up into mere lakes and rivers. No one's using $1,000 bills to light cigars in the kingdom anymore. After all, why be wasteful? A ten or a hundred will do just as well.

Obviously, I'm joking, but behind the joke there's a point that I want to make. Three points, in fact:

- Even though things have settled down a bit, the Saudi cultural attitudes that gave rise to the Western perceptions (of corruption, waste, and so on) haven't gone away.

- It wasn't just Saudi cultural attitudes that gave rise to those perceptions. The easy availability of excess cash helped promote wasteful consumption, which (probably inevitably) also arose from the sudden leap that the Saudis made during that turbulent period.

- Like the cultural attitudes, the excess cash and the tendency toward waste haven't entirely gone away either, though they've certainly diminished from their earlier peaks.

The Importance of Being Well Connected

Earlier I told you that Saudis don't draw a line between what Westerners think of as "business" and "personal" relationships. For Saudis, all relationships are personal, and personal affection and trust are essential for any business relationship. Keep this in mind, because it's the key to understanding the Saudi approach to business.

The personal nature of doing business in the kingdom makes knowing the right people even more important here than in other places. Whether you're a Westerner or a Saudi, doing business in the kingdom depends almost completely on who you know. For an outsider, in fact, just getting into the country is usually a matter of knowing someone. Saudi Arabia doesn't issue tourist visas, and in order to enter the country on a visitor's visa you must have a Saudi sponsor, who takes responsibility for your behavior while inside the country. (Your alternative is an expensive "approved" tour, with official guides who keep a tight lid on your activities.) The sponsor can be an individual or a company. Similarly, a foreigner who wants to run a business inside Saudi Arabia must have a Saudi partner.

The Saudi partner might do no more than give official cover to the business, but he might also act as the foreigner's sponsor, or as an agent who has access to influential Saudis. Remember, it's all about who you know. Having a good product won't help you if you don't have a good relationship with the right person, but establishing the right relationship will help you sell your product—in many cases, even if it's inferior or unneeded. This should give you a good idea of how waste might occur, along with the charges of corruption commonly made by Western journalists accustomed to a different business environment.

Business Ethics

The bottom line is that what a Western observer would call bribery or influence peddling doesn't necessarily have the same taint to a Saudi. For the Saudi, providing a personal connection is viewed as a legitimate business service, for which it is natural to expect to be paid. In the past, payment has meant whatever the market would bear—in other words, whatever you can get away with. But in recent years, the Saudi government—sensitive to Western cries of corruption—has regulated agents' "fees" more closely.

I'll let you decide whether you think this sort of thing is corrupt or not. For some observers, "corrupt" means departing from locally accepted norms of behavior, in which case the Saudis are merely following their own cultural traditions. Such practices, indeed, are common throughout the Middle East. You might have a less forgiving view, but that's your business. Literally.

Politics Without Votes

Politics and business are closely intertwined in the kingdom, although, of course, Saudi Arabia isn't the only place where knowing a high-level official in the right ministry will help you land a lucrative contract. In Saudi politics as in Saudi business, personal connections are everything, and all relationships are based on personal affection and trust. Also as in business, family connections work best, and family loyalty will always play a leading role if it's involved in any way. This is most obvious in the complex workings of the Al Saud dynasty, which is a big enough subject to deserve its own chapter. I'll cover it separately, in Chapter 19.

Technocrats and Royals

However, as pervasive as they have been and still are in the corridors of power, the Al Saud can't do it all. Increasingly, they have relied on the help of competent civil servants from outside the royal family. In Chapter 6, I introduced you to one of the best-known of these technocrats, Sheik Ahmed Zaki Yamani, King Faisal's highly able oil minister.

Since Sheik Yamani's day (he was oil minister from 1962 to 1986), the role of non-royal technocrats in the government has grown more and more pronounced. Positions of power in the government—ministries and other key offices—are occupied either by Al Saud princes or by these highly educated commoners, who work hand in hand with the Al Saud. (For information on the government itself, go to Chapter 12.) Many have graduate degrees from prestigious American or European universities. In some ways, the technocrats have replaced tribal leaders as the Al Saud's power base, though traditional tribal politics haven't been totally eclipsed.

Sheik-Speak

Shura means "consultation," and you see it for example in the name "Majlis as-Shura," or "Consultative Council," which I've given you background on in Chapters 9, 10, and 12. **Ijma** means "consensus," which is defined as a group's overall opinion on a particular issue. Together, shura and ijma represent the two basic parts of the Saudi political process. They are related: consensus (ijma) is the end result of consultation (shura).

To a limited degree then, the technocrats make up a political group that counterbalances the Al Saud on the political scene. In general, they tend to be moderate modernizers, though there are exceptions. You'll find them well represented in the Council of Ministers and the Majlis as-Shura (Consultative Council), for example, the two bodies that make up the backbone of the Saudi government. By including the technocrats, the Al Saud have basically created a bureaucratic version of the two traditional components in the Arab style of rule: *shura*, or consultation, and *ijma*, or consensus.

Together, shura and its end result, ijma, are the two basic ways that the Al Saud give their hold on power an aura of political legitimacy. Few important decisions are made without an effort at consensus by the Saudi monarch, both within the Al Saud and among the technocrats. If the decision touches on religion (most do), then the consensus must also include the Wahhabi conservatives. In many ways, Saudi Arabia's kings are more like executive consensus builders than absolute rulers in the familiar, Western sense. This is why they so often seem to end up as a moderate voice between the extremes represented by the modernizers and the conservatives.

No Room at the Top

Over the last few decades, then, the Al Saud have created a large governmental bureaucracy, headed and staffed at the upper levels by their own family members and by competent technocrats. This bureaucracy has successfully replaced the old-style system of tribal rule, but the problem now is that the technocrats have gone as far as they can within this system. The influential positions in the civil service are filled by technocrats who are still relatively young men. They sit on the Council of Ministers or the Majlis as-Shura. Yet every year the universities pump out hundreds of educated, technically competent younger men, who find themselves excluded from the political process. They're joined by young businessmen and other educated professionals.

Sound familiar? It's very similar to the situation in the religious establishment that I've described elsewhere (in Chapter 13, for example). Lots of eager young men are ending up very frustrated, because they're being shut out of a system that has no room at the top. The difference is that instead of advocating religious terrorism, these frustrated young men (along with many young women) are calling for democratic reforms. Since the system gives them no role, they're standing outside it demanding to participate in a real way. It's these would-be reformers who may well tip the balance from consultation (with only informal, advisory checks on hereditary rulers) to democracy (with real, binding checks on elected leaders).

National Reform Document

It's too soon yet to know how the reformers will do, but they won a significant victory early in 2003, when Crown Prince Abdullah agreed to meet with 34 of them. The meeting came after they and 69 others signed a "National Reform Document" that they then sent to the Crown Prince, in which they called for basic democratic and human rights reforms. As a result of the meeting, in May 2003 Abdullah announced the formation of an independent committee to monitor human rights in the kingdom.

Desert Dates

January 20, 2003: Crown Prince Abdullah holds an unprecedented three-hour meeting in Riyadh with 34 leading Saudi critics of the country's political system. The 34 are drawn from a list of more than 100 pro-democracy reformers who signed the "National Reform Document" sent to Abdullah earlier in the month. The document calls for a written constitution, elected regional and national legislatures, universal suffrage (including votes for women), an independent judiciary, and comprehensive human rights reforms.

Keep these recent developments in mind. They arose partly in the context of the 2003 U.S. invasion of Iraq, and may represent a resurgence of the modernizing liberals against the dominance of the religious conservatives that followed the first Gulf War. I'll be returning to these questions later, especially in the final chapter of this book. At that point, I'll offer my parting assessment of the chances for real democratic reform in Saudi Arabia.

The Saudi Media

So far, I've made several references to the Saudi media, and to the strange system of partly self-imposed censorship that governs all public discourse in the kingdom. For example, in Chapter 15 I talked about the 2002 girls' school fire in Mecca, and the unparalleled newspaper criticism of the Religious Police that followed the deaths of the 15 schoolgirls. Now I'll give you the full picture on Saudi newspapers, books, and TV and radio, along with Internet use.

Newspapers

Saudi Arabia has 11 major daily newspapers and 3 major weekly publications. All are privately owned. Three of the dailies (*Arab News*, *Saudi Gazette*, and *Riyadh Daily*) are published in English and are directed at the large expatriate community. They include local and foreign coverage, but exclude anything that may be objectionable to the Saudi government or to the religious conservatives.

That doesn't leave much real news, so expatriate Westerners have become adept at smuggling papers and magazines into the country for themselves and their friends. Any foreign publications available for purchase in the kingdom are left with gaping holes—literally. Political censors cut out articles deemed sensitive or unfavorable to the government, while religious censors cut out articles and photos they find offensive (including almost all ads featuring women models, scantily clad or otherwise).

Nowadays, however, news starvation is largely a thing of the past, since expatriates with computers can go online to read foreign newspapers.

Desert Dates

1964: King Faisal decrees the so-called Press Law, which puts all publications in the kingdom under the indirect supervision of the Ministry of Information. The law says that each privately owned newspaper must be overseen by a 15-member committee, which will exercise editorial and financial control over the paper. The members of the committees are to be approved by the Ministry of Information. In addition, the Ministry of Information has the power to fire editors who don't toe the party line. It still exercises that power regularly.

Among the eight major Arabic-language dailies, the largest are *Al Riyadh*, published in Riyadh, and *Al Jazirah*, published in Jiddah. Mecca, Medina, and Dammam also have their own dailies. The three main weeklies are *Al Daiwa* (Riyadh), *Al Yamama* (Riyadh), and *Ekkra* (Jiddah). In addition, there are a number of smaller weekly magazines and periodicals, including several in English. Within the confines of the unwritten rules, Saudis go in for a fair amount of public self-examination and hand wringing. The newspapers often run articles assessing Saudi ways and contrasting them, favorably or unfavorably, to those of other cultures. Earlier I mentioned articles against domestic violence, which are a good example of this.

Censorship of the domestic press in Saudi Arabia isn't a matter of running news articles by an official, who then accepts them or bans them. It's more a matter of indirect government supervision, with editors and reporters expected to follow a whole set of largely unwritten rules. When they don't, they often get fired.

In February 1992, for example, the highly respected editor in chief of the *Arab News*, Khaled al Maeena, was fired after he published an Associated Press story featuring an interview with the infamous "blind sheik," Omar abdel Rahman. (The well-known Egyptian fundamentalist exile was living in New Jersey at the time; he was later imprisoned for planning the 1993 World Trade Center bombing.) Later that year, the editor in chief of a smaller daily, *An Nadwah*, was fired for printing a story about religious extremists in Saudi Arabia. More recently, in May 2003 Jamal Khashoggi, editor in chief of the leading liberal daily *Al Watan*, was fired after publishing articles critical of the kingdom's religious institutions, including the Religious Police. More on this story in Chapter 20.

Books

In contrast with newspapers, book publishing in the kingdom is subject to prepublication censorship. The result is that books don't get published or sold in Saudi Arabia unless they have titles like *King Fahd: the Man and His Legacy*, *Wildflowers of the Empty Quarter*, or *Dress and Adornment: the Purifying Tradition*. (The last title, an import published in Cairo, tells women how to dress modestly—and runs to some 700 pages.) So while a relatively high level of public soul-searching goes on in the newspapers, books in the kingdom are mostly restricted to a narrower range: technical volumes, religious tracts, patriotic or pro-Arab polemics, and literary efforts like acceptable novels and poetry.

TV and Radio

TV is still more restricted, since both channels are owned by the government. That's right, there are only two channels, Arabic and English. Religious programs get the lion's share, predictably enough, with extensive special programming for Ramadan, the hajj period, and other religious holidays. Even programming that isn't overtly "religious," however, has to conform to the requirements of the religious conservatives. There are, however, some programs about Saudi culture and Arab culture in general, as well as dramas, entertainment, and music—all of which your average North American viewer would find tame and lame beyond belief. Ditto for "news" and "current events" programs, which have as their highest goal the avoidance of anything that might conceivably be considered controversial by anyone.

Radio, too, is government-owned, and is also dominated by religious programming, with long readings from the Koran being the most common thing you'll hear. Foreign language broadcasting is aimed at "Islamic solidarity," and at converting Christians and others to Islam. And that's the moderate religious programming. There's a whole station—the Call of Islam station—that's devoted to defending Wahhabism against "hostile ideologies." Other stations feature education, childcare, and health. Music programming on the radio basically means military marches.

The Internet

Internet access from the kingdom is extensively blocked by government-installed filtering systems, which run on proxy servers that all web traffic in the kingdom is funneled through. The government's Internet Services Unit (ISU), which operates the proxy servers, describes its goals in filtering the Internet as preserving the kingdom's "Islamic values" and preventing exposure to "the materials that contradict with our beliefs or may influence our culture." At its website, the ISU states that its policy aims at filtering "the absolute minimum possible number of web pages possible to fulfill its duties."

What does that mean exactly? Jonathan Zittrain and Benjamin Edelman of Harvard Law School did a recent study of Saudi Internet blocking that you can find on the web (see Appendix C). The Saudis' primary concern, it appears, is to block pornographic and other sexually explicit sites. (To Wahhabi eyes, this includes swimwear catalogues and the like.) Outside of sexual content, though, the study examined 63,762 other kinds of sites, and found 1,353 blocked. Prominent among them were many sites that are heavily visited by people in other countries.

Aside from sexual content, areas in which websites were blocked included the following:

- ◆ Religion (at least 246 pages in Yahoo's Religion category were found to be blocked)

- ◆ Human rights (for example, Amnesty International and Human Rights Watch pages about Saudi human rights abuses)

- ◆ Middle Eastern politics and activism

- ◆ Women's issues (including the "Women in American History" section of *Encyclopedia Britannica Online*)

- ◆ Humor (81 pages, including a site featuring Monica Lewinsky jokes)

- ◆ Education, reference, and health

- ◆ Gay and lesbian sites

- ◆ Entertainment, music, and movies

- ◆ Sites that let you get around blocking and gain access to blocked sites (like megaproxy.com)

Interestingly, among those that weren't blocked were news sites and foreign government web pages.

Decisions, Decisions, Decisions

So how are such things decided? In Chapter 13 we examined some of the cultural assumptions behind the ways that Saudis think. That should give you an idea of the "whys" of Saudi thinking. In this chapter I've already talked a bit about *how* Saudi business and government leaders make their decisions. Now let's go into a little more detail on the "hows" of Saudi decision-making.

It's Personal

So far, the aspect I've spent most time underscoring is how personal considerations influence nearly all areas of Saudi behavior. One way that this can affect decision-making

Sandra Mackey, who lived in Saudi Arabia for several years in the 1980s, tells a wonderful story in her insightful and often humorous book, *The Saudis*. She asks two policemen for directions on the street one day. They give her completely different answers, and the grand finale is when they stand there pointing in opposite directions.

is that Saudis tend to avoid saying "no" or "I don't know" at all costs. Sometimes this is because they don't want to offend, other times it's because they don't want to lose face.

In general, when they answer a question, Saudis are more concerned with how the answer will affect the person doing the asking than with what Westerners would call "the truth" of the situation. They'll want to please the other person, in other words, rather than risk offending him or her with an unpleasant reality.

Mirage Ahead _____

Just because they don't like to say "no," don't expect Saudis to say "yes" when they don't want to. Generally, if they don't wish to say "yes," they'll just sort of very politely hem and haw without promising anything. Business and political negotiations with Westerners have sometimes dragged on pointlessly for years, because the Westerners don't understand that the Saudis simply don't want to come out with a definitive "no"— even though from the start they never had any intention of agreeing. The other side of the coin is that a Saudi will expect you to hem and haw politely, too, and may take even a regretful "no" as an insult.

Mental Compartments

Observers also note another pattern in Saudi thinking, one that's often described as compartmentalization. What this means is that Saudis tend to see a choice from only one point of view at a time, and to ignore its possible consequences in different areas.

Compartmentalization is especially clear when it comes to public policy. A classic example is the decision in the 1970s to use water from Saudi Arabia's nonrenewable aquifers to irrigate large new wheat fields. As I explained earlier, the idea was to make the kingdom more agriculturally self-sufficient, by ending its reliance on imported wheat. It was part of a big push to jump-start Saudi agriculture, a push that in many ways was a matter of national pride more than anything else. Sadly, because no one considered the inevitable environmental impact of the decision, the aquifers are now more or less depleted.

Two Trumps

Though it won't come as a surprise to you by now, there are two potential "trumps" when a Saudi faces any decision—two considerations that, if relevant, will override any others. They are, of course, family loyalty and religious ideology. That raises the obvious question of which one would come out on top if they should clash, but to that I'll have to give the unsatisfying answer that it would depend on the situation. Usually they won't clash, since family loyalty would apply more to personal and business decisions, while religious ideology would apply more to public policy and political decisions.

Arabian Almanac

Saudi Arabia's political ideology is based on the writings of the fourteenth century Hanbali jurist Taqi ibn Taymiyya, who lived during the decline of the Abbasid Caliphate. (For the Abbasids, see Chapter 3.) As petty rulers sprang up and took power from the declining Abbasids, they would get local religious scholars to issue legal decrees legitimizing their rule. Ibn Taymiyya rejected this practice, arguing that only strict adherence to Islam's fundamental teachings could give a ruler political legitimacy. Ibn Taymiyya's teachings were taken up in the eighteenth century by Muhammad ibn Abdel Wahhab, and form the basis of the Wahhabi political outlook.

This explains why the Al Saud's religious credentials are so important to their political authority. Furthermore, Ibn Taymiyya has also been a seminal inspiration for modern Islamic extremists, including Osama bin Laden. Ibn Taymiyya's writings are thus more widely influential today than when he put them down on paper, and his reach extends from the fourteenth century into the age of global terror.

The Least You Need to Know

- Business and politics in the kingdom both largely come down to personal connections.

- Pressure for democratic reform is coming from young, educated Saudis who resent being shut out of political power in a country with no elections whatsoever.

- Much self-censorship in the Saudi media is motivated by a desire to avoid stirring up controversy, inciting lust, or causing anyone to lose face.

- Saudi decision-making is often shaped by personalization and compartmentalization.

Part 4

Saudi Arabia in the Age of Global Terror

In Part 1 and Part 2, I took a historical approach to Saudi Arabia, filling you in on the political, religious, and cultural currents that shaped the country's past. Then in Part 3, I gave you a "snapshot" of Saudi culture today. In Part 4, I want to blend these two approaches, applying "historical" thinking not so much to the past as to the present and even the future. In other words, we're facing some big questions—both about the world, and about Saudi Arabia's place in it. To answer them, we have to try to look at Saudi Arabia and its role in the world the way a historian of the future might.

Earlier I called the Gulf War the first global conflict of the post-Cold War age. I treated the decade that followed—the 1990s, basically—as a sort of interim period, putting it in its own category, "Recent History." Now it's becoming clear what followed this interim period. The 1990s amounted to a transition between the Cold War and the Age of Global Terror.

And the country at the epicenter of the new age? You guessed it: Saudi Arabia.

Chapter 17

September 11, 2001: The Saudi Connection

In This Chapter

- ◆ The opening shots in a new war go largely unanswered
- ◆ Why 15 Saudis helped kill over 3,000 Americans
- ◆ Europe's unexpected role in the events of 9/11
- ◆ The money trail leads back to Saudi Arabia

September 11, 2001 will remain stamped in our memories for a long time to come, but most of us today are no closer to understanding why the hijackers acted than we were at the time. I took that question as a starting point for this book, in the Introduction, when I pointed out that 15 of the 19 hijackers were Saudis. Yet Saudi Arabia is supposed to be a friendly ally of the United States. So, I asked, what's up with that? How did citizens of one of America's "allies" end up so twisted with hatred that they gave up their own lives to kill Americans?

At the time, I sketched a brief explanation, but I couldn't really go into much detail. Now it's time to return to those events, and to explore that question more fully. So in this chapter we come full circle. The difference is that now you have the knowledge that you'll need to make sense of it all.

I'll start this chapter with a quick review of al Qaeda's activities before 9/11, showing how both the American and Saudi governments failed to respond adequately to the new threat posed by the global terror network. Then I'll give you a concise account of the attack itself, along with details on the mostly Saudi hijackers. From there we'll investigate how the hijackers were recruited, organized, and financed, focusing on how Saudi Arabia's social and economic ills contributed to their motivations. Finally, I'll describe the legacy of anger and distrust that's eroded the U.S.–Saudi relationship since September 2001.

Prelude

In Chapter 10, I outlined the rise of al Qaeda in the context of two wars: the Afghan jihad against the Soviet Union, and the U.S.–led Gulf War to reverse Iraq's occupation of Kuwait. Now let's catch up on al Qaeda's activities between the end of the Gulf War in early 1991 and the catastrophic attack on American soil just over a decade later.

Al Qaeda Declares War

In retrospect, it's easy to see that the 1990s marked an escalating campaign of terror against American targets, one that reached a climax on 9/11. It's equally easy to see—also with 20/20 hindsight—that neither the Americans, the Saudis, or anyone else truly realized the depth of Osama bin Laden's commitment or the scope of his organization, al Qaeda.

Arabian Almanac

In his public pronouncements to Muslims, Osama bin Laden selectively draws on—and often distorts—"traditional" elements of Islamic belief to encourage hatred and violence against Christians (especially Americans), Jews (especially Israelis), and Muslims he doesn't like (especially the Al Saud). For example, he stresses the Islamic idea of ongoing conflict between *Dar al Islam*, the House of Islam, and *Dar al Harb*, the House of War, which traditionally means everything outside the Islamic world. Unlike the traditional view, though, which dates from Islam's earliest years, bin Laden's Wahhabi-inspired, intolerant version of Dar al Islam embraces only those who agree with him. By the same token, his version of Dar al Harb includes other Muslims, "apostates" like the Al Saud, that he accuses of betraying their faith by allying with the West.

At the same time, bin Laden ignores all Koranic messages that encourage peaceful coexistence between Muslims and non-Muslims. Such messages are as much a part of "Islamic tradition" as the idea of division between Dar al Islam and Dar al Harb. For further discussion of religious traditions and how they can be used to further destructive agendas by the power-hungry, see Chapter 14.

Here's a timeline of the important developments during the 1990s, including al Qaeda's major terrorist strikes.

- **September 1991:** Osama bin Laden takes up residence in the Sudan after being expelled from Saudi Arabia. He calls on Muslims to attack U.S. forces in Saudi Arabia, Yemen, and Somalia.

- **December 1992:** In its first terrorist strike, al Qaeda detonates a bomb in a hotel in Yemen, killing one tourist. The bomb is intended for American soldiers deployed in the U.S. humanitarian mission to Somalia.

- **February 23, 1993:** A truck bomb explodes in the underground parking structure of the World Trade Center in New York City, killing 6 and injuring more than 1,000 people. The strike is planned by al Qaeda operative Ramzi Yousef, along with the exiled Egyptian fundamentalist cleric Sheikh Omar Abdel Rahman (the "Blind Sheikh").

- **October 3–4, 1993:** After extensive training by bin Laden and al Qaeda starting the previous year, Somali fighters attack U.S. Marines in Mogadishu, Somalia, killing 18 and injuring many others.

- **November 1995:** An al Qaeda truck bomb explodes in a Saudi military facility in Riyadh, killing five U.S. soldiers and two Indians.

- **May 1996:** Forced out of the Sudan, bin Laden is invited to Afghanistan by the new Taliban government.

- **June 1996:** An al Qaeda truck bomb explodes at Khobar Towers in Dhahran, Saudi Arabia, killing 19 U.S. soldiers and wounding many others.

- **August 1996:** From Afghanistan, bin Laden issues his "Declaration of War Against the Americans Occupying the Land of the Two Holy Mosques." He calls on Muslims to join in jihad against Americans and Israelis, later declaring that it is the duty of all Muslims to kill Americans and their allies, civilians, and soldiers alike.

- **August 7, 1998:** Two truck bombs explode minutes apart at U.S. embassies in Kenya and Tanzania, killing 301 (including 12 Americans) and injuring more than 5,000 others. The United States retaliates a few weeks later with cruise missile attacks. The missiles hit al Qaeda training camps in Afghanistan and a pharmaceutical plant in the Sudan that was (probably mistakenly) thought to be used for making chemical weapons.

- **July 1999:** President Clinton imposes economic sanctions on the Taliban government for harboring bin Laden and al Qaeda. Later the same year the United Nations follows suit, banning trade with Afghanistan by its members.

- **December 14, 1999:** Al Qaeda operative Ahmed Ressam is arrested while entering the United States with explosives. The arrest foils his planned attempt to blow up Los Angeles International Airport at midnight, January 1, 2000.

- **October 5, 2000:** A suicide team of al Qaeda *martyrs*, operating in a rubber dingy, blows a gaping hole in the USS *Cole* at harbor in Aden, Yemen, killing 17 sailors and wounding 39.

Sheik-Speak

Like other Islamic terrorist leaders, Osama bin Laden has perfected the art of bravely getting gullible young people to kill themselves for his cause. While mainstream Islamic thinking rejects suicide as a sin, it does bless as martyrs those who die fighting against invaders of Muslim lands. Maintaining that America's presence in Saudi Arabia amounts to invasion, bin Laden has incited young men to undertake suicide missions by promising them a worldly paradise after death, including a boundless supply of beautiful young virgins. Bin Laden exhorts his followers to love death, not life.

That takes us to the eve of 9/11, but before we move on to that horrific event, let's take a moment to assess the response to al Qaeda's terror campaign up to this point on the part of the United States and its ally, Saudi Arabia.

A Threat Ignored

On the American side, President Clinton—who came into office shortly before the massacre at Mogadishu and left office shortly after the USS *Cole* bombing—grew steadily more preoccupied with stopping bin Laden. But bin Laden proved elusive, evading American cruise missile strikes. And the United States was embarrassed by the apparently mistaken strike on the Sudanese pharmaceutical plant that intelligence experts had claimed was manufacturing chemical weapons. Short of invading Afghanistan, American options were limited, especially since the American public continued to ignore a threat that so far hadn't touched them directly.

On the Saudi side, the Al Saud publicly maintained that bin Laden was merely a minor irritant who posed no threat to them. Within Saudi Arabia, Saudi officials repeatedly blocked U.S. attempts to investigate al Qaeda. This was despite the fact that bin Laden had openly targeted the "outlaw" Saudi regime and called for its overthrow. However, some experts believe that, after revoking his citizenship in 1994, the Saudi government made at least one attempt to assassinate bin Laden in the mid

1990s. And yet, as later investigations revealed, wealthy and influential Saudis continued to pump millions of dollars—knowingly or unknowingly—into Islamic charity organizations that ultimately funneled the money to al Qaeda. A report commissioned by the U.N. recently estimated that Saudi sources have given some $500 million to al Qaeda over the last decade. There's been no attempt by the Saudis to interrupt the flow of money supporting the terrorist network, even though that network had now openly declared war on the Saudi government as well as on all Americans.

Arabian Almanac

In addition to its successful operations in the 1990s, al Qaeda also had a string of failed attacks. The failures included repeated attempts to blow up American airliners over the Pacific, as well as botched assassination attempts on several world leaders (U.S. President Clinton and Philippine President Fidel Ramos in Manila, Egyptian President Hosni Mubarak, Pope John Paul II).

9/11

The attacks on September 11, 2001 changed the American perspective forever, shocking the American public to awareness of the al Qaeda threat. A corresponding awakening on the part of the Saudis would be much slower in coming.

The Killing

The details of the attacks themselves are, I'm sure, familiar enough that I don't need to go into them too deeply here. Four airliners are taken over by four squads of suicide hijackers. Two of the planes are flown into the Twin Towers of the World Trade Center in lower Manhattan, at 8:48 and 9:03 A.M., causing the collapse of both buildings with the loss of some 3,000 lives. Shortly after the first impacts, the third plane dives into the Pentagon, destroying a huge section of the building and killing all 58 passengers onboard and 120 people on the ground. A few minutes later, the fourth plane crashes into a rural field near Pittsburgh, Pennsylvania, killing everyone on board—apparently after passengers overpowered the hijackers, diverting the plane from its intended target, thought to have been the Capitol building.

It is the deadliest terrorist attack ever to strike the United States. And on each plane, all or nearly all the hijackers were Saudis.

The Hijackers

The hijackers' identities became known with remarkable speed in the weeks following the attack, along with a fairly good picture of their activities leading up to it. They were all young men who were originally from Islamic countries. There was an overall leader, an Egyptian in his early thirties named Mohamed Atta, as well as a team leader/pilot for each plane. Some members of the teams had lived for up to almost two years in the United States on student visas, and the team leaders had attended flight school in several states. Only one of the team leaders was a Saudi, and I'll have more to say about that interesting fact in a moment.

Here are the hijackers' names and nationalities as reported in *The New York Times* of November 4, 2001, with each team leader/pilot listed first.

♦ American Airlines Flight 11 (Boston-Los Angeles) hits the North Tower at 8:48 A.M. The hijackers are Mohamed Atta (Egyptian), Abdulaziz Alomari (Saudi), Waleed Alsheri (Saudi), Wail Alsheri (Saudi), and Satam al-Suqami (United Arab Emirates).

♦ United Airlines Flight 175 (Boston-Los Angeles) hits the South Tower at 9:03 A.M. The hijackers are Marwan al-Shehhi (United Arab Emirates), Fayez Ahmed (Saudi), Ahmed Alghamdi (Saudi), Hamza Alghamdi (Saudi), and Mohand Alsheri (Saudi).

♦ American Airlines Flight 77 (Washington-Los Angeles) hits the Pentagon at 9:45 A.M. The hijackers are Hani Hanjour (Saudi), Khalid al-Midhar (Saudi), Nawaq Alhazmi (Saudi), Salem Alhazmi (Saudi), and Majed Moqed (Saudi).

♦ United Airlines Flight 93 (Newark-San Francisco) crashes in rural Pennsylvania at 10:10 A.M. The hijackers are Ziad Jarrahi (Lebanese), Ahmed Alhaznawi (Saudi), Ahmed Alnami (Saudi), and Saeed Alghamdi (Saudi).

In addition to the team leaders, the same *New York Times* article reports, FBI investigators divided the remaining hijackers into two further categories: "support staff" (those who had helped rent apartments and take care of other logistical details), and 12 "soldiers" (those recruited purely to provide "muscle" for the hijackings themselves, which were carried out with box-cutters). The support staff also doubled as muscle once the hijackings were underway.

Anatomy of a Mass Murder

Investigators also quickly determined that most—possibly all—of the hijackers had spent time in al Qaeda training camps in Afghanistan. Having shown their willingness and ability, it is thought, they were presented with the basic plan by top al Qaeda leaders.

The man investigators believe actually devised the plan was a Kuwaiti lieutenant of Osama bin Laden's named Khalid Sheikh Mohammed (captured in Pakistan in early 2003). Investigators also believe that Mohammed may have been inspired by the 1993 attack on the World Trade Center, together with a scheme hatched by Ramzi Yousef, architect of the earlier attack, to fly a plane into CIA headquarters.

To unscramble the sequence of events that led up to the attack, and to help get a fix on the hijackers' motives, *New York Times* columnist Thomas Friedman divides them into two groups: "the Europeans" and "the Saudis." Using Friedman's labels for them (which will become clear in a moment), let's look at "the Europeans" first.

"The Europeans"

In making the distinction between "Europeans" and "Saudis," Friedman draws on an article by Adrian Karatnycky in the November 5, 2001 issue of the conservative magazine *National Review*. The article, entitled "Under Our Very Noses," points out that three of the four leader/pilots in the 9/11 terror team, while originally from Islamic countries, had lived for significant lengths of time as university students in Hamburg, Germany, during the late 1990s. It was in Hamburg, investigators discovered, that the plan's details were ironed out before the young men came to America. In fact, Karatnycky wrote, it turns out that the rapidly growing Muslim communities in European countries are a rich breeding ground for Islamic extremism and a major source of manpower for al Qaeda recruiters.

The most surprising part is that the three young men—Mohamed Atta, Marwan al-Shehhi, and Ziad Jarrahi—do not seem to have been particularly religious before they came to Europe. They came from relatively affluent, well-educated families, and were enrolled in Hamburg University. So what turned them into fanatical terrorists?

Arabian Almanac

Many notorious al Qaeda operatives are thought to have been radicalized in European countries by anti-Muslim discrimination. They include Zacarias Moussaoui, a French-Moroccan arrested in the United States shortly before 9/11, when a flight school instructor grew suspicious of his behavior. He's believed to have been the "twentieth hijacker." Another was Richard Reid, the "shoe bomber," whose grandfather immigrated to Britain from Jamaica, and who was converted to radical Islam while in a British prison. European prisons are full of young Muslim men, and European investigators have found a prison sentence to be a common path to radical Islam.

Short answer: the poor reception they got in Europe. Europe has turned into a land of immigrants over the last several decades, and many of those immigrants came from Islamic lands that were once under European colonial domination. Europe now has millions of Muslims and thousands of mosques. Yet the Muslims live in poor, segregated areas, discriminated against by their host societies, and the mosques have become centers of radical fundamentalism fed by economic frustration. Witnessing their fellow Muslims being rejected by the new society, these young men reacted by embracing an extremist version of the old one.

Unlike North America, where society is used to assimilating immigrants, Europe has so far rigidly excluded its immigrants from mainstream life. I say so far, because one thing that's clear from recent events is that this has to change if the war on terror is to be won. Earlier I talked about Saudi xenophobia, or fear and hatred of foreigners. Obviously, such feelings are not confined to the Saudis. European countries—Britain, France, Germany, Belgium, and Denmark, to name the worst offenders—must develop ways of assimilating their Muslim immigrants into their societies.

Otherwise, young men like Mohamed Atta will go on experiencing the feeling of being outcasts, and being driven into a radicalism they never felt in their homelands. In the hate-filled sermons of the anti-Western clerics, they'll continue to find a new and destructive direction in life.

"The Saudis"

So much for "the Europeans," who basically made up the leadership and support staff of the terror team. Now for "the Saudis," who essentially provided the muscle. For this part of the equation, Friedman relied partly on his own travels in the kingdom, and partly on Charles M. Sennott of the *Boston Globe*, who filed a ground-breaking three-part story from Saudi Arabia that was published in the *Globe* from March 3 to March 5, 2002.

Sennott noted that of the 15 Saudi hijackers, 12 came from the same economically depressed region in southwestern Saudi Arabia, especially the province of Asir. Like "the Europeans," these young Saudis were from the middle class, even the upper-middle class. They were from educated, fairly affluent families, not from the growing ranks of the Saudi poor. Nor were they known for being especially devout. But, like many of their generation, they were unemployed, bored, and increasingly bitter about it. On top of that, with its moderate climate the Asir is a center for tourism, both by wealthy Saudis and by Westerners. It's full of luxury hotels and laughing outsiders living the high life. This made the bitter young men especially vulnerable to the anti-American rantings of the radical clerics.

Hani Hanjour, whose family Sennott interviewed in the Asir, was the only one of the Saudis who was a team leader/pilot, rather than part of the muscle. As a young man he had dreamed of being a pilot for Saudia, the Saudi national airline. Since Saudia pilots had to be FAA-certified, Hanjour came to America in 1999 to receive his certificate, but when he went back home he still couldn't get a job with Saudia. Over the next year or so, he grew depressed and bored, spending endless hours in the Internet café owned by his family. Eventually Hanjour began listening to taped sermons, attending radical mosques, and reading religious texts. In December 2000 he returned to the United States, and less than a year later he piloted American Airlines Flight 77 into the Pentagon.

Especially heavily represented among the muscle was the Alghamdi tribe, one of the Asir region's largest and most influential. Three of the Saudi hijackers bore the name Alghamdi on their visas, and a fourth, Ahmed Alhaznawi, was also from a branch of the tribe.

Sennott describes how, in late 1999, Alhaznawi approached his father, a cleric who was in charge of a local mosque, and asked permission to join the jihad in Chechnya. The elder man refused, advising his son instead to wage "the higher form of jihad," by which he meant the spiritual effort to live a good Muslim life. (For the two traditional forms of jihad, see Chapter 1 or Appendix D.) Alhaznawi disobeyed his father, leaving for Afghanistan the following year, where he attended an al Qaeda training camp. It's not known whether he made it to Chechnya, but he was back in Saudi Arabia by late 2000, where he recruited at least two of his distant Alghamdi cousins. One cousin, Hamza Alghamdi, was especially easy to recruit, since he felt stuck in a dead-end job as a poorly paid stock boy in a local shop.

Mirage Ahead

While economic factors like unemployment played a big role in fomenting the hijackers' eagerness to wage jihad, don't forget about the power of indoctrination. Saudis encounter messages of hatred from their school years into adulthood, and those messages come directly from the Saudi system. Charles Sennott's *Boston Globe* article of March 4, 2002 quotes a widely used tenth-grade textbook called "Monotheism" that incites hatred and violence against Jews and Christians. Describing "Judgment Day," for example, the book declares, "The hour will not come until Muslims will fight the Jews, and Muslims kill all the Jews." The Wahhabis send the same hate messages out to Saudi-funded mosques and religious schools in places like Pakistan, Europe, and America.

I wouldn't want you to think that unemployment and boredom are enough by themselves to explain 9/11. The Saudi system bears a huge responsibility, both within the kingdom and outside it.

Alhaznawi returned to Afghanistan with his cousins, where they all trained at al Qaeda's Al Farouk camp near the city of Khost. There they were chosen for the 9/11 mission by the top al Qaeda leader Mohammed Abu Zubaidah.

The Money Trail

I've mentioned a number of times that al Qaeda's funding has come largely through donations given to Islamic charity organizations by wealthy Saudis. Now let's look at this aspect of things more closely.

The first thing to point out is that the Saudi banking system is murky to say the least, so don't expect too many exact figures and amounts. That being said, a *New York Times* article of December 1, 2002 suggested that about 300 Saudi charities hand out as much as $4 billion a year total. The same article had Saudi officials putting the number much lower, around $200 to $300 million a year. Between those amounts—whichever is correct, if either—it's impossible to get a clear idea of how much finds its way into al Qaeda's coffers. But most experts estimate it's somewhere in the neighborhood of tens of millions of dollars, at least.

As early as 1996, U.S. anti-terrorism experts came up with a list of 31 Saudi charities they suspected of funneling funds to al Qaeda. The list is classified, but here are a few of the major Saudi charities that anti-terrorism experts are known to have put in their sights.

- **The Muwafaq Foundation.** U.S. officials claim that this supposedly "humanitarian" organization funneled millions of dollars to Osama bin Laden. Its $20 million endowment came from a close associate of the Al Saud, a prominent Saudi banker named Sheik Khalid bin Mahfouz. In October 2001, the Treasury Department froze the assets of the foundation's head, wealthy Saudi businessman Yasin al Qadi. Both Mahfouz and al Qadi are named in the 9/11 survivors' lawsuit, which I'll describe in a moment.

- **Al Haramain.** With branches in Bosnia, Somalia, and Southeast Asia, this charity claims to support Islamic schools and orphanages. Interrogated by the CIA in the summer of 2002, al Qaeda's Southeast Asia chief said that the charity funded the network's activities there.

- **Benevolence International Foundation.** According to the *Times* article, in November 2002 "federal prosecutors in Chicago charged the head" of this Saudi charity "with running a criminal enterprise that supported al Qaeda."

◆ **The SAAR Foundation.** Suspected of helping finance Hamas and Palestinian Islamic Jihad, which sponsor Palestinian suicide bombers.

◆ **International Institute for Islamic Thought (IIIT).** Also suspected of funding Hamas and Palestinian Islamic Jihad. Congressional investigations in August 2002 revealed that IIIT employee Tarik Hamdi gave Osama bin Laden batteries for his cell phone.

◆ **International Islamic Relief Organization (IIRO).** This charity's Philippine office was run by Osama bin Laden's brother-in-law from 1986 to 1994. Another IIRO employee was implicated in plans to blow up two U.S. consulates in India.

The last three groups were among five Saudi-funded charities whose offices in northern Virginia were raided by U.S. Treasury agents in March 2002. In addition to suspect charities, well-connected private companies are thought to have funneled money as well, some of it in the form of solicited donations. For example, in 2002 Spanish investigators charged Mohamed Zouaydi, owner of a Saudi trading and investment company operating in Spain, with raising money for an al Qaeda cell whose reach extended from Spain throughout Europe and the Middle East. The officials said that the Saudi company sent almost $700,000 to Spain, and that about $105,000 of it went to al Qaeda, through a courier named Mohamed Bahaiah.

Desert Dates

November 2002: The money trail heats up when a story breaks that two of the Saudi hijackers, Khalid al-Midhar and Nawaq Alhazmi, had been provided with funds that could ultimately be traced to Princess Haifa bint Faisal, daughter of King Faisal and wife of the Saudi ambassador to the United States, Prince Bandar bin Sultan. For several years, the princess had sent about $2,000 a month to the family of Osama Basnan, a Saudi living in America, to help with medical expenses. Basnan passed some of it on to his friend, Omar al-Bayoumi, and al-Bayoumi in turn passed several thousand dollars of the money to the two al Qaeda terrorists when they arrived in San Diego. Al-Bayoumi appears to have helped the two establish themselves in America, right down to assisting them in signing up for flying lessons.

Spokesmen for the Al Saud said that, like other royal family members, the princess has a long list of charitable contributions that she regularly makes, including many to needy private individuals who have approached her. Don't forget about zakat, one of the Five Pillars of Islam, which enjoins the obligation of charitable giving on all devout Muslims. My read on this scandal is that the princess was simply being generous—if perhaps careless in the unsavory targets of her generosity.

Mutual Anger, Mutual Suspicion

Thomas Friedman, the *New York Times* columnist I referred to earlier, has traveled extensively in Saudi Arabia since 9/11. He reports many angry and frustrating encounters with everyone from people on the street to editors and reporters at major newspapers whose newsrooms he visited. The Saudis, he says, simply don't want to acknowledge openly that their system might be even partly to blame for creating the situation that led to the attacks. Yet a few, he adds, are ready to admit it privately.

Blanket public denials have also been issued by the Al Saud, who at first refused to acknowledge that the 15 hijackers were even Saudis. As you'll see in the next chapter, the Al Saud put out repeated lies and evasions, blocking U.S. investigators and stalling attempts to uncover the truth.

The atmosphere of mutual suspicion and anger deepened in the months following the attack. Further tension was injected into the relationship in August, 2002, when nearly 3,000 relatives of the victims filed a lawsuit seeking $1 trillion in damages against 186 defendants. The defendants named in the case include several members of the Al Saud, other wealthy Saudis, Islamic charities, and foreign banks, and the suit alleges that they knowingly helped al Qaeda terrorists.

The Least You Need to Know

- ◆ Al Qaeda declared war against America in the 1990s, but few in America took the threat seriously.

- ◆ Most of the Saudi 9/11 hijackers served as "muscle," while most of the leaders were non-Saudi Muslims recruited to al Qaeda in Europe.

- ◆ The plan for 9/11 was conceived by al Qaeda leaders in Afghanistan and developed by Mohamed Atta and others in Hamburg, Germany.

- ◆ Investigators believe that most of al Qaeda's funding comes from Islamic "charity" organizations, which are supported by donations from wealthy Saudis.

Chapter

Afghanistan, Iraq, and Beyond: The Continuing Threat

In This Chapter

- The Taliban and Saddam go bye-bye
- Osama goes underground—literally
- W. goes nation building after all
- Al Qaeda goes on the offensive again
- The Saudis come out of denial and go into shock

In this chapter I'll lay out the immediate aftermath of 9/11 as it relates to Saudi Arabia. (The long-term aftermath, as you know, is still unfolding.) I'll take the story up to June 2003, when this is being written. It starts with three U.S. wars, each of which has a strong bearing on Saudi Arabia. The first war was the U.S. invasion of Afghanistan in the fall of 2001, leading to the overthrow of the unpopular Taliban regime and the killing, arrest, or dispersal of thousands of al Qaeda personnel. The second war was another

U.S. invasion, of Saudi Arabia's neighbor Iraq, in early 2003. The third war is the continuing war on terrorism itself, in which the Saudis also figure prominently (and not in a good way).

Those three wars make up the U.S. response to 9/11. Next we'll explore the Saudi response, which is less well-defined—even after terror comes home to Riyadh in a big way in the spring of 2003. And finally, we'll take another hard look at al Qaeda itself, concluding with a summary of the terror network's activities since 9/11.

The U.S. Response: Three Wars

Although al Qaeda's responsibility for the 9/11 attacks was amply confirmed within days, the United States held off for nearly a month before taking retaliatory action. In the days after the attack, however, U.S. President George W. Bush surprised observers by stating boldly that his administration would consider any state harboring terrorists to share full responsibility for the terrorists' actions. This was a policy shift. The U.S. president had issued a clear warning not only to al Qaeda's Taliban hosts in Afghanistan, but also to other states (such as Iran and Libya) which had long supported terrorism.

Afghanistan

When action did come, it was measured and mindful, with careful attention paid to marshalling international support and minimizing civilian casualties. On October 7, 2001, the United States launched air strikes on Afghanistan, targeting al Qaeda training camps, Taliban bases, and selected sites in the Afghan capital of Kabul. A few days later, American ground troops and aircraft were deployed to Pakistan, whose leader General Pervez Musharraf had extended full cooperation to the Americans. Pakistan became the main staging area from which U.S. forces carried out the war.

By December, U.S. and allied forces had occupied Kabul and other major cities, and an interim government had been set up in the Afghan capital. After bombing the fortified cave complexes in the Tora Bora mountains where bin Laden was believed to be holding out, U.S. troops were unable to close in on the al Qaeda leader. In March 2002, the U.S.–led Operation Anaconda engaged in the heaviest ground fighting of the war, in the Shahi-Kot Valley, where fighting continued into April. Thousands of Taliban and al Qaeda fighters were killed or arrested, but thousands more fled east into Afghanistan or west into Iran. Osama bin Laden remained at large, and his survival would be confirmed by messages to his followers videotaped later.

Arabian Almanac _____

Pakistan, a strongly Islamic country, played a key role in the U.S. war in Afghanistan. Indeed, Pakistan is a critical player in the overall war on terror. Before 9/11, Pakistan and Saudi Arabia had been the Taliban regime's only international allies. Pakistan's leader, General Pervez Musharraf, had been regarded as an Islamist. Yet after 9/11 he threw his lot in with the United States, gambling on being able to control anti-American sentiment among his people.

Pakistan has a large ethnic Pashtun population living along its border with Afghanistan, and Pashtuns also comprise one of the biggest ethnic groups in Afghanistan, where they formed the backbone of Taliban support. After the U.S. invasion of Afghanistan, many Taliban and al Qaeda fighters found refuge over the mountainous, rugged border in Pashtun-controlled regions of Pakistan, where the Pakistan government had little authority. When news footage shows angry mobs of bearded Pakistani men burning American flags and wearing Osama bin Laden T-shirts, Pashtun territory is usually where they are.

The U.S. war in Afghanistan added further tension to the U.S.–Saudi relationship, which was already strained by angry public reactions in the United States to the Saudi role in the 9/11 attacks. At first, the Saudis barred U.S. planes from flying through Saudi airspace to launch strikes on Afghanistan. While they backed down on that issue, they upheld their refusal to let the United States launch air strikes from Prince Sultan Air Base, where dozens of U.S. fighters were headquartered.

They did let U.S. commanders use the air base for command and control in the Afghan campaign, "but only if the Pentagon keeps quiet about it," *The New York Times* reported on March 10, 2002. The reason they wanted it kept quiet, of course, was the resentment inspired by the U.S. presence—and the leverage it gives to the Wahhabis and the terrorists. At that time, the *Times* story went on, "No one is suggesting that all 5,000 American troops will pack up and leave here." Actually, Osama had been "suggesting" it for a decade. And within a year, that's exactly what would happen. But before it happened, there was a new U.S. war to be fought.

> **Desert Dates**
>
> **January 2002:** The United States moves several hundred suspected al Qaeda prisoners captured in Afghanistan to the U.S. Navy base in Guantanamo Bay, Cuba. News sources report that about two thirds of the prisoners are Saudi nationals. In his State of the Union address, President Bush labels Iran, Iraq, and North Korea an "axis of evil." The speech doesn't mention Saudi Arabia.

Iraq

Even before 9/11, influential members of the Bush administration had set their sights on the Saddam Hussein regime in Iraq. As military operations in Afghanistan wound down over the late spring and early summer of 2002, these officials won the president over to the view that Saddam should be the administration's next target. Over the rest of the year, the U.S. administration's increasingly obvious determination to topple Saddam Hussein presented even more problems for the Saudis than the war in Afghanistan. Or rather, it intensified the problems that already existed, plus creating a few new headaches for both sides.

Mirage Ahead

Polls taken just before the United States invaded Iraq found that over 50 percent of Americans erroneously believed that Iraqis had been among the 9/11 hijackers. It was also widely accepted that Saddam Hussein had had something to do with the plot, or that he had supported al Qaeda. On the contrary, however, there is no firm evidence of any link between Saddam and Osama, despite the Bush administration's media blitz to the contrary. Too many Americans lapped up the administration's unproven assertions that Saddam and Osama were working together. Don't be one of them—at least not until some evidence is presented.

The central problem was still that old chestnut, the American troop presence, with its related issues of what role if any the kingdom would play in facilitating a U.S. attack. But the prospect of a U.S. invasion of Iraq also raised the following new and unsettling questions for the Saudis:

♦ **What sort of Iraq would emerge after Saddam?** Despite the American involvement in Afghanistan, candidate Bush had been famous for his denigration of "nation building." So would the United States have what it takes to ensure continuity and stability after toppling Saddam? An unstable, strife-torn Iraq right next door would be a security nightmare for the kingdom. And if Iraq became a democracy, how would that threaten the far-from-democratic regime in Saudi Arabia? The Al Saud had no love for Saddam Hussein, but as they discovered during the first Gulf War, the idea of a new regime in Iraq opened some very unattractive possibilities.

♦ **How much anger would a U.S. invasion stir up inside Saudi Arabia itself?** In the larger Arab world? A short war might be survivable, but a long war or a protracted U.S. occupation would give the Wahhabis and other anti-American elements plenty of ammunition. It was a bad time for a war that promised to turn even more Saudis against the already shaky regime. And, of course, any attack on Arabs by the United States would boost al Qaeda's credibility on the "Arab street" in places like Egypt and Jordan.

♦ **Finally, what impact would an American war and victory in Iraq have on the U.S.–Saudi relationship?** If the Saudis helped too much, they'd lose even further support at home. But if they helped too little, they'd risk losing the American support that came with the special relationship.

In short, a U.S. war in Iraq looked like a no-win situation from the Saudi point of view, and accordingly the Saudis spent much of 2002 lobbying hard against it. During most of that time, they publicly waffled back and forth over the question of whether they'd allow the Americans to use Saudi bases. By September, however, U.S. negotiators had secured the use of the huge Al Udeid Air Base, at Doha in neighboring Qatar, for war games later that fall.

Desert Dates

1995: Qatar's pro-American emir, Sheikh Hamad bin Khalifa, overthrows his father in a bloodless coup and undertakes significant democratic reforms in Qatar. At the same time, he begins construction on a massive air base, much larger than anything Qatar could possibly ever need, near the capital city of Doha. This is like hanging a big "Welcome, Uncle Sam" sign on the front door. The United States didn't waste much time offering its assistance, and Qatar became America's new best friend in the region. The relationship was consummated in March 2003, when the United States used the Qatari base as its headquarters for the successful invasion of Iraq.

While tiny, wealthy Qatar is the only Arab country other than Saudi Arabia to adhere to the Wahhabi form of Islam, it has a looser and more tolerant version of Wahhabism than its larger neighbor. Alcohol is permitted, and women can drive cars, walk around in public without veils, and even vote. The liberal, progressive Qatari government also encourages a free press and sponsors the hugely popular Arab satellite TV network, Al Jazeera. Many more Saudis watch Al Jazeera than watch Saudi TV. For the limitations of Saudi TV, see Chapter 16; for more on Al Jazeera, see Chapter 20.

By the time the war games began in November, U.S. general Tommy Franks had chosen Al Udeid as the nerve center for any invasion of Iraq. Between November and February 2003, the Saudis continued lobbying against such an invasion. They also worked behind the scenes in Iraq, encouraging Iraqi generals to overthrow Saddam Hussein in exchange for amnesty from war crimes prosecution. By the end of February, however, Saddam Hussein remained in power and the U.S. troop build-up in Kuwait, the major U.S. staging post, was complete.

Mirage Ahead

It's true that Saddam Hussein had few friends—but for many Arabs, to see U.S. tanks in downtown Baghdad wounded them more deeply than to see years of his bloody dictatorship.

The invasion of Iraq did indeed come in March 2003, and like everyone else the Saudis breathed a big sigh of relief when Saddam's army failed to put up any significant resistance. In just a few weeks, the United States had occupied Baghdad, Iraq's ancient and fabled capital city, and mopping-up operations were concluding in the rest of the country. And for the time being at least, the Saudis seemed to have succeeded in walking the fine line between too much and too little support for the Americans.

The Saudis quietly assisted the U.S. invasion and occupation of Iraq in five ways:

- They allowed U.S. forces to fly over Saudi airspace.

- They made Prince Sultan Air Base available for command-and-control operations.

- They agreed to increase oil production to make up for any shortfall caused by Iraqi oil going offline.

- They agreed to supply extra oil to Jordan, which was extending support to the United States.

- The Saudi army sent a small contingent of 3,300 soldiers into Kuwait to assist in defending against any Iraqi attack.

In exchange, the United States secretly put an unknown number of isolated Patriot missile batteries out in the desert, near the border with Iraq, to guard against any Iraqi missile attack on Saudi territory. Additional numbers of U.S. forces were secretly stationed for "defensive and humanitarian" purposes along the border.

Only after the war was over did both sides announce that nearly all of the 5,000 American troops stationed in Saudi Arabia would be withdrawn. The success of the war made this seem less like a concession to Osama bin Laden, and more like a natural outcome of neutralizing the Iraqi threat. Besides, the United States now had Qatar. But, as you'll see in a moment, the withdrawal of American troops from Saudi soil didn't exactly bring a peace offer from Osama bin Laden. Somewhere along the way, the stakes had changed.

There was a single big plus for Saudi Arabia in the U.S. invasion of Iraq: It temporarily let the kingdom off the hook in the war on terror. For nearly six months, first during the drawn-out diplomatic maneuvering leading up to the war and then during the war itself, the Western press was almost completely preoccupied with Iraq. This had the effect of taking issues like the financing of al Qaeda and the hatred-inciting Saudi system off the table. But, as I said, this was only temporary.

The War on Terror

Long before the tanks rolled into Baghdad, critics of the Bush administration were taking it to task for ignoring the war on terror in the headlong rush to get rid of Saddam at any cost. They pointed out that, contrary to President Bush's public pronouncements, no demonstrable links existed between the Iraqi tyrant and Osama bin Laden or al Qaeda. They also complained that the single-minded focus on Iraq had diverted valuable resources and manpower from the hunt for Osama bin Laden and the campaign against al Qaeda.

American contributions to the war on terror have come mostly in two ways, both primarily through military campaigns. First, U.S. forces have killed al Qaeda leaders and personnel in bombing campaigns and combat (like Mohammed Atef, bin Laden's second-in-command, killed by American bombs in Afghanistan in November 2001). Second, U.S. forces have captured al Qaeda personnel in combat, and have been able to gather intelligence by interrogating them. The intelligence can then be shared with other security services to assist in tracking down terror cells. Most of the interrogation has taken place at the U.S. Navy base at Guantanamo Bay, Cuba, where close to 700 alleged al Qaeda and Taliban detainees are being held as of June 2003. Their lengthy detention without charges or trial has been strongly criticized by international human rights groups and by American civil rights organizations, as has the decision to try them in military rather than civilian courts.

U.S. intelligence did score a well-publicized high-tech success in October 2002, when the CIA used a missile fired from an unmanned Predator aircraft to kill a senior al Qaeda leader, Qaed Salim Sinan al Harethi, in Yemen. At home, the FBI has conducted raids on alleged al Qaeda cells in Buffalo, Detroit, and Portland, although as of this writing it's unclear whether the arrests have netted bona fide al Qaeda members.

The Bush administration was able to point to some major successes in the international war on terror. Indeed, while it was true that Osama bin Laden himself and his top aide Ayman al Zawahiri remained at large as of June 2003, a number of other al Qaeda leaders have been captured. However, as the administration's critics pointed out, it's also true that the United States has often taken little part in their capture.

A leading role has been played by the security forces of Pakistan, where many of the most important captures have taken place—and American attempts to take credit for them haven't always sat well with the Pakistanis. Key al Qaeda leaders captured in Pakistan include Ramzi bin al-Shibh and Khalid Sheikh Mohammed, who together conceived the plan for 9/11, and Mohammed Abu Zubaidah, who chose the hijackers. However, scores of other arrests have been made by security services in Europe, Asia, and the Middle East.

Saudi participation in the war on terror has been virtually nil, since until very recently the Saudis have been locked in denial that the problem had anything to do with them.

The Saudi Response

Indeed, as I suggested earlier, far from helping the war on terror, the Saudis have generally done everything they could to hinder it. Long before 9/11, Saudi officials refused to allow U.S. investigators to follow up leads in the kingdom as they looked into terror attacks like the U.S. embassy bombings in East Africa and the attack on the USS *Cole*. Similarly, the Saudis refused to extradite 13 Saudi citizens indicted in the United States for the 1996 Khobar Towers bombings. Such obstruction was a major source of friction between the Clinton administration and the Saudi government, and it has also caused similar problems during the Bush administration, as FBI agents investigated after 9/11. News reports have described FBI agents as complaining privately that the Saudis refused hundreds of requests for background information on the 15 Saudi hijackers.

As earlier with the Clinton administration, the Bush White House gave the order to back off, frightened by the specter of the oil weapon. In President Bush's case, another reason was the hope of Saudi cooperation in the war plans against Iraq.

Desert Dates

November 2000: A car bomb kills Christopher Rodway, a British hospital engineer working in the kingdom, as he drives his jeep through a Riyadh suburb. Other attacks on Westerners followed, in what was clearly a sustained al Qaeda campaign. Incredibly, Saudi officials rounded up six Britons, claiming that they had carried out the bombings as part of a turf war between rival expatriate bootlegging operations. The six were convicted in a series of transparently rigged show trials. Two of the men were sentenced to be publicly beheaded, while the other four got 18-year prison sentences. In a TV appearance, all six showed clear signs of torture. This shocking episode demonstrates the lengths that the Saudis were willing to go to to deny any al Qaeda presence on Saudi soil. In May 2003—after that month's al Qaeda bombings in Riyadh finally shattered the Saudis' long denial—it was rumored that the six would soon be released.

Why did the British government basically abandon its six wrongfully imprisoned citizens? You'll learn about one nasty possible reason in the next chapter.

Denial and Evasion

The Saudi record of denial and evasion after 9/11 starts with repeated refusals to accept that any of the hijackers were in fact Saudi citizens. There's been some heavy competition, but Prince Naif, the powerful Interior Minister, has to take the prize. As late as December 8, 2001, he told reporters he still didn't believe that any of the hijackers were Saudis. In its issue of January 14, 2002, *U.S. News and World Report* quotes Naif as saying, "It's true that Saudi citizens were on the planes, but who can be certain whether they were behind the attacks?"

Naif's comments were part of a media offensive that the Al Saud undertook in December 2002 to counteract "slanderous" American media coverage of the hijackers' Saudi connection. "We have pain for what happened in America. We are condemning what happened. You guys are refusing to accept us," Prince Bandar, the Saudi ambassador to the United States, was quoted as saying in the *New York Times* of December 21. As commentators like Thomas Friedman pointed out, however, nowhere did any of the Al Saud attempt to account for Saudi participation in the hijackings. Nowhere was there anything resembling an apology, or an acknowledgment that the Saudi system may have played some role in fomenting the hatred that drove the hijackers. And nowhere did anyone try to explain why many Saudis openly rejoiced after the attacks, or why they continued to support bin Laden.

Arabian Almanac

By the summer of 2002, the Saudis were reportedly paying millions of dollars to well-connected Washington lobbyists and high-powered American PR firms to polish their tarnished image among Americans. Yet in August a national poll by Fabrizio, McLaughlin, and Associates showed that 63 percent of Americans had a negative opinion of Saudi Arabia—up from 50 percent in May.

Desert Dates

October 2001: New York Mayor Rudy Giuliani wins kudos for handing back a $10 million check that Saudi Prince Alwaleed bin Talal has offered to help the victims of 9/11. Touring Ground Zero, the prince had declared that it was time to get at the "roots" of terrorism—by stopping Israel from "slaughtering" Palestinians.

Among the Saudi public, denial continued to be the order of the day as well. Osama bin Laden wasn't involved, Western reporters were often told. Or if he was involved, he was led astray by his Egyptian advisors. One popular theory says that the Mossad, the Israeli intelligence service, carried out the attacks to spark enmity towards the Saudis. A variant of this theory maintains that thousands of Jews escaped death when they were warned not to show up for work at the World Trade Center that day. Another common theory says that the CIA did it. Thomas Friedman has reported hearing all these and more during his visits to the kingdom. In his *New York Times* column of February 10, 2002, Friedman describes a Saudi journalist asking him in all seriousness, "Are Jews in the media behind the campaign to smear Saudi Arabia and Islam?" It's a question, Friedman says, that's "everywhere" in the Arab world. But Friedman also writes that conspiracy theories about Jewish domination of the world are more deeply embedded in Saudi Arabia than anywhere else he's ever been. (And he's been all over the Middle East in his distinguished career.)

It's all part of the fatalistic streak in Arab culture I described earlier, which encourages Arabs to believe that they themselves have no share in shaping their own destiny, and no responsibility for their own actions. It also has to do with saving face. First comes denial: We didn't do anything. And if denial gets pierced, evasion follows immediately on its heels: It may have happened, but it's someone else's fault. As Friedman says, this pattern can be found throughout the Arab world, but it's strongest with the Saudis.

And yet … in the final chapter of this book, I'll tell you how a few Saudi voices have started to question this sort of response.

Crown Prince Abdullah's Peace Plan

Right now, though, I want to cover another important part of the Saudi response to 9/11, which is Crown Prince Abdullah's plan for an Israeli-Palestinian peace settlement. This is an especially good place to mention it, since I've been citing Thomas Friedman, who actually played a part in bringing it to light. (You can read about it in his 2002 book, *Longitudes and Attitudes*.) The *New York Times* columnist was meeting with the Crown Prince in February 2002, and mentioned a column he'd written recently suggesting that President Bush propose a peace plan. The terms of Friedman's suggested plan were simple: Israel withdraws to its pre-1967 borders, allowing an independent Palestinian state in the West Bank, in exchange for peace and full normalization of relations with all Arab League nations.

The Crown Prince asked jokingly if the journalist had broken into his desk, claiming that he had just such a plan all ready to go. He then authorized Friedman to write a column detailing the simple idea and putting his, the Crown Prince's, name to it. And that's what happened. The column was published on February 17, 2002, under the headline "An Intriguing Signal from the Saudi Crown Prince." In it, Friedman underscores the importance of such a proposal coming from a major Arab leader, one of the "big boys" (that is, Egypt or Saudi Arabia).

Fast-forward to a year later, when President Bush is trying to draw a bead on Saddam and wants to boost his credibility in the Arab world with his own peace plan. He introduces the "Road Map To Peace"—basically, the same as Abdullah's plan, which was the same as Friedman's plan. A Jewish-American journalist, an Arab prince, and a born-again Christian president—maybe it's just crazy enough to work. We can only hope.

> **⚠ CAUTION**
>
> **Mirage Ahead** _____
>
> Don't forget that the biggest issue inflaming the Arab world is the ongoing conflict between the Israelis and the Palestinian Arabs. (For background, see Chapters 5 and 7.) Remember Prince Alwaleed's comments when he presented the $10 million check to Mayor Giuliani? Though Alaweed's comments may have seemed deeply inappropriate from the perspective of many Westerners, they do reflect a real Arab mindset. The root of Arab terrorism, as Arabs see it, is the conflict with the Israelis.
>
> Of course, that begs the question: If peace is achieved, will it really end the terror?

Al Qaeda Resurgent?

Finally, I want to bring you up to date on the activities of al Qaeda since 9/11. The U.S. invasion of Iraq gave many in the West a bad case of the jitters. But the period of heaviest fighting, March 2003, passed without any terror strikes. Just when some Western commentators were suggesting that al Qaeda was a broken reed, however, the terror network struck again. In May 2003, deadly suicide truck bombers struck not only in Riyadh, but also in Morocco and elsewhere. Suddenly, the commentators were talking about the "revival" of al Qaeda.

Al Qaeda Attacks Since 9/11

It seems more likely, though, that al Qaeda never really went away. Here's a timeline of al Qaeda's major attacks since 9/11:

- **April 11, 2002:** The firebombing of a Tunisia synagogue kills 19, injures 22.

- **May 11, 2002:** A suicide car bomb at a Karachi, Pakistan, hotel kills 14.

- **June 14, 2002:** A suicide car bomb outside the U.S. Embassy in Karachi kills 12, injures 45.

- **October 6, 2002:** A suicide attack is carried out on the French supertanker *Limburg* off the coast of Yemen.

- **October 8, 2002:** An attack on U.S. soldiers in Kuwait kills one, wounds another.

- **October 12, 2002:** A Bali, Indonesia, nightclub bombing kills 212, mostly vacationing Westerners.

- **October 28, 2002:** U.S. diplomat Laurence Foley is gunned down in Amman, Jordan.

- **November 28, 2002:** An Israeli-owned hotel in Mombasa, Kenya, is bombed, killing 15, injuring 40. Minutes earlier, two surface-to-air missiles barely miss an Israeli holiday jet on takeoff from Mombasa airport.

- **May 12, 2003:** Three separate suicide bombings against Western targets in Riyadh kill 34, wound at least 160.

- **May 18, 2003:** Five separate suicide bombings against hotels and Jewish targets in Casablanca, Morocco, kill 43 and wound hundreds of others.

In addition, during that same week in May 2003, suicide bombers killed more than 50 people in Chechnya, 18 explosions ripped through Shell gas stations in and around Karachi, and a bomb destroyed a courtroom in Yemen where a terrorist had recently received the death sentence for the murder of 3 U.S. missionaries. At the same time, Britain's intelligence service warned its citizens against traveling to seven African countries, and the United States issued warnings about South East Asia. Behind it all, observers believed, lay a massive global stirring of al Qaeda.

Help Wanted?

The Riyadh bombings, as I've said, finally seem to have pierced through the veil of denial that made the Saudis pretend that al Qaeda was someone else's problem. Although—you've got to hand it to him—Prince Naif tried once again. "Where do the terrorists spring from? Other countries," he said on Abu Dhabi TV four days after Riyadh was paralyzed by the three blasts. A few days later, he was forced to admit that the 3 dead suicide bombers had been among 19 men who escaped a police raid in Riyadh less than a week earlier. Of the 19 men, all thought to be al Qaeda operatives, 17 were Saudis. Rumors have it that Naif is not long for his job as interior minister. (Maybe they could give it to that guy who was Saddam Hussein's information minister.)

The fact is that the Al Saud, and the country as a whole, were still in shock. It's too soon to say what the outcome will be, though I'll talk about some possibilities in the final chapter. As of late May, the FBI planned to send 60 investigators. True to form, good old Prince Naif was impossible to pin down when Western reporters asked him if the Saudis would finally cooperate: "We welcome them here to inspect the site and location of the bombs." Hmm, that sounds helpful.

But at least the Saudis know now that they, too, have a problem. Correction: They always knew it, but now they *acknowledge* it.

The Least You Need to Know

- The U.S. war in Afghanistan put the Saudis in a tight spot.

- The U.S. war in Iraq put them in an even tighter one.

- After the U.S. invasion of Iraq, only 3 percent of Saudis had a favorable view of the United States.

- Also after the invasion, the United States and Saudi Arabia announced that American troops would be leaving Saudi soil.

- Al Qaeda struck in Riyadh (and elsewhere) anyway, in May 2003, finally piercing the Saudi blanket of denial.

Chapter 19

Blood Lines in the Sand: Inside the House of Saud

In This Chapter

- Intrigue and rivalry among 5,000 (or so) Saudi princes
- Shocking royal scandals
- The House of Saud meets the House of Bush

By now, of course, you already know a lot about the Saudi royal family, the Al Saud. You'll remember, for example, that the family got its start in the middle of the eighteenth century, when its founder, Muhammad ibn Saud, established the dynasty. You know that its power was revived early in the twentieth century by King Abdel Aziz, later known as Ibn Saud, who founded the modern state of Saudi Arabia. You've also met the sons of Ibn Saud who've succeeded to the throne, as well as some of those who've held other positions of authority in the Saudi state.

In this chapter, I'll fill out that picture, giving you a more intimate and detailed portrait of the Saudi royal family. You'll find out how the various factions have jockeyed for position in the past—and how they're doing so now, as the elderly and ailing King Fahd approaches death. I'll also offer up some juicy and shocking royal scandals, before examining the long and close relationship between two oil dynasties, the House of Saud and the House of Bush.

Al Saud Basics

The first thing you need to know is that not all of the estimated 30,000 members of the Al Saud are technically considered royalty, even though they're all descended from Muhammad ibn Saud. In fact, the designation "royal" is officially reserved only for those descended from a great-great-grandson of Muhammad ibn Saud, Faisal ibn Turki.

The Al Faisal

You can read about Faisal and other early Al Saud rulers in Chapter 4. Ruling as an emir in Riyadh during the middle of the nineteenth century, Faisal greatly expanded Al Saud power and is credited with creating the second Saudi state. In recognition of his achievements, his descendants are called the *Al Faisal*, and they are considered the true "royalty" of the Al Saud—the cream of the crop, as it were. All subsequent Saudi rulers have come from Faisal's bloodline.

Sheik-Speak

The **Al Faisal** are the main branch of the Al Saud and the only branch that's officially considered "royalty." In 2003, Al Faisal princes were estimated to number about 5,000. Ibn Saud and his descendants in turn comprise the main branch of the Al Faisal, but there are collateral Al Faisal bloodlines as well.

Only males in the Al Faisal line of the Al Saud are entitled to call themselves emir, or prince. In 2003, Al Faisal princes were estimated to number about 5,000. Ibn Saud and his descendants comprise the main branch of the Al Faisal, but there are collateral Al Faisal bloodlines as well. Faisal was Ibn Saud's grandfather, or the father of Ibn Saud's father, Abdel Rahman. The most important collateral branch of the Al Faisal is called the al Kabir branch and consists of the descendants of Abdel Rahman's brother Saud.

Here's a selected family tree showing the Al Faisal branch and other main branches of the Al Saud.

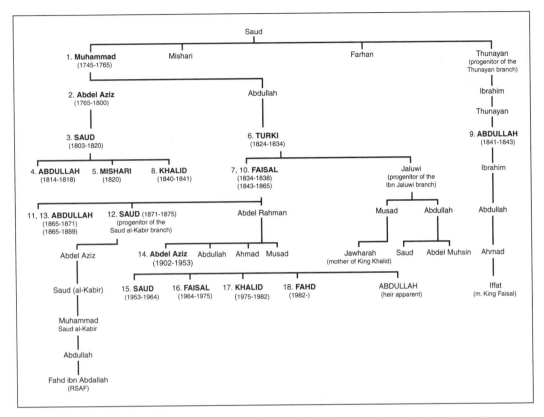

The main branches of the Al Saud family tree, including the Al Faisal, the Ibn Jaluwi, and the Al Thunayan branches. Numbers and dates indicate rulers and the period of reign.

The Sons of Ibn Saud

As you know, since Ibn Saud's death the throne has passed among his sons in succession, starting with the oldest but skipping several who either declined to rule or were judged unfit by the rest of the family. You're already well acquainted with those who have ruled so far, so I'll just give you a quick review of their names and the dates of their reigns: Saud (1953–1964), Faisal (1964–1975), Khalid (1975–1982), and Fahd (1982–present). (If you want a more detailed review of their careers and accomplishments, go back to Chapter 6.)

Fahd is now 81 and barely hanging on to life after a series of crippling strokes starting in the mid 1990s. Yet Crown Prince Abdullah, Fahd's designated successor, is himself 79 years old. The "younger" brothers are also aging by now, too. Here's a breakdown of the major players among Ibn Saud's remaining sons, starting with Abdullah:

- **Crown Prince Abdullah ibn Abdel Aziz, age 79.** He's run the country since Fahd's incapacitation. In addition to being designated as the next king, he's long commanded the Saudi National Guard, charged with protecting the royal family. Once viewed as anti-Western and a religious conservative, he's recently taken steps toward both greater openness with Western governments and toward religious reform. In 2002, he issued statements calling for greater "self-examination" by Saudi society. His once firm support by the Wahhabis has suffered as a result, but he retains an aura of piety and popularity that Fahd never enjoyed. He thinks for himself and is a strong leader with good instincts. His health is reported to be okay, but he's no spring chicken.

- **Prince Sultan ibn Abdel Aziz, age 78.** As second deputy prime minister, he's officially next in line after Abdullah. Sultan has long been the minister of defense and aviation, and has arranged the purchase of billions of dollars of military equipment by the kingdom, mostly from the United States and Britain. He's known as "Mr. 10 Percent," supposedly because he's amassed great wealth from taking bribes and kickbacks from Western arms firms.

- **Prince Naif ibn Abdel Aziz, age 69.** The powerful minister of the interior has the reputation of being hard-as-nails, and is probably the man most responsible for Saudi Arabia's dismal human rights record. According to Amnesty International, Saudi prisoners are routinely tortured, beaten, whipped, deprived of sleep, and drugged. Naif is the one I quoted in the last chapter as questioning the guilt of the Saudi hijackers. He's also in charge of a government committee that gives money to the families of Palestinian suicide bombers.

- **Prince Salman ibn Abdel Aziz, age 66.** The long-serving governor of Riyadh, Salman has taken on the role of arbitrator in many family disputes. He has a high reputation among foreign diplomats, and some Saudi watchers think he may be chosen by the family to succeed Abdullah, leap-frogging his older brother Sultan. He is a strong but calm leader, and has been a major player behind the scenes in the family. One black mark: He's named in the lawsuit filed by the families of the 9/11 victims, who accuse him of financing charities linked to al Qaeda.

◆ **Prince Nawaf ibn Abdel Aziz, age 69.** Nawaf is considered to be an ally of Abdullah, who appointed him to succeed their nephew Turki ibn Faisal as head of the Saudi foreign intelligence service just before 9/11. But Nawaf suffered a stroke in March 2002, and it's not clear how much weight he pulls in the family now.

Those are the major players among Ibn Saud's sons; you can get a visual fix on them in the following family tree. Abdullah's successor, and the next few Saudi monarchs, will almost certainly be chosen from their ranks. My money says keep your eye on Salman.

Arabian Almanac

Among the various sons of Ibn Saud by his many wives, alliances tend to be strongest between whole brothers. The most powerful faction in the Al Saud is the block of seven whole brothers called "the Sudairi Seven," after the family of their mother, Hassa bint al Sudairi. Hassa herself, revered throughout the country, is probably the most respected woman in Saudi Arabia. The Sudairi Seven (oldest to youngest) are Fahd, Sultan, Abdel Rahman, Naif, Turki, Salman, and Ahmed. Faisal, who had no whole brothers, allied himself with them, much to his advantage.

Abdullah has often found himself at odds with them, and especially with Sultan, the next in line. The two reportedly despise each other. Abdullah's problem right now is that until Fahd dies, he can't finalize his own grip on power, especially against the two of his Sudairi half-brothers who are the most significant threats to him, Sultan and Naif. If he wants to go ahead with reforms, as he seems to, it's important that he do so from a secure power base. Right now, the Sudairi Seven stand in the way of that—especially Sultan and Naif.

The Grandsons of Ibn Saud

The big question facing the family is what will happen when, as it will inevitably, the throne has to pass to the next generation—the grandsons of Ibn Saud. There are hundreds of them, and they're spread throughout the armed services and the government. Since Ibn Saud continued having children into his seventies, his oldest grandchildren are as old as some of his younger children. Many were educated abroad, especially at British or American schools and universities.

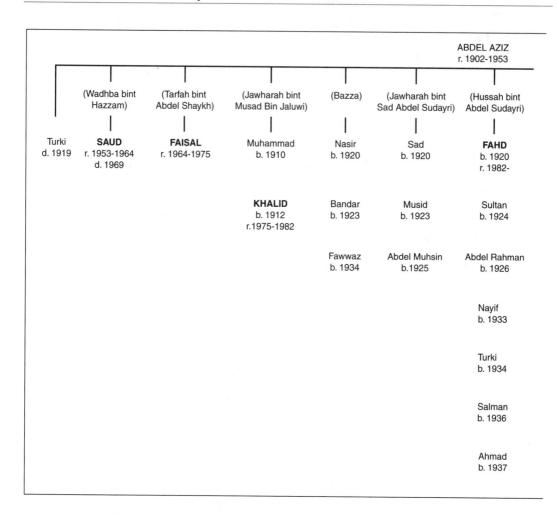

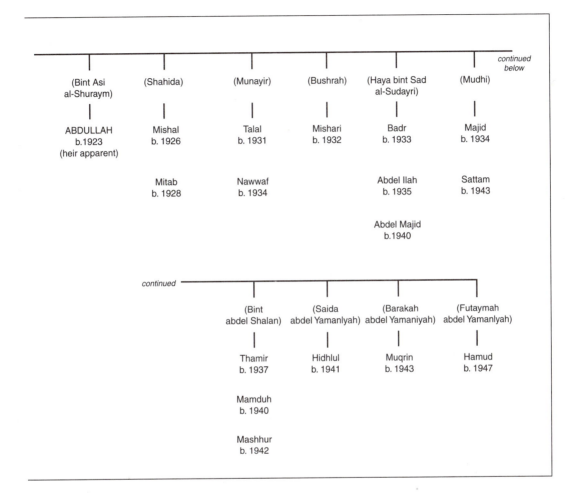

A selected family tree showing some of Ibn Saud's sons.

Here are the most powerful of Ibn Saud's grandchildren:

♦ **Prince Bandar bin Sultan, age 52.** As the Saudi ambassador to the United States for over 25 years, Prince Bandar is the well-known face of Saudi Arabia to many Americans. He's been a close consultant to both Democratic and Republican presidents, but he's most intimate with the Bushes, who truly consider him family. His mother was a concubine from the Asir province, and as an illegitimate child Bandar had little contact with his father, Prince Sultan (though he enjoyed full legal recognition, as Islamic law provides). Raised by his widely revered grandmother Hassa bint al Sudairi from the age of 11, Bandar proved himself in British military school and as a hot-shot fighter pilot in the Saudi air force.

He's married to his cousin, Haifa al Faisal, the youngest daughter of the late king—the princess whose checks ended up in the bank accounts of two al Qaeda operatives, as I detailed in the previous chapter. If the couple weathers that scandal, the sky's the limit. The thoroughly Westernized Bandar has played a key role in many top-secret negotiations. He's smooth, capable, dedicated, and highly intelligent. More on Bandar and the Bushes in a moment.

♦ **Prince Saud al Faisal, age 61.** Bandar's older cousin and brother-in-law, and son of the late King Faisal, Saud is the kingdom's Princeton-educated foreign minister. Regal to the point of stuffiness, he's married to Crown Prince Abdullah's granddaughter. Reportedly, his once secure position with the crown prince is now shaky, since he's done little to improve the Saudi image in the United States after 9/11.

♦ **Prince Turki al Faisal, age 57.** Saud's younger brother, Turki was head of foreign intelligence for 25 years before being appointed ambassador to Britain after 9/11. He's the guy who made Osama bin Laden what he is today, selecting bin Laden and funding the jihad in Afghanistan in the 1980s. He, too, is named in the lawsuit filed by the 9/11 victims' families, which claims that he paid off the Taliban to ensure that bin Laden didn't strike Saudi Arabia. Others say that Turki attempted to induce the Taliban to surrender bin Laden in 1998, but that Mullah Omar, the Taliban leader, went back on the deal.

♦ **Khalid bin Sultan, age 53.** Bandar's brother and the son of the defense minister, Khalid won his spurs commanding Saudi forces during Operation Desert Storm. The rakeoffs he took during and after the war reportedly shocked even his father, and Khalid eventually resigned, only to be reappointed recently as his father's deputy minister.

- **Muhammad ibn Fahd, age 52.** Governor of the oil-rich Eastern Province, Muhammad by all accounts is incredibly wealthy. He's the most visible and ambitious of King Fahd's sons, and it's reported that he has his eye on the throne. The question is whether his influence can outlast his father's death.

- **Abdel Aziz ibn Fahd, age 29.** Muhammad's younger brother and the kingdom's minister of state, Abdul Aziz is another one of Fahd's highly visible sons whose future depends on outlasting his father's demise. Unstable and ambitious, he's been courting Wahhabi support in an effort to improve his chances of eventually winning the throne. In 1997, he helped arrange a $100 million aid package for the Taliban, which was sheltering Osama bin Laden at the time.

So far, these princes' ambitions have ridden largely on the luster of their fathers' reputations and status. For example, all of Faisal's sons have benefited from the reverence in which Saudis continue to hold the late king. Similarly, King Fahd's sons will likely loose status when their father, who isn't so widely respected, passes away. The sons of the Sudairi Seven will continue to act as a block and will be influential for that reason. Here's a family tree for Ibn Saud's grandsons, as well.

(Saud)	(Faisal)	(Khalid)	(Nasir)	(Fahd)	(Abdallahh)	(Sultan)	(Abdel Muhsin)	(Naif)	(Salman)
Sayf al-Islam *Minister of Interior*	Saud *Foreign Minister*	Sultan *Navy Lt.*	Turki *General, Air Force*	Faisal *Director, Youth Welfare*	Mitib *General, National Guard*	Khalid *General, Army*	Saud *Deputy Amir, Makkah*	Fahd Ibn Turki *great-grandson* *Ministry of Interior*	Sultan *former astronaut* *Director, Agency for* *Disabled Children*
Muhammad *Amir of Baha*	Khalid *Amir of Abha*			Muhammad *Amir of Eastern Province*	Faisal *Captain,* *National Guard*	Bandar *Ambassador to the U.S.*			
	Bandar *Air Force*			Sultan *Deputy, Youth Welfare*		Fahd *Amir of Tabuk*			Abdel Aziz *Deputy Minister* *of Petroleum*
	Turki *Director, GID*			Saud *Deputy, GID*					
				Abdel Aziz *Royal Counselor*					

A selected family tree of Ibn Saud's grandsons—the third generation of Saudi Arabia's rulers.

When the crunch comes, seniority will likely play a role, but the family will also make its choice based on personal qualities. Whoever is chosen will have to be savvy and strong enough to make his own mark. My money says keep your eyes on the sons of Faisal.

The Recent Turning Point: Fahd's Strokes

The biggest recent turning point for the family came when Fahd suffered his first debilitating stroke in 1995. Up to then, Abdullah, despite his role as crown prince and head of the National Guard, had been relatively isolated within the family. Not only was he without any full brothers, but he also had the stigma of being descended on his mother's side from the Rashids, the Al Saud's traditional enemies (see Chapter 4). Like Faisal, another one of Ibn Saud's sons without whole brothers, Abdullah spurns his half-brothers' extravagant ways; he's more at home in a simple tent drinking camel's milk than in a penthouse condo sipping champagne. Sticking to a modest and conservative Bedouin lifestyle has made him popular with the people but less so inside the family.

Abdullah has also made no secret of his intentions to pursue democratic reforms, rein in the religious conservatives (despite his own strong conservative credentials), and break the long Saudi military dependence on the United States. Worst of all, he has long opposed the rampant corruption and extravagance of the royal family. These convictions rankled even more with most of his relatives than Abdullah's Bedouin simplicity.

So when Fahd had his first major stroke in 1995, writes former CIA analyst Robert Baer in the May 2003 *Atlantic Monthly*, the other senior princes were more worried about keeping him alive at all costs than they were about his actual well-being. As long as Fahd was warm and breathing, Abdullah could be kept from the throne. Hopefully, Abdullah himself would die before Fahd, and they could continue with business as usual. This block was led by Sultan, Salman, and Naif, who positioned themselves firmly against Abdullah. But the anti-Abdullah faction has problems of its own, the major one being Fahd's son Abdel Aziz (whom I just mentioned in the list of Ibn Saud's grandsons). He's been working to exclude his uncles Sultan and Naif from power, in hopes of switching succession away from them and toward himself. And there are disagreements, too, between Sultan, who is very pro-American, and Naif, who is less so, over issues like Naif's stonewalling of U.S. attempts to investigate the Khobar and other bombings.

Exploiting this and other weaknesses in the opposition's unity, Abdullah managed to consolidate his position somewhat against Sultan and the others by 1998, after Fahd had had further strokes. But, as I said a moment ago, until Fahd dies and Abdullah officially becomes king, he remains vulnerable.

Scandal!

For a family that prizes secrecy and privacy over all else, the Al Saud have been at the center of many international scandals over the years. Here are a few of the juiciest and most shocking.

The Saud Files

Remember poor old King Saud, booted into exile in 1964 after he made a mess of the kingship? Well, he continued to make a mess of things even after his exile. For five years, until his death in 1969, the ex-king stirred up one embarrassing scandal after another for the Al Saud, first with political troublemaking, and then with his glitzy, debauched lifestyle. Saud was the royal family's first experience with international scandal, and it took years afterward for them to even be comfortable acknowledging his name in public.

First the disgruntled ex-king was caught by the CIA hiring mercenaries and buying old military aircraft—apparently with the absurd intention of invading Saudi Arabia and mounting a coup. The staging area was Portugal, where, after being tipped off by the CIA, the police confiscated Saud's private air force of 23 planes. Coup over.

Next, in the fall of 1966, Saud approached his former enemy Gamal Abdel Nasser, the Arab nationalist president of Egypt, who welcomed him in Cairo. A few months later, Saud popped up in Yemen, where Nasser was fighting his proxy war against Saudi Arabia. (You'll find background on the proxy war in Yemen in Chapter 6.) There, in the capital of Sana, Saud publicly denounced his brother Faisal as an imperialist lackey of the West, praised Nasser, and ostentatiously contributed a million bucks to the revolutionary cause—capping the performance by declaring himself to be Saudi Arabia's rightful ruler. Both of these debacles—the abortive coup and the Yemen fiasco—were well-chronicled in the Arab and Western press.

By 1967, however, Saud was ill and becoming increasingly feeble. Nasser, embarrassed not just by Saud but also by the disastrous 1967 war with Israel, was forced to make up with the Al Saud and other Arab rulers he had offended in the past. So Saud, no longer welcome in Cairo, moved on to Athens, where he and his 50-odd sons lived in a series of luxury hotels, occupying entire floors. Saud was now pretty much laid up, but that didn't stop him from throwing money around. His sons had to have their Ferraris, their women, and their parties. This, too, was all fully recorded by the paparazzi of the tabloid press. In 1968, the last full year of his life, Saud reportedly ran through some $10 million in living expenses alone. He died in February 1969, a broken man in body, mind, and spirit. When Faisal laid his older brother's body to rest in Riyadh, it must have been with mingled sadness and relief.

Death of a Princess

The shenanigans of ex-King Saud may have embarrassed his royal family mightily, but they were nothing compared to the hurricane of publicity that hit the Al Saud just over a decade later, in the spring of 1980. The storm—much of which the Al Saud brought on themselves—arose over a British documentary film entitled "Death of a Princess," about events that had happened almost three years earlier, in the summer of 1977.

The princess in question was named Mishail, and she was a granddaughter of Ibn Saud's oldest surviving son, Prince Muhammad ibn Abdel Aziz. Married as a young girl to a much older relative who ignored her, the bored Mishail had started an adulterous love affair with a young man named Khalid Mulhalhal, who was the nephew of an influential Saudi general. The couple tried to leave the country but were caught, and Prince Muhammad—in accordance with Islamic law—decreed the death penalty for both his adulterous granddaughter and her lover. One day in July 1977, they were duly led out into a parking lot next to a royal building in Jeddah, where she was shot and he, after being forced to watch her execution, was himself beheaded.

The events themselves caused minor international protests at the time. But Western governments were still reeling over the Arab oil embargo of 1973 and 1944, and no one was ready to risk an oil shut-off over something that was an "internal" Saudi matter, not to mention a done deal. And after all, such things happened on a regular basis in the kingdom without an international ruckus being raised. The real trouble came when an independent film producer named Antony Thomas came to Saudi Arabia. Pretending to be interested in the changing role of women in the kingdom, he actually went around interviewing people about the princess's story. He got a bunch of conflicting stories, and—unable to persuade people to appear on camera—used the interviews as a script for hired actors, who played the interviewees. It was, in fact, TV's first "docudrama."

The film was scheduled to be shown in April 1980 on Britain's BBC television network, and then a month later on the public television network PBS in the United States. Both broadcasts brought livid protests and strong diplomatic, economic, and political pressure from the Saudis. Having failed to get the British showing cancelled, King Khalid expelled the British ambassador from Saudi Arabia while the enraged Saudi press fulminated at the "Zionist" BBC. Attention then shifted to the other side of the Atlantic, where PBS officials endured a month of mounting pressure from corporations and politicians bought with Saudi money or scared by Saudi threats. The Mobil Oil Corporation, a major PBS sponsor with vast Saudi interests, took out a full-page ad on the *New York Times* op-ed page opposing the film and declaring that it jeopardized U.S.–Saudi relations.

Desert Dates

May 12, 1980: The American public television network PBS airs the controversial film "Death of a Princess," already aired a month earlier (April 11) in Britain by the BBC. PBS went ahead with the broadcast over strenuous objections from the Saudis, pressure from the U.S. State Department (nervous about oil), and a public campaign against showing the film by the Mobil Corporation, an oil company with Saudi interests and a major PBS sponsor. Bowing to corporate pressure, many local PBS affiliates choose not to carry the broadcast. The film didn't just expose Saudi Arabia's harsh legal and social system. It also examined political instability in the kingdom, making reference to an unsuccessful coup attempt by officers in the Saudi air force, a number of whom were afterward executed.

Interestingly, calls to PBS stations recorded an overwhelming majority against showing the film. Those opposed to it argued that it might make the Saudis cut off America's oil supply again, as they had during the oil embargo of the early 1970s. So when faced with a choice between free speech or cheap gas, cheap gas won hands down.

In the end, PBS appeased the Saudis by later running two other programs. The first, broadcast immediately afterward, was a pro-Saudi "discussion" of the film. The second, shown in early June, presented a flattering portrait of the role of women in Saudi culture.

Al Yamamah

Between 1986 and 1988, Saudi Arabia and Britain signed the top-secret al Yamamah arms deal, which an article in the London *Observer* of May 18, 2003, called "probably the biggest weapons sale in history." Details are sketchy, but the multi-billion dollar transactions were arranged to stretch decades into the future, and are still going on. So are the questions.

Remember in the last chapter when I told you about the British men wrongly detained, tortured, and imprisoned for the car bombing of a British engineer in Riyadh in 2000? At the time, I promised to offer one possible reason why the British government has turned a blind eye to their treatment. In an article of May 18, 2003, the *Observer* of London talks about the six men, going on to suggest that concern over the al Yamamah arms deal has led the British government "to downplay fundamentalist turmoil" in Saudi Arabia, and to try to silence relatives of the six men in Britain itself. The article also notes that "by the mid 1990s, Saudi Arabia ... was accounting for 75 percent of total UK arms sales." Without the deal, in other words, "there wouldn't be much of a British arms industry."

And while al Yamamah never caused that much scandal inside Saudi Arabia, it sure made a mess in Britain. In 1989, after the *Observer* accused Saudi royal family members and "British citizens with close contacts to the government" of both giving and taking bribes over the deal, the British government opened an investigation. The findings were never released. And when Jonathon Aitken, the British government minister in charge of the deal, sued the *Guardian*—the *Observer*'s sister paper—for libel, he himself was convicted of perjury, or lying in court.

The *Observer* and the *Guardian* continue to champion the six imprisoned men, and to demand that the results of the secret government investigation be released.

Two Oil Dynasties

Given that both families are in the oil business as well as in politics, it shouldn't come as a huge surprise that the Al Saud's favorite presidents have been the two George Bushes, father and son. The first President Bush, of course, is hailed as the victor of the Gulf War and the kingdom's protector against the aggression of Saddam Hussein. The second President Bush, however, while still popular, hasn't had quite so warm a reception with the Al Saud.

The Bandar Conduit

The strongest link between the two dynasties is Prince Bandar bin Sultan, who has been the Saudi ambassador to the United States since he was in his twenties. (I profiled him earlier in the chapter, along with the Ibn Saud's other grandchildren.) In the early 1980s, while still new at the job, Bandar starting lunching regularly with the first George Bush, who was then the vice-president in the Ronald Reagan administration. Bush knew that King Fahd relied on Bandar for frequent advice, and in turn the vice-president relied on the young prince to act as a special conduit to the Saudi king.

The relationship deepened into a close personal bond after Bush was elected president in 1988, and Bandar and his wife Haifa both came to look on the elder Bushes as family. When Bush lost his reelection bid to Bill Clinton in 1992, Bandar said that he felt like resigning his position. However, he stayed on, continuing to act as a conduit to the Saudi throne during the Clinton years. He also became a close partner and trusted go-between in the Clinton administration's attempts to broker a peace plan between the Israelis and the Palestinians. However, the conservative Bandar missed Bush's presence. While he admired Clinton's grasp of the issues, he was less at home with the White House's more liberal outlook during those years.

A Long Road to Crawford

When the second President Bush was elected, glad tidings rang out big time in the House of Saud. Much of his father's old team returned, including Colin Powell, with whom Bandar had played racquetball starting in the 1970s. The two have been close ever since. But from the start, the second George Bush had far less interest in the Middle East and its problems than his father had.

When the Saudis realized just how little interest the new president had in Middle Eastern affairs, they used diplomatic channels to express their displeasure. In August 2001, according to a story by Elsa Walsh in *The New Yorker* of March 24, 2003, the Crown Prince sent Bandar to Washington with a sharp message for the administration: "Starting today, you go your way and we will go our way." It was an abrupt policy shift, and as Secretary of State Colin Powell said, it put "the fear of God" into the Bush White House. Bush saved the situation by telling Abdullah—through Bandar—that he, Bush, basically supported the idea of an independent Palestinian state, and by agreeing to make that position public. That was around the first week of September, 2001. Before the announcement could be made, 9/11 happened, and the emerging news that 15 of the hijackers were Saudis rapidly began to erode the delicate rapprochement.

> **Desert Dates**
>
> **May 2001:** Crown Prince Abdullah publicly turns down an invitation to the White House. He tells reporters that he is frustrated by the administration's lack of interest in the Middle East, especially in the ongoing Israeli-Palestinian conflict. A deeply compassionate man, Abdullah has been disturbed by photos and news footage of Palestinian children and old people being killed by Israeli soldiers.

In February 2002 (as I related in the last chapter), Abdullah announced his own peace initiative, but to Saudi eyes Bush seemed to be more and more one-sided in Israel's favor. In early April, the *New Yorker* article says, Bandar declared in a public speech that he was "frustrated" in dealing with the White House. Later that month, the White House announced that Abdullah would visit the president at his ranch in Crawford, Texas. Bush was seeking support in his bid to topple Saddam Hussein. By this time, according to Walsh, "Abdullah's opinion of Bush was increasingly unfavorable."

In addition to the president and the crown prince, the Crawford meeting included Bandar, Vice-President Cheney, Secretary of State Powell, and Secretary of Defense Donald Rumsfeld. It did not go well. Abdullah wanted to focus on Israel and the Palestinians, while the Bush team wanted to talk smart bombs and regime change.

The president, one of his own aides warned Bandar, didn't know a thing about what was going on in the region anyway. Powell and Bandar argued—a rare occurrence—but after two hours of one-on-one between Abdullah and Bush, the meeting ended on a hopeful note. Over the coming months, despite press coverage of the Saudi hijackers, the money trail to the Saudi charities, and the survivors' lawsuit, Bandar continued to be a special conduit between his uncle, the crown prince, and the president of the United States.

Recycling—and We're Not Talking Trash

Of course, if Abdullah has his way, it's not just Sultan and the other arms supershoppers and profiteers in the royal family who will suffer. American politicians and corporate leaders—often one and the same these days—will also take a hit. For decades, generous streams of Saudi oil money have been channeled back into American weapons, construction, and communications companies, not to mention drilling and petroleum processing firms. Because so much Saudi money came out of American pockets in the first place, this is called "recycling," but don't let that fool you into thinking it's going back to those who originally paid it out.

Oh, no. Instead, much of it is ending up in the pockets of Washington insiders who've made a career out of going around and around through the "revolving door" between politics and high-paying corporate or lobbying positions. Two corporations stand out in having a long and profitable tradition of recycling: the Carlyle Group and Halliburton, both of which have also been in the news recently for landing lucrative contracts in the rebuilding of Iraq. The boards of these corporations read like a who's who of the Reagan, Clinton, and both Bush administrations. Just to take one example, Halliburton was headed by Dick Cheney between his jobs as secretary of defense under the first President Bush and vice-president under the second President Bush. In 2001 Halliburton was awarded a $140 million contract by the Saudis to develop a new oil field.

So here's the real "oil weapon": Saudi Arabia gives these and other big American companies billions of dollars worth of contracts each year, not to mention the frequent "gifts" and other considerations that routinely go to politicians and influential insiders. On top of that, the Saudis have somewhere around a trillion dollars invested in Wall Street.

And you wonder why President Bush and other U.S. leaders have tiptoed around Saudi participation in terror attacks?

The Least You Need to Know

- The big crunch for the Al Saud will likely come when the throne passes to the third generation, Ibn Saud's grandsons.

- The Al Saud loved the first President Bush, who remains especially close to Prince Bandar, the Saudi ambassador to the United States.

- Crown Prince Abdullah doesn't have a whole lot of time for the second President Bush.

- Washington politicians have been in bed with the Al Saud for years—and have been paid millions for it.

Chapter 20

The Immediate Future: Which Way Saudi Arabia?

In This Chapter

- ◆ Winds of change start to blow in the kingdom
- ◆ The question of the succession
- ◆ The future of the Saudi–U.S. relationship
- ◆ The chances for democracy in Saudi Arabia

So far in Part 4, I've focused partly on the events leading up to the tragedy of 9/11, but mostly on its short-term aftermath. We've examined the role that Saudi Arabia has played in bringing on the age of global terror, how global terrorism has influenced Saudi Arabia itself, and also how it has eroded the relationship between Saudi Arabia and the United States.

Now, in the final chapter of this book, it's time to turn from the past and the present towards the future, and to see if we can discern the shape of things to come. Probably not! History has a way of confounding predictions. But it can't hurt to try, and we may just pick up an insight or two along the way.

I'll start with one or two very recent developments that tie in with some things we've looked at earlier, like the signs of growing discontent with a system that constantly incites hatred of outsiders. Then I'll weigh some different possibilities for the succession, the survival of the Al Saud, and the relationship with America. In addition, I'll give you a nutshell summary of the possible impact that the recent U.S. invasion of Iraq might have, both on the region and on Saudi Arabia. Finally, as promised, I'll offer my parting assessment of the chances for democracy in the kingdom. Why bother? Because that, I'd argue, is the biggest question of all.

New Questions, New Answers

In Chapter 18, I said that the May 12, 2003 Riyadh bombings had finally pierced the veil of denial that made the Saudis pretend for so long that al Qaeda was someone else's problem. That goes for the public statements of the Al Saud—what they're willing to acknowledge in the glare of publicity. But other Saudis have been able to admit for some time that something is broken in their system. Indeed, Saudis have been asking new questions of themselves since 9/11, and they've been coming up with some new answers as well.

From 9/11 to 5/12: Questioning Hate

In that sense, the May 12, 2003 bombings furthered a process that started on September 11, 2001, and has been marked by milestones like the March 2002 girls' school fire in Mecca (see Chapter 14). A few months after the fire, and almost a year before the May bombings, the *New York Times* of July 12, 2002, carried an article by Neil MacFarquhar describing "the cautious debate" within Saudi society over its hostile, intolerant attitudes. A small number of journalists, academics, intellectuals, and religious scholars have begun to openly question the impact of hate, MacFarquhar wrote. "We have to confront a lot of things that we thought were normal," said Khaled M. Batarfi, managing editor at the liberal paper *Al Madina*. "Before Sept. 11, it was just an opinion, 'I think we should hate the others.' After Sept. 11, we found out ourselves that some of those thoughts brought actions that hurt us, that put all Muslims on trial."

Yet others—like the Wahhabis and a few Al Saud princes—dismissed any such connection between hate and violence. "Well, of course I hate you because you're a Christian, but that doesn't mean I want to kill you," the *Times* article quotes an Islamic law professor in Riyadh as saying, apparently seriously. One of Ibn Saud's younger sons, Prince Sattam, the 61-year-old governor of Riyadh, echoed the sentiment. As he explained it, though they may have been Saudis, the 15 hijackers "were in Afghanistan, they took their ideas not inside Saudi Arabia, but outside Saudi Arabia."

Arabian Almanac _____

Earlier, in Chapter 14, I traced a connection between fear and hatred. What do you think about the connection I'm tracing now, between hatred and violence? Certainly, Saudi Arabia is not alone in experiencing cultural violence that can be seen as driven by hatred and, ultimately, fear. The developed world has only recently awoken to the dangers of hate—it took World War II and the Holocaust to dramatize just how profoundly evil hate's consequences can be. Most developed countries now have laws against "hate crimes," for example.

In the United States, overwhelming public condemnation of hate and hate crimes came only with the Civil Rights Movement of the 1950s and 1960s, as white hate crimes against peacefully protesting black Americans were captured on film and in photos. Saudi Arabia may seem backward. But remember how recently legalized hate ruled in the United States, during the era of segregation, before Jim Crow was toppled by the Civil Rights Movement.

What the May 12 bombings did was make it harder for those who want (or need) to maintain this fiction. It's been suggested in the Western press that perhaps this is because the May attacks killed Saudis for the first time, rather than only Westerners (earlier bombings in the kingdom wounded a few Saudis but didn't actually kill any). Whether that's true or not, I couldn't say. I can say that the bombings of 5/12 changed the terms of what, a year earlier, Neil MacFarquhar had called a "cautious debate." The debate is no longer cautious, in other words. It's now urgent. And that can only be a good thing for Saudi Arabia—in the long term, that is. In the short term, it's bound to be a disturbing and unstable process. The religious conservatives won't give up their grip on society without a fight.

The Press

The Saudi press will be at the forefront of this struggle. In Chapter 16, I mentioned a well-known newspaper editor and columnist named Jamal Khashoggi, who was fired in May 2003 for writing columns critical of the Religious Police and other conservative religious institutions. His story illustrates how tense things have gotten, since before he was fired, guards had to be stationed at his office in order to protect him. This level of tension is a recent phenomenon, and it shows that the battle is heating up. The liberals are now on the offensive again.

Desert Dates

May 27, 2003: Jamal Khashoggi, editor of the leading liberal daily *Al Watan*, is summoned to the Ministry of Information and told that he's been fired. According to an article by Brian Whitaker in the *Guardian* (London) of May 29, 2003, Mr. Khashoggi's firing comes the day after a leading cleric, Abdullah al Jabrein, issued a fatwa, or religious decree, against the newspaper and commanded Saudis to boycott it. The *Guardian* article describes a recent cartoon in the paper as depicting "a suicide bomber with rolled up fatwas attached to his waist, as if they were sticks of dynamite." However, the paper's biggest offense, Whitaker suggests, is a recent article with a headline asking, "Who is more important—the nation, or Ibn Taymiyyah?" Ibn Taymiyyah, you'll remember from Chapter 16, was the fourteenth-century Islamic jurist whose teachings form the basis of Wahhabi theology.

Take a column in Khashoggi's former newspaper, the liberal daily *Al Watan*, by Abd Al-Qadr Tash. In reaction to the May bombings, Tash wrote, "The time has come for us to admit the bitter truth—the phenomenon of violence and terror has a domestic dimension … in our social culture, and primarily in its religious part." (The translation was provided by the Middle Eastern Media Research Institute, or MEMRI. At its invaluable website, memri.org, you'll find a treasure trove of translations from Arabic language newspapers.) Only months ago, saying something like this would have been almost inconceivable, but now it's representative of positions the emboldened liberals are taking.

Of course, the press has its share of conservatives, too. Right next to the preceding quote from *Al Watan* at the MEMRI website, for example, I found the following, written by Abed Khuzindar in the popular daily *Okaz*: "The truth is that these terrorists—and bin Laden who stands behind them—although Saudis—did not graduate from Saudi Arabia's schools and universities as terrorists; they came from abroad, primarily from Afghanistan, from schools established by American intelligence."

Arabian Almanac

Fanning the flames of controversy is the well-known Arab satellite TV network *Al Jazeera*, which broadcasts from Qatar. It's the most widely watched network in the Arab world, including in Saudi Arabia. It's almost always first with Osama bin Laden's videotapes, which it broadcasts, but it's best known for showing hours upon hours of Israeli soldiers brutalizing Palestinians.

The People

So where do the Saudi people stand in all this? Trying to answer that question is one of the most baffling things about the kingdom. A lot of the answer depends on who you're talking to. To hear the Al Saud describe it, "the people" are the most conservative element in society, and the royal family is the progressive element. In the last chapter, for example, I cited a *New Yorker* article about Prince Bandar by Elsa Walsh from March 24, 2003. In it, Walsh quotes Bandar as saying, "The reality is that we are the only government system where the leadership is more forward-looking than the public, and that is a big problem."

There's certainly some truth in that, but is it the whole picture? Unfortunately, it's next to impossible to say for sure what's up with the Saudi people. I'm not sure *they* know. All that does seem certain is that within Saudi society—and probably within most individual Saudis—there's a battle of values going on: between "traditional" and "modern," between "Arab" and "Western," between "Islamic" and "infidel."

The problem, as Saudis see it, is how to move forward without giving up their identity as Arabs and Muslims. It's a problem that's shared, more or less, by the rest of the Arab world, which is currently in a state of what you might call catastrophic cultural implosion. I have my own ideas about that implosion and the challenge it represents, but let me wait a moment before I tell you what they are.

Some Likely Scenarios

Before I get to that, I want to offer some possible scenarios for Saudi Arabia's future. We'll cover two areas of interest: the succession, and the relationship with the United States.

The Succession

In the last chapter, I suggested that the biggest crisis facing the Al Saud will come when the torch is passed to the next generation, that of Ibn Saud's grandchildren. While that's true, there are two other crises that will come sooner, and they may also prove to be risky for the Al Saud. The first crisis will be Fahd's death, and the second will be Abdullah's. They may come close together, since at 79 Abdullah is only a couple of years younger than Fahd.

- ◆ **Fahd's death.** This is the easiest one to call, since Abdullah already went through the struggle to succeed Fahd in the mid 1990s, when Fahd suffered his strokes. Facing off against the Sudairi Seven (see the previous chapter), Abdullah secured his power base in the family, probably with the support of the religious conservatives. He shouldn't have any trouble finalizing his orderly accession to the throne.

- **Abdullah's death.** This is where it gets tricky. Abdullah managed to balance various factions in the family against the Sudairi Seven, and the question is what will happen without his presence. If Abdullah's alliance falls apart, one of the Sudairi Seven will likely become king, probably Sultan (the senior prince next to Abdullah) or Naif (the next in line). However, if Abdullah's alliance holds up, it's possible that the family might have to settle on a compromise candidate, or a younger Sudairi such as Salman, the family mediator. Most likely, though, is the boring option: Sultan, who is after all the designated next-in-line, followed duly (and dully) by Naif.

It's not outside the realm of possibility, however, that the family might bite the bullet and make the jump to the third generation on Abdullah's death. I think that's unlikely (they're not known for biting bullets), but if they do, I'd put my money on one of Faisal's sons, probably Saud, the eldest. This would represent a victory for Abdullah's camp, since Saud al Faisal—the regal, Princeton-educated foreign minister—has been closely allied with Abdullah.

The Relationship with America

There's a wild card in the deck, though. Actually, the whole deck is made up of wild cards, but there's one in particular I'm thinking about: the relationship with the United States. If the relationship with America sours, it will hurt the Sudairi Seven, who have aligned themselves most strongly with Westernization. It will especially hurt Sultan, who has been the strongest supporter of the alliance with the United States and Britain. (And the biggest beneficiary of massive, bloated, totally unnecessary arms deals with them.) A clean break with the United States might—I say *might*—throw the succession forward to the third generation sooner rather than later. And put it, most likely, with the sons of Faisal, again probably Saud.

Why, you ask, do I bring this up? Remember in the previous chapter, when I said that Abdullah sent Bandar to the White House in 2002 with a message that basically said, "You go your way, we'll go ours"? Well, that's what I predict for Saudi Arabia's future: a definitive split with the United States. There are four reasons why I think the Saudis will, probably gradually, make a break with America over the next few years.

- It was in the cards even before 9/11. Abdullah is a strong nationalist, but not in the familiar "Arab nationalist" sense. He's a Saudi Arabian nationalist, who has long called for nonalignment, a Cold-War term that means avoiding strategic alliances with either of the superpowers. He has also pushed to reduce arms expenditures, and he knows that Saudis are tired of seeing billions of dollars spent on arms and equipment that will probably end up lying around rusting to death. This is especially true since the money has dried up, a fact that Sultan and the other weapons super-shoppers seem to be unaware of.

◆ If Abdullah wishes to reform the hate system—which he does—he's going to need to do everything he can to keep the support of the religious conservatives in other areas. The best way to do this is to publicly turn his back on the United States.

◆ Don't forget about 9/11 and all the damage it's done to the relationship, on both sides. The Saudis need to get their act together, but it's hard to do that with a big bully breathing down your neck. A break in the Saudi–U.S. relationship could be the best thing for both sides.

◆ Finally, if 9/11 started the process, the 2003 U.S. invasion of Iraq has pushed it further along. Public resentment of the United States is now the highest in Saudi Arabia that it's ever been. At the same time, the threat from Saddam Hussein is gone (a big reason for keeping the relationship strong), and Saudi relations with Iran are improving. The Saudis need America less, and if America has Kuwait and Qatar (and who knows, maybe a friendly Iraq), it needs the Saudis less, too. The relationship was always founded on mutual need, not mutual affection. Let's face it, folks, mutual affection was never strong, even in the relationship's heyday.

CAUTION

Mirage Ahead

If the long alliance between the United States and Saudi Arabia comes to an end, you'll probably hear a lot of doom-saying about the "oil weapon." Forget about it—the oil weapon's a dud. Refusing to sell oil would hurt the Saudis more than it would hurt anyone else. In the long term, oil isn't a weapon, as the Saudis learned after the oil embargo of 1973-4. It's more like a boomerang: It comes back and bites the person wielding it. Remember, the embargo shocked Americans, but it also encouraged them to conserve fuel (in other words, to invite the Japanese to invent the economy car) and find alternate energy sources. And that's a real doomsday scenario for the Saudis. The "oil weapon" may occasionally be an effective threat, but only for those faint-hearted enough to cower. U.S. policy makers need to get over their fear of it.

Bottom line: The Al Saud may have to end their long alliance with the United States in order to survive in power. I don't foresee any kind of overthrow—the family is too broadly and deeply entrenched for that—but they do have to respond to public opinion.

The American Invasion of Iraq

So what about the invasion of Iraq? I've already said what I think it means for the U.S.–Saudi relationship. But what does it mean for the Saudis outside of that?

First, let's talk about oil. One reason the Saudis lobbied so hard against the invasion was the convenient oil embargo that had been imposed on Iraq by the U.N. ever since the Gulf War. A new Iraq, whatever form it takes, will be putting its vast oil reserves back online soon, and that will hurt the already-strapped Saudis.

Additionally, public resentment of America doesn't just threaten the U.S.–Saudi relationship, it also undermines the stability of the Al Saud and the country in general. The invasion ratcheted up the sense of public tension in Saudi Arabia, which the bombings of May 12 have brought to a fever pitch. Of course, a lot depends on how long the Americans stay in Iraq, and what kind of Iraq they leave behind when they go. As I've already suggested, a democratic Iraq would be bad news for the Al Saud— but it could only be good news for Saudi Arabia in the long term.

What about the rest of the region? What is the regional impact of the American occupation of Iraq likely to be? Let's look briefly at how the occupation will affect some of Saudi Arabia's neighbors.

- **Jordan.** Jordan is basically in the same boat as Saudi Arabia. It's a monarchy, and although its King Abdullah is progressive and pro-Western, he has a strongly radicalized, heavily Palestinian population to deal with. There's lots of anti-American feeling on the "Arab street" in Jordan, and a prolonged U.S. occupation of Iraq will no doubt exacerbate it. At the same time, a democratic Iraq has the same disadvantages for monarchical Jordan as it does for monarchical Saudi Arabia. Or rather, for their ruling families.

- **Egypt.** Some of the same considerations apply to Egypt, which, while not a monarchy, does have an oppressive, authoritarian regime. As America got ready to invade Iraq in early 2003, anti-American demonstrations in Cairo attracted more than 100,000 Egyptians. Despite the regime's ties to America, Egypt's nearly 70 million people were heavily radicalized and anti-American already, and the invasion and occupation notched it up (it's no coincidence that Ayman al Zawahiri, Osama bin Laden's top lieutenant, is Egyptian). In response, the government has had to take steps to further suppress the militants. A democratic regime in Iraq is the last thing the Egyptian ruler, Hosni Mubarak, needs or wants.

- **Syria.** Like Jordan and Egypt, Syria also has an authoritarian government with strong economic ties to the old Iraq, and it suffered heavy economic damage from the U.S. invasion. It's thought that Syria illegally imported several hundred thousand barrels of inexpensive Iraqi oil a day during the last years of the Saddam Hussein regime. Losing that will definitely hurt. And, of course, the same disadvantages to having a prosperous, democratic neighbor apply to Syria's oppressive Assad regime as to the other Arab autocrats.

- **Kuwait.** After Kuwait's liberation by the United States in the first Gulf War, America's best friend right now in the Middle East—Israel aside—is Kuwait, which gladly offered its territory as the main staging area for the invasion of Iraq. Kuwait is the country in the region most likely to gain significant short-term benefits from the occupation of Iraq, as friendly economic and cultural ties resume between the two neighbors. Yet Kuwait does have a strong Islamist movement simmering under its pro-Western regime, and a number of American soldiers have been gunned down there since the occupation of Iraq began. As with Egypt, Kuwait is also strongly represented in al Qaeda. For example, Khalid Sheikh Mohhammed, the mastermind of 9/11 who was captured in March 2003, is a Kuwaiti.

- **Qatar.** Progressive, pro-American, and very wealthy, Qatar has gained the most after Kuwait from the occupation of Iraq. Most importantly, it now looks as though Qatar will replace Saudi Arabia as an important "forward base" for American troops and aircraft in the Gulf region. (That role will also be played by Djibouti, on the horn of Africa.) But Qatar's friendlier version of Wahhabism does harbor some radical clerics, and there have been anti-American sermons in some mosques. There were also unconfirmed reports of a failed coup attempt in October 2002, by army officers unhappy with the emir's pro-American stance.

- **Bahrain.** Another U.S. supporter, Bahrain also stands to benefit strategically and economically from the American presence in Iraq. Bahrain, which hosts the U.S. Navy's Fifth Fleet, has recently undertaken democratic reforms, but five Baharainis were arrested in February 2003 for planning terrorist strikes against U.S. targets.

- **Yemen.** Poor old Yemen, Saddam's ally from the first Persian Gulf war, has been left out in the cold. Economic stagnation, a 27-year-rule by the autocratic President Ali Saleh, and militant unrest offer a bleak picture. There was little to celebrate in Yemen before the invasion, but even less after it. There were strong anti-American demonstrations before the U.S. invasion of Iraq.

One thing to keep in mind that I didn't mention (I would have had to repeat it for each country): First and foremost, all of these Arab regimes want a peaceful, dignified resolution to the Israeli-Palestinian conflict. That ugly, despair-ridden situation keeps the pot boiling, especially in the populous, poor countries like Egypt and Jordan.

The Last, Last Word: Democracy

Why do I keep harping on democracy, you might ask? Well, for one thing, as I explained in Chapter 14, I want to refute King Fahd's claims that Islam and democracy are incompatible. Islam is a way of life, like any other religion; democracy is a political system.

But more than that, I want the Saudis to succeed in shaping for themselves a society that isn't always being twisted and deformed by the constant pressures of fear and hate. We in the West will certainly benefit if they do. For one thing, their hate is terrorizing us. But in the end, it can't really hurt us: All the 9/11s in the world won't overthrow our secular, democratic society. Meanwhile, though, it's poisoning them, and that's a tragedy on top of the body count at Ground Zero. For their own sake if for no one else's, the Saudis need to embrace tolerance. I believe the only way they will be able to do that, at least in this modern world, is by undertaking democratic reforms. And the good news is, there seems to be a growing number of Saudis who think so, too.

Enforcing Tolerance

But, you say, look how conservative the rest of the people are. Given a chance, won't the Saudis just vote themselves into a totalitarian Wahhabi state? What if that's what the majority wants? You'd barely have time for one election and bam, no more democracy. After all, that came close to happening in Algeria in the early 1990s. When radical Islamists won the election, the government ended up canceling the results rather than have the democratically elected Islamists take over and turn the state into an Islamic theocracy. What happens when the people don't want democracy? You can't exactly shove it down their throats, after all. That's not democratic!

The key to resolving this apparent dilemma is to understand that democracy is not—repeat NOT—simply about elections. Nor is it simply about majority rule. Democracy, at least as we know it in the modern world, is just as much about protecting the rights of minorities as it is about respecting the will of the majority. It's a constitutional system of checks and balances, not a collection of voting booths. Of course, voting is central to making the system work, but there's got to be a workable constitution in place to give the votes meaning.

Above all, democracy is about tolerance, about enforcing tolerance if need be, so that minorities—racial, ethnic, religious, whatever—are protected by the system. A democracy *can't* vote itself away democratically, since any vote that votes democracy away is not a democratic vote at all, but an example of the majority tyrannizing the minorities. Majority rule can be as undemocratic as anything else, and that's why the secret of democracy lies in respecting minorities, not obeying majorities.

Mirage Ahead _____

I'm not claiming that democracy is perfect. Quite the opposite, in fact, and that's precisely its glory. Totalitarian states are the ones that always need to pretend they're perfect. Like the Al Saud, their claim to power lies in preserving an unruffled mask of public perfection. Democracy, by contrast, is all over the place. It's messy, it's inefficient, and it's often undignified. As the old saying goes, democracy is the worst system of government the world has ever known, except for all the others. Don't expect perfection!

The public expectation of perfection is one that Arab rulers tend to feel burdened by, and for that reason it's been a hidden force against democracy in the Arab world.

If democracy is about enforcing tolerance, that makes it sound very much like what Saudi Arabia could use: a system that ensures protection against hate. If hate is the problem, democracy is the solution. There are other undemocratic societies where hate hasn't rotted the social fabric the way it has in Saudi Arabia—maybe they can do without democracy for a while. But make no mistake, the Saudis need democracy if they're going to make it through the twenty-first century. That doesn't mean they have to do it exactly like the West. But it does mean they have to work out some form of government in which the people enjoy representation in government and the rights of minorities are secured by law.

Reinventing Tradition

A common objection you often hear from Arab leaders who reject democracy is that it's not part of the Arab cultural tradition. My answer to that one is simple: So what? Who cares? If it works, use it! Make it part of the tradition!

During the Golden Age of Islamic Learning, Arab and Muslim scholars absorbed the wisdom of ancient Greek, Indian, and other cultures, weaving them into a wonderful new cultural tapestry of their own. I talked about that in Chapter 3, remember? Those scholars didn't worry about whether math and science were part of their "tradition"! They were interested in learning, and they were driven to improve their culture, not fossilize it.

At least, until the mullahs got hold of them around about the twelfth century, when the philosophers and scientists were ordered to get rid of their books and instruments. Such things, they were told, were "foreign" and "non-Islamic." Those very same ideas, transmitted to the West partly by the Arab scholars, eventually gave rise to the rationalism of the Enlightenment in seventeenth-century Europe—and thus to secular democracy. Yet liberal Arab intellectuals today are being told the same thing by the mullahs: such ideas are "foreign" and "non-Islamic."

But Arab and Islamic culture does indeed have a tradition of openness, a great one. It just needs to rediscover it.

A Matter of Time

Besides, who are the Saudis fooling? It's only a matter of time. The Internet, satellite TV, instant global communication—all of these things have already exposed the Saudis to ideas that, like the genie of Arabian lore, can't simply be stuffed back into the bottle. All you need to do to know that is to read a few of the recent articles by liberal Saudi journalists. So what is my parting assessment of democracy's chances in Saudi Arabia? 100 percent. The only question is when.

The Least You Need to Know

- The May 2003 bombings in Riyadh gave the Saudi liberals a chance to go back on the offensive in their public debate with the religious conservatives.

- From 9/11 to the 2003 U.S. invasion of Iraq, recent events have severely eroded the U.S.–Saudi alliance.

- It's likely that the Saudis will turn their back on the United States over the next few years.

- That's also likely to be a good thing for both, at least for the time being.

A

FAQs About Saudi Arabia

Q: *What's the difference between Arabs and Muslims?*

A: Arabs are an ethnic or linguistic group—basically, people who speak Arabic are considered to be Arabs. They live mostly in a broad swath from the Middle East to North Africa. Muslims are a religious group—those who follow Islam. Nearly all Arabs are Muslims, but, at around 280 million, Arabs make up only about 20 percent of the world's 1 billion plus Muslims. So while most Arabs are Muslims, most Muslims aren't Arabs. Yet because Islam was born in Arab culture—its prophet, Muhammad, was an Arab, and its sacred texts are written in Arabic—Arabs feel a certain pride of place as the most "authentic" Muslims. And Saudi Arabia, where Muhammad and Islam were both born in the seventh century, is at the center of that feeling.

Q: *I've noticed that Arab names are spelled all sorts of different ways in English. There's Muhammad and Mohammed, for example, or Abdullah and Abdallah. What's with that?*

A: Arabic is written without the vowel sounds inserted between the consonants. So when you read something in Arabic, you have to supply the vowel sounds yourself. Depending on what part of the Arab world you come from, the vowels may come out sounding different. There's a lot of variation in Arab pronunciation from one place to the next (sometimes Arabs have a lot of trouble understanding one another). You say Abdullah, and I say Abdallah … In this book, I've tried to be consistent with spelling, choosing the forms that look the most familiar in English: Koran, for example, rather than the more academic Quran. The biggest variation you'll see in this book is between ibn and bin, which both mean "son of." It's the same word, and in Arabic it's spelled "bn." Thngs gt prnncd dffrnt wys whn yv gt t sppl th vwls yrslf.

Q: I'm confused about the "al" thing. What does "al" mean?

A: *Al* has two different meanings. The first is simply "the," as in al Qaeda, literally "the Base." The second meaning is "family of" or "House of," as in Al Saud, the "House of Saud." You'll see the initial "a" of both capitalized elsewhere, and you'll also see both in lowercase. To distinguish between them in this book, I've put the "a" in al Qaeda ("the") in lowercase, and capitalized the "a" of Al Saud ("family of").

Q: Are Saudi women oppressed? If so, why do they seem to go along with it?

A: Next question, please.

Q: Oh, come on, don't be such a wimp.

A: Tough crowd. Okay, since you push me so rudely, I'm not even going to try to be diplomatic. Saudi women *are* oppressed, certainly by Western standards—but also by their own, since many of them have publicly and privately confirmed that they feel oppressed. So there's no doubt that many Saudi women resent the stringent restrictions placed on their lives. Equally, however, there's no doubt that many are content and don't know any different way of doing things. That's a powerful thing. So much for diplomacy and tact.

Q: Are women more oppressed in Saudi Arabia than elsewhere in the Arab world?

A: I see you're determined to make me reveal what I really think. Okay, the answer is yes. It's worse in Saudi Arabia. In neighboring Iraq, for example, women don't have to wear head scarves or veils and can work and mix freely with men in public. Women tend to have greater freedom in Arab countries, like Iraq, that flirted with socialism in the 1960s. Egypt is another example, though many women there voluntarily wear the veil as a sign of religious devotion.

Q: What about the men? Are those headdresses religious?

A: No, they're an Arab thing, not an Islamic thing, part of the Arab national costume, although Islam does say that the top of the head should be covered while praying. But the men's clothing is an adaptation to the needs of desert life. For example, the headdress—called the *ghutra*, by the way, a square of cotton cloth secured with a doubled cord around the head—can be brought up over the mouth to keep out blowing sand. The men wear a light, loose-fitting, ankle-length white cotton shirt called the *thobe* that's also designed for comfort in the heat. It's only the women who have to wear the heavy, black robe called the *abaya*, along with the headscarf and veil (*hijab*), when they go out. This is so that a glimpse of skin or hair, or even the outlines of their bodies, won't drive men to the outer limits of passion right there on the street. Come to think of it, maybe that's why the women are content to stay home—black robes and desert sun can't be a great combo.

Q: *What about Arab food? What do Saudis like to eat?*

A: Food in Saudi Arabia is similar to that elsewhere in the Arab world, and in the Mediterranean, for that matter. The main thing to know is that Islamic law forbids eating pork or drinking alcohol. Arabs eat unleavened bread—made without yeast—called *khobz* with most meals. Coffee and tea are popular, and drunk very sweet, the tea often being served with mint. Falafel (ground chick peas fried in little balls), grilled chicken or lamb, and a paste of fava beans flavored with garlic and lemon (*fuul*) are other staples.

If you live in a metropolitan area, such as New York City, you may sample Middle Eastern food at many restaurants, including especially Lebanese, Syrian, Yemenite, Egyptian, and other national cuisines. All very similar, and all delicious, too!

Q: *How do Saudis like to relax?*

A: In a country without bars, clubs, movie theaters, music, or any of the other venues where men and women commonly hang out, your options for relaxation and recreation can be a little limited. For women, you stay home, or go to a friend's house to hang with the sisters, or nowadays maybe the mall. But you have to have a male relative drive you, although these days more Saudi women are getting away with hired male drivers. Maybe the inconvenience started to get to the men. Anyway, hired male drivers are more common than they used to be, although it's still not quite considered respectable. The most proper thing is to have your husband (if you're married) or father or brother (if you're single) take you out any time you leave the house. For men, you basically go to the corner coffeehouse, where you will probably drink tea, and smoke the "hubbly-bubbly," a waterpipe filled with tobacco spiced with apple. There you hang out and chat with other men.

Q: *Sounds like a blast.*

A: What can I say? It's not about fun, it's about preserving your honor, and the honor of "your" women.

Q: *Yikes.*

A: Indeed.

Q: *Is it possible to travel to Saudi Arabia as a tourist? What if I am invited to visit a Saudi friend? Or an American who is working there?*

A: Unlike most other countries, the government of Saudi Arabia doesn't issue tourist visas. But if you're invited to visit a Saudi friend, or an American working in the kingdom, it's certainly possible to do so with a minimum of red tape. You'll probably have to get your friend to act as a sponsor for you, though, by vouching for your good behavior while in the kingdom.

Q: *Does Saudi Arabia have a national culture? Or is it all a part of general Arab world culture?*

A: Since Saudi Arabia was founded only about 70 years ago, there hasn't been time for a strong national identity to develop there. Some national feeling has arisen, but traditional regional, tribal, or family loyalties generally remain stronger. By the same token, Saudi Arabia doesn't yet have a strongly defined national culture, as distinct from the larger Arab culture that it's part of. That's one reason that I spend so much time in this book talking about the larger Arab world.

An Arabian Timeline from Before the Birth of Islam to the Present

c. 1000 B.C.E.	Arabs domesticate the camel, allowing the rise of camel nomadism and trade routes using camel caravans.
224 C.E.	The Sassanid dynasty begins in Persia. Zoroastrianism is revived as the state religion.
330 C.E.	The Roman emperor Constantine converts to Christianity. The pagan Roman empire begins the transformation into the Christian Byzantine empire.
c. 550	Mecca has become an important trade and religious center for the pagan Arab tribes.
c. 570	Muhammad is born in Mecca.
c. 610	Muhammad begins experiencing the visions that would be recorded in the Koran. He shares his visions with a few followers.
614–631	Holy war between Byzantium and Persia results in the exhaustion of both empires.
622	Muhammad and his followers flee from Mecca, taking refuge in Medina (the *hijra*). Islam's foundation is dated from this event.
630	Muhammad and a Muslim army take Mecca without bloodshed.

632	Muhammad dies, having brought virtually all of Arabia under his control. After his death, his successors begin the conquest of Byzantine and Persian lands in the Middle East.
636	Arabs shatter the Byzantine army at the battle of Yarmuk, north of Jerusalem, opening Palestine to Arab occupation. Further to the east, victory over the Persians at Qadisiyyah opens Persia to Arab expansion. A century of Arab conquest ensues, as Muslim Arab armies found an empire stretching from India to Spain.
661	The murder of the last "Rightly Guided" caliph, Ali, leads to a split between Shiites, loyal to Ali, and Sunnis, who accept his successor Muawiya. Muawiya founds the Umayyad dynasty, moving the capital of the Arab empire from Medina to Damascus, Syria.
732	The Arabs are defeated by Charles Martel at the battle of Poitiers, in central France.
750	The Abbasids overthrow the Umayyads, moving the capital further east, to the newly founded city of Baghdad in Mesopotamia. Baghdad becomes the center of the Arab world during the Golden Age of Islamic Civilization, which lasts until the twelfth century.
1055	The Seljuk Turkish ruler Toghril takes over in Baghdad, demoting the Abbasid caliph to figurehead and ruling in his name.
1071	The Seljuk Turks defeat the Byzantines at Manzikert, allowing Turks to settle Asia Minor (now Turkey).
1095–1099	The First Crusade launched by Pope Urban II. Christian Crusaders conquer Jerusalem (1099), and establish four Crusader kingdoms in the Middle East.
1146–1148	The Second Crusade fizzles.
1188–1192	The Third Crusade saves the Crusader kingdoms from recapture by the Muslims.
1202–1204	The Fourth Crusade captures Constantinople from the Byzantines, holding it until 1261.
1217–1221	The Fifth Crusade fails to capture Egypt.
1258	The Mongols sack Baghdad, ending the weakened Abbasid dynasty.
1288	Ottoman dynasty founded in Asia Minor.
1307–1453	The Ottoman empire expands, conquering Byzantine lands in Asia Minor and Europe, and extinguishing the Byzantine empire by capturing Constantinople in 1453. The city is renamed Istanbul, becoming the new capital of the Ottoman empire.
1453–1666	The height of the Ottoman empire.
1671	Ottoman defeat by combined European forces at Lepanto (near the Gulf of Corinth) marks the beginning of the Ottoman decline.

1744	Muhammad ibn Saud, founder of the Al Saud, marries the daughter of Muhammad ibn Abdel Wahhab, the founder of Wahhabism. This marks the beginning of the partnership between the Wahhabis and the Al Saud. Wahhabism inspires the fierce desert warriors under the command of the Al Saud.
1765	Death of Muhammad ibn Saud, who by now has conquered most of the Najd in central Arabia.
1803–1813	The Al Saud's Wahhabi warriors conquer the Hijaz from the Ottomans.
1811–1814	Muhammad Ali recaptures the Hijaz for the Ottomans, defeating the Wahhabis and destroying the first Saudi state.
1824	Turki Al Saud founds the second Saudi state, reconquering the Najd.
1843–1865	Faisal ibn Turki expands Saudi domains, bringing the second Saudi state to the height of its power.
1891	After Faisal's death brings decline to Al Saud power, his son Abdel Rahman is forced into exile in Kuwait.
1901	Oil is discovered in Iran by the British.
1902	Abdel Rahman's son Abdel Aziz (Ibn Saud) captures Riyadh.
1902–1921	Ibn Saud conquers the Najd, using a special corps of fanatical Wahhabi soldiers called the Ikhwan.
1913–1932	Ibn Saud conquers other lands in Arabia.
1914–1918	World War I. The Ottoman empire, allied with Germany, goes down in defeat.
1916–1921	Arab revolt against Ottomans is led by Lawrence of Arabia and the Hashemite Sharif Husayn of Mecca.
1924	Ibn Saud captures the Hijaz from Sharif Husayn, ending Hashemite rule in the Hijaz.
1928	Ibn Saud dissolves the rebellious Ikhwan.
1932	Foundation of the Kingdom of Saudi Arabia.
1938	Oil is discovered in Saudi Arabia by the American oil company Socal, which splits its Saudi operation off as Casoc.
1939–1945	World War II.
1943	America aids Saudi Arabia under the Lend-Lease Program.
1944	Casoc becomes Aramco.
1945	Ibn Saud meets with President Franklin Delano Roosevelt, sealing the new alliance between the United States and Saudi Arabia.
1945–1990	Cold War between the United States and the Soviet Union.
1948–1949	Israel's War for Independence against the Arabs. Palestinian refugees become the most urgent political issue in the Arab world.
1952	Saudi oil revenues hit $212 million after Ibn Saud negotiates a 50–50 split with Aramco.

1953	Death of Ibn Saud, accession of King Saud.
1956	Suez Crisis, Suez-Sinai War between Israel and Egypt.
1960	Organization of Petroleum Exporting Countries (OPEC) founded.
1964	King Saud deposed; accession of King Faisal. Modernization drive begins.
1967	Israel defeats combined Arab forces in the Six-Day War.
1973–1980	Saudi Arabia completes the purchase of Aramco, which becomes Saudi Aramco.
1973	Combined Arab forces attack Israel in the October (Yom Kippur) War.
1973–1974	Arab oil embargo.
1975	King Faisal is assassinated by a deranged nephew; accession of King Khalid.
1979	The Iranian Revolution installs an Islamic fundamentalist regime under the Ayatollah Khomeini. In November, Islamic militants seize the Great Mosque in Mecca. In December, the Soviet Union invades Afghanistan, prompting a call for jihad that results in the formation of al Qaeda.
1980–1988	Iran-Iraq War leaves over one million dead.
1982	King Khalid dies; accession of King Fahd.
1989	The Soviet Union withdraws from Afghanistan; al Qaeda begins the transformation from guerrilla force to terror network.
1990	Iraq under Saddam Hussein occupies Kuwait and threatens Saudi Arabia. U.S.–led coalition responds with Operation Desert Shield.
1991	Operation Desert Storm liberates Kuwait (Persian Gulf War).
1992	Osama bin Laden and al Qaeda call for overthrow of Al Saud and jihad against America. King Fahd promulgates the Basic Law.
1993	Al Qaeda truck bomb explodes in World Trade Center; al Qaeda-trained Somali fighters kill 18 American marines in Somalia.
1995	King Fahd suffers the first of several debilitating strokes. Al Qaeda truck bomb in Riyadh.
1996	Osama bin Laden goes from the Sudan to Afghanistan. Al Qaeda truck bomb at Khobar Towers in Dhahran, Saudi Arabia.
1998	Two al Qaeda truck bombs explode minutes apart at U.S. embassies in Kenya and Tanzania. Crown Prince Abdullah consolidates his grip on power after Fahd's incapacitation.
2000	Al Qaeda suicide team strikes USS *Cole* at harbor in Yemen.
2001	On September 11, al Qaeda hijackers fly four American airliners into U.S. targets, killing over 3,000. Of the 19 hijackers, 15 are Saudis.
2003	In a span of a single week in May, al Qaeda strikes multiple targets in Riyadh and elsewhere in the Arab world.

C

Magazines, Websites, and Books

Magazines

Saudi Arabia and the Islamic world are frequently in the news these days. You'll find stories about both appearing regularly in the major newsmagazines, as well as in other publications.

Alter, Jonathan. "The End of the Double Game." *Newsweek*. January 13, 2003.

Baer, Robert. "The Fall of the House of Saud." *Atlantic Monthly*, May 2003.

Borger, Gloria, and others. "The Road to Riyadh." *U.S. News & World Report*. December 9, 2002.

Lewis, Bernard. "The Revolt of Islam." *The New Yorker*. November 19, 2001.

Mayer, Jane. "The House of Bin Laden." *The New Yorker*, November 12, 2001.

Omestad, Thomas. "The Kingdom and the Power." *U.S. News & World Report*. November 5, 2001.

Surowiecki, James. "The Oil Weapon." *The New Yorker*. February 10, 2003.

Walsh, Elsa. "The Prince." *The New Yorker*. March 24, 2003.

Websites

Websites can be useful and fun, but you've got to take a lot of the information you find on them with a grain of salt. They are definitely not as reliable as print sources, so use them with caution. Make sure you know who's behind the "facts" you're coming across, and be aware that they might have an axe to grind.

www.cia.gov/cia/publications/factbook/geos/sa.html
This is the online address for the *CIA World Factbook 2002* chapter on Saudi Arabia. It includes all the latest facts and figures. Dry reading, but useful for research. Good on oil industry info.

cyber.law.harvard.edu/filtering/saudiarabia
This is where you can find the article on Internet filtering by Saudi authorities that I cited in Chapter 16. The article is by Jonathan Zittrain and Benjamin Edelman of the Berkman Center for Internet & Society at Harvard Law School.

www.hrw.org
This is the website for Human Rights Watch, which monitors human rights abuses around the world.

www.memri.org
This is the website of the invaluable translation service MEMRI (Middle East Media Research Institute). Here you can find a full menu of translated excerpts from news sources throughout the Arab world and the Middle East. This one is a must—if there's one website you check out, this should be it.

www.saudhouse.com
This is posted by a group of Saudi dissidents, and it has a lot of provocative things to say about human rights, corruption, and politics in the kingdom. It also has hot links to human rights groups like Amnesty International and Human Rights Watch, where you can find information on Saudi prisoners of conscience. The site's authors seem dedicated and scrupulous, but use this site with some care.

www.saudiembassy.net
At the other end of the spectrum, this website offers the "party line" and gives a happy picture of life in the kingdom. You won't find a lot about human rights here, but it's helpful to see what the Saudi government wants Americans to think. Use with caution.

www.saudinf.com
Another Saudi government site, this one offers "more than 2,000 pages of information on every aspect" of Saudi Arabia. Saudi government "information" is notoriously unreliable, however. Use with caution.

www.saudi-pages.com

This site is put out by NetComm, and offers a wide range of information on everything from cultural events in the kingdom to weather and travel tips. It also includes Saudi and international news sources. If you plan to travel to Saudi Arabia, make this one of your stops before you leave. It should be fairly reliable.

www.un.org/Publications

This is a website of the United Nations, where you can find U.N. publications. It's worth logging on to check out the U.N.'s Arab Human Development Report 2002, which gives a comprehensive status report on economic and social issues affecting the Arab world.

Books

Armstrong, Karen. *Islam*. New York: Modern Library, 2000.

Dawood, N. J. (trans.) *The Koran*. London: Penguin, 1997.

Field, Michael. *Inside the Arab World*. Cambridge, MA: Harvard University Press, 1995.

Friedman, Thomas. *Longitudes and Attitudes: Exploring the World After September 11*. New York: Farrar, Strauss, and Giroux, 2002.

Gunaratna, Rohan. *Inside Al Qaeda*. New York: Columbia University Press, 2002.

Halliday, Fred. *Islam and the Myth of Confrontation: Religion and Politics in the Middle East*. New York: I. B. Tauris, 1996.

Hitti, Philip K. *The Arabs: A Short History*. Princeton: Princeton University Press, 1943.

Hourani, Albert. *A History of the Arab Peoples*. Cambridge, MA: Harvard University Press, 1991.

Kepel, Gilles. *Jihad: On the Trail of Political Islam*. Cambridge, MA: Harvard University Press, 2002.

Lacey, Robert. *The Kingdom*. New York: Harcourt Brace Jovanovitch, 1981.

Lewis, Bernard. *Islam and the West*. Oxford: Oxford University Press, 1993.

———. *What Went Wrong? The Clash Between Islam and Modernity in the Middle East*. New York: Perennial, 2002.

Long, David E. *The Kingdom of Saudi Arabia*. Gainesville: University Press of Florida, 1997.

Mackey, Sandra. *The Saudis: Inside the Desert Kingdom.* (Updated edition.) New York: Norton, 2002.

Mernissi, Fatima. *Islam and Democracy: Fear of the Modern World.* Reading, MA: Addison-Wesley, 1992.

Metz, Helen Chapin. *Saudi Arabia: A Country Study.* Washington: Federal Research Division, Library of Congress, 1993.

Nydell, Margaret K. (Omar). *Understanding Arabs: A Guide for Westerners.* (Revised Edition.) Yarmouth, ME: Intercultural Press, 1996.

Polk, William R. *The Arab World Today.* Cambridge MA: Harvard University Press, 1991.

Schwartz, Stephen. *The Two Faces of Islam: The House of Sa'ud from Tradition to Terror.* New York: Doubleday, 2002.

Thesiger, Wilfrid. *Arabian Sands.* New York: Dutton, 1959.

Yergin, Daniel. *The Prize: The Epic Quest for Oil, Money & Power.* New York: Simon & Schuster, 1991.

Wolfe, Michael. *One Thousand Roads to Mecca: Ten Centuries of Travelers Writing about the Muslim Pilgrimage.* New York: Grove, 1997.

Glossary

Abbasids   The Arab dynasty that overthrew the Umayyads in 750 C.E., founded the city of Baghdad, and ruled until the middle of the thirteenth century, when they were succeeded by the Seljuk Turks.

abaya   A robe-like garment, usually black, worn by traditional Saudi and other Muslim women. Its loose folds are supposed to conceal women's bodies and prevent male lust.

Achaemenids   This powerful dynasty ruled the first ancient Persian empire, which lasted from about the sixth century B.C.E. to the fourth century B.C.E.

adilla   These "agents" assist Muslim pilgrims who travel to Medina after completing the pilgrimage rites in Mecca.

Afghans   A national grouping made up of various ethnic groups whose members live in Afghanistan.

Afghan Arabs   The Saudi nickname for Arabs who went to join the jihad in Afghanistan in the 1980s and 1990s.

Afghan Service Bureau   A guerrilla group run by Osama bin Laden and his mentor Abdullah Azzam to assist the jihad in Afghanistan. Often known by its Arabic initials, MAK, it's the organization that eventually became al Qaeda.

Allah   Arabic for "God."

Arab-Israeli Wars   A series of wars fought between the Israelis and Arabs between 1948 and 1973.

Arab nationalism   A secular political movement that flourished in the 1950s and 1960s, Arab nationalism sought to celebrate Arab identity and to unify Arabs from different countries in a greater Arab nation. Also known as "pan-Arabism," its greatest proponent was the Egyptian president Gamal Abdel Nasser.

Arabia Felix   Ancient name for southern Arabia (today's Yemen).

Arabs   Originally an ethnic group thought to have come from the Arabian peninsula, Arabs are now considered to be all native Arabic speakers. They have mostly lived in the Middle East and North Africa, though Arabia is still considered the homeland. There are an estimated 280 million Arabs in the world today. The vast majority of Arabs are Muslims, though there's a significant Christian minority.

Aramco   The Arab American Oil Company, now Saudi Aramco. Founded by Socal (later Chevron), Aramco was eventually owned by a cartel of American oil companies before being purchased by the Saudis in the 1970s.

Arsacids   The second incarnation of the ancient Persian empire came under this dynasty, which lasted from the fourth century B.C.E. to the third century C.E.

Asir   Region of southwest Saudi Arabia, bordering Yemen.

Balfour Declaration   Britain issued this public statement in November 1917. It expressed Britain's support for "a national home for the Jewish people" in Palestine, and played a crucial role in encouraging Jews to immigrate there. Thus, it was instrumental in the process that ultimately resulted in the foundation of the state of Israel in 1948. Arabs, especially those who lived in Palestine and were displaced by incoming Jews, felt that the Balfour Declaration betrayed promises the British had made to them. *See* Sykes-Picot Agreement.

Bedouin   Nomadic Arabs, many of whom live in Saudi Arabia. In the past, the traditional Bedouin lifestyle centered around the camel, although sheep and goats were also herded. The Bedouin are mostly settled now, but the image of the lean, warlike desert-dwellers is as important for Arabs as the image of the cowboy is for Americans.

Byzantium   The continuation of the Roman empire into the Middle Ages—but with Christianity as the state religion, and the city of Constantinople (later Istanbul) as the new capital.

caliph   Literally, "successor" in Arabic. The Caliphs were the rulers of the Arab empire who succeeded Muhammad, the founder of Islam. Later the term was appropriated by other Muslim rulers.

Central Plateau Saudi Arabia's largest geographical feature, a huge expanse of desert upland in the middle of the country. The Najd, the Al Saud's traditional stronghold, is located here.

clan A social unit made up of several extended families. Several clans in turn make up a tribe.

Cold War The long, global ideological confrontation between the United States and the Soviet Union that followed World War II, lasting from 1945 to the collapse of the Soviet Union in 1990.

concession In the oil industry, the temporary purchase of exploration and development rights to a specified area. The seller usually receives an annual fee that maintains the concession, plus royalties or a percentage of the profits.

Consultative Council *See* Majlis as-Shura.

Council of Ministers The body made up of government ministers; with the Consultative Council, it's one of the main organs of the Saudi government.

Crusades A series of armed expeditions encouraged by the Popes and carried out by Medieval Western European knights and other wanderers into Arab and Turkish lands in the Middle East. The aim was to recapture the Holy Lands that had been conquered by the Muslims centuries earlier. The five major Crusades took place between 1095 and 1221 C.E.

Custodian of the Two Holy Places The preferred title of Saudi monarchs. The "Two Holy Places" are the Great Mosque in Mecca and the Prophet's Mosque in Medina, Islam's two holiest sites.

Dahna A long, narrow ribbon of sandy desert that runs along the eastern and southeastern edge of the Central Plateau in Saudi Arabia. It forms the border between the plateau and the Empty Quarter, or Rub al Khali.

Dar al Harb, Dar al Islam Respectively, "the House of War" and "the House of Islam," traditional ways of distinguishing the Islamic and non-Islamic worlds.

Death of a Princess A dramatized documentary film about the Saudi penal system that stirred great controversy when it was aired by the BBC and PBS in 1980.

Desert Shield U.S.–led military operation to protect Saudi Arabia after Saddam Hussein invaded Kuwait in 1990.

Desert Storm U.S.–led military operation to liberate Kuwait from Iraqi occupation in 1991. Also called the Gulf War, the Persian Gulf War.

downstream The consumer's end of the oil-refining process.

embargo   Refusal to trade with another party or parties. The most famous one is the Arab oil embargo of 1973–1974.

emir   Arab title, usually translated as "commander" or "governor." Also spelled "amir."

Empty Quarter   A huge expanse of sandy desert in southern Saudi Arabia, along the border with Yemen. In Arabic, Rub al Khali.

"Europeans"   In quotation marks, used in this book to mean the 9/11 hijackers who had spent time in Europe, and who played leadership roles in the hijacking.

Faisal, Al   The royal branch of the Al Saud, comprising the descendants of the eighteenth-century Saudi ruler Faisal bin Turki. All Saudi monarchs have been from this branch of the family.

fatalism   The philosophical attitude that says everything that happens was preordained by God, so why bother trying to do anything about it.

Fatimids   Several Shiite Arab dynasties took this name, after Muhammad's daughter Fatima.

fatwah   An Islamic religious decree.

Five Pillars of Islam, The   The five religious obligations of all Muslims: the declaration of belief (shahada), prayer five times daily, charity (zakat), fasting during Ramadan, and pilgrimage (hajj). *See* shahada, Ramadan, and hajj.

fossil water   Nonrenewable water deep underground, which has accumulated since prehistoric times. Most of Saudi Arabia's water is fossil water, and it's almost gone.

fundamentalism   A type of religious movement, common to all world religions, that purports to get back to a pure, "fundamental" version of the faith.

Golden Age of Islamic Civilization   Between the eighth and twelfth centuries, Arabs led the way in science, math, philosophy, and other forms of learning. By the twelfth century, however, Islamic religious authorities shut down the spirit of rationalistic inquiry as threatening to Islamic beliefs. Arab culture is still under their influence.

Great Mosque   The huge mosque complex in Mecca that houses the Kaaba, which is the central object of Muslims' prayers. In Arabic, the Great Mosque is called the "Haram."

guilt culture   A type of culture—like most Western cultures—in which limits on behavior are generated from within the individual. *See* shame culture.

Gulf War   The war to liberate Kuwait from Iraqi occupation in 1991. *See* Desert Storm.

hadar   Arabic word for settled farmers or city dwellers.

Hadith   The Traditions, or written reports of Muhammad's words and deeds. One of Islam's two sacred texts; *see* Koran.

haji   A Muslim who has performed the pilgrimage to Mecca.

hajj   Pilgrimage to Mecca, the culmination of a Muslim's spiritual life and a sacred obligation for all Muslims who are able to perform it. *See* Five Pillars of Islam, The.

Hanafi   A branch of Islamic law practiced in Turkey, Syria, Iraq, Central Asia, and India.

Hanbali   The branch of Islamic law practiced in Saudi Arabia.

Haram   *See* Great Mosque.

harem   The part of a Muslim family's home in which the women spend most of their time. Men are not allowed in the harem.

Hasa   An oil-rich region in eastern Saudi Arabia, also called the Eastern Province.

Hashemites   The family, believed to be descended from the Prophet Muhammad, that now rules in Jordan. In the past, they ruled the Hijaz, where Mecca and Medina are located.

hijab   The veil worn over the face by many traditional Muslim women.

Hijaz   The region in Saudi Arabia that contains Mecca and Medina. It runs along the shore of the Red Sea, and the ancient trade routes to Arabia Felix (Yemen) go through it.

hijra   Muhammad's flight with his followers from Mecca to Medina in 622, taken as the beginning of the Muslim calendar.

id al adha   The "feast of sacrifice," a ritual feast during the hajj that represents Abraham's willingness to sacrifice Isaac to God.

ifada   *See* nafra.

ihram   The state of purity in which a Muslim performs the hajj rites.

ijma   Arabic for "consensus," an important political concept in the Arab world and the end product of "consultation" or shura. *See* shura.

Ikhwan   Arabic for "the Brotherhood," the corps of Wahhabi fighters that Ibn Saud used to consolidate control over the lands that became Saudi Arabia.

Iran-Iraq War   From 1980 to 1988, Iran and Iraq waged a bloody and inconclusive war that cost more than a million lives.

ird   A woman's honor, which is totally contained in her chastity, and which reflects on the men in her family.

inshallah   A common Arabic expression that means "If God wills it."

Islam   The religion proclaimed by the Prophet Muhammad in the early seventh century. The word means "submission" and is related to "Muslim," which means "one who submits." *See* Muslim.

Jaluwi, Ibn   The branch of the Al Saud named after an uncle of Ibn Saud, Jaluwi.

jamaras   The three pillars that are ritually stoned during the hajj.

jihad   Arabic for "holy war," jihad traditionally has two meanings: inner spiritual struggle, or armed struggle against non-Muslims.

Kaaba   The cube-shaped shrine in the Great Mosque that houses the famous Black Stone (believed to be a meteorite). The Kaaba is the object of Muslims' prayers.

Koran   The revelations that Muslims believe were given to Muhammad by God, as written down and collected in book form. The Koran is Islam's main sacred text, along with the Hadith. Also spelled Quran.

majlis   Arabic for "council," a traditional forum for a leader to meet with his people and advisors.

Majlis as-Shura   The Consultative Council created by King Fahd in 1992, now one of the main arms of the Saudi government. The other is the Council of Ministers.

Maliki   The branch of Islamic law followed in North Africa, Central Africa, and West Africa.

Mamluks   Dynastic Muslim rulers in Egypt and elsewhere between the thirteenth and nineteenth centuries, the Mamluks were descended from slaves, and were mostly Turkish in origin. Also spelled "Mamelukes."

martyrs   Islamic teachings say that those who die defending the faith will be transported to a paradise of worldly pleasures.

Mecca   Islam's holiest city, site of the Great Mosque and place of Muhammad's birth.

Medina   Islam's second-holiest city, where Muhammad fled in the hijra and where he founded Islam. Originally named Yathrib, after the hijra, it's been called simply "Medina," Arabic for "the city," as a token of its central role in the rise of Islam.

Mesopotamia   Essentially, ancient Iraq, a fertile area between the Tigris and Euphrates rivers that was home to early civilizations. The name means "between the rivers" in Greek.

monotheism   Belief in a single, all-powerful God.

Mosque   A Muslim's place of worship.

muezzin   The caller who summons Muslims to prayer at a mosque.

mujahidin   Those who fight in jihad; often used of the fighters of the Afghan jihad in the 1980s.

Muslim   A follower of Islam; literally, "one who submits" (to the will of God).

mutawaffin   The guides who help Muslim pilgrims in getting to Saudi Arabia and also in performing the complex hajj rites in Mecca.

Mutawain   The independent government body officially called the Committee for the Propagation of Virtue and the Prevention of Vice; also known in the West as the Religious Police.

Muwahiddin   Literally, "unitarians," this is how the Wahhabis refer to themselves. The name emphasizes their core belief in the unity of the one God.

nafra   Literally, "the rushing," a rite in the hajj in which pilgrims rush from the plain of Arafat to the town of Muzdalifa. Also called the *ifada*, or "pouring forth."

Nafud   Literally, "desert," a region in northern Saudi Arabia. Sometimes called the "Great Nafud" to distinguish it from the kingdom's other deserts.

Najd   Region in central Saudi Arabia. Riyadh is located there, and most of the Saudi ruling class, including the Al Saud, are Najdis.

National Reform Document   Signed by 103 reformist leaders, this document was presented to Crown Prince Abdullah in early 2003.

neutral zone   Areas of joint jurisdiction with its neighboring states along much of Saudi Arabia's borders, the neutral zones were abolished by treaty in the 1960s and 1970s.

nomads   Herders who live an ambulatory life, moving from pasture to pasture. *See* Bedouin.

oasis   A watered place in the desert that supports plant and animal life. Most Saudi towns grew up around oases.

Organization of Petroleum Exporting Countries (OPEC)   This organization was founded by leading oil exporters in 1960 to increase their bargaining leverage against the Western oil companies. Saudi Arabia was instrumental in founding it; other founding members are Venezuela, Kuwait, Iraq, and Iran.

Ottoman Empire Turkish-ruled Islamic empire that dominated the Middle East starting in the fifteenth century, and dismembered in the early twentieth century after a long decline.

pagan Follower of any non-monotheistic religion.

Persia The ancient name for Iran, and the site of many powerful empires before being absorbed by Islam starting in the seventh century. Persia officially took the name Iran in the twentieth century.

petroleum Literally, "rock oil," the valuable substance from which gasoline, kerosene, and other products are refined. Saudi Arabia has more of it than any other country.

polytheism The belief in many gods.

Press Law Decreed by King Faisal in 1964, the Press Law gives the Saudi government control over all newspapers in the kingdom.

price hawks OPEC members who push for high prices.

production quotas The set levels of oil exports that OPEC members are not supposed to exceed.

qadi An Islamic judge.

Qaeda, al The terror network founded by Osama bin Laden that has declared war on the United States and the Al Saud. In Arabic, literally "the Base."

qiblah The direction in which a Muslim faces for prayer, which Muhammad changed from Jerusalem to the Kaaba in 624.

Quraysh The Arab tribe, centered in Mecca, that the Prophet Muhammad belonged to.

Ramadan The ninth month in the lunar Muslim calendar (which revolves through the seasons) and the Muslim holy month, during which Muslims are to fast from sunrise to sunset. Fasting during Ramadan is a religious obligation for Muslims. *See* Five Pillars of Islam, The.

Rashidun The first four "Rightly Guided" Caliphs, Muhammad's immediate successors.

Rub al Khali *See* Empty Quarter.

Sassanids The third and last dynasty of ancient imperial Persia, the Sassanids ruled from the third century until being conquered by the Muslim Arabs in the seventh century.

Saud, Al   Saudi Arabia's royal family, which has ruled (on and off) in partnership with the Wahhabi sect of Islam since the eighteenth century.

say   Literally, the "running," a hajj rite in which pilgrims run seven times between two hills near the Zamzam Well in Mecca.

secularism, secularization   Secularism is the separation of religion from government and civic life, and is commonly seen in the West as essential to the democratic process.

Seljuks   Turkish dynasties that ruled from the eleventh to the fourteenth centuries in much of the Middle East.

Shafii   The branch of Islamic law practiced in Egypt, the southern Arabian peninsula, East Africa, and Southeast Asia.

shahada   A Muslim's profession of faith: "There is no God but God, and Muhammad is His Prophet." *See* Five Pillars of Islam, The.

shame culture   A type of culture (like Saudi culture) in which limits on behavior are generated outside the individual, by direct social pressure or "shaming." *See* guilt culture.

sharaf   A man's honor, which resides largely but not entirely in the sexual chastity of the women under his protection.

Sharif   Honorary title denoting descent from the Prophet Muhammad.

Sharia   Islamic law.

sheikh   An informal, non-hereditary title of respect.

Sheikh, Al   The descendants of Muhammad ibn Abdel Wahhab, the founder of Wahhabism. *See* Wahhabism.

Shiites   Muslims who split off from mainstream Islam over a succession dispute concerning the Caliphate in the seventh century. Saudi Arabia has a significant Shiite minority that is downtrodden by the Sunni majority. *See* Sunnis.

shura   Literally, "consultation." *See* ijma.

Sunnis   Mainstream Muslims, who form the majority in Saudi Arabia and most Muslim countries (Iraq and Iran being the most important exceptions). *See* Shiites.

suras   Chapters in the Koran, Islam's holy text.

Sykes-Picot Agreement   In November 1917, a secret accord came to light that proposed splitting up the Middle East among Britain and other European colonial powers. Though it was never implemented, the Sykes-Picot Agreement deeply angered the Arab world. Like the Balfour Declaration, it seemed to break promises that Britain had made to the Arabs. *See* Balfour Declaration.

Taliban   Islamic fundamentalists who ruled Afghanistan from 1997 to 2001. In Pashtu, literally "the students" (singular *talib*).

tawaf   Literally, "the turning," a hajj rite in which pilgrims walk en masse in a circle around the Kaaba, in the courtyard of the Great Mosque in Mecca.

Third Country Nationals (TCNs)   Workers from developing nations who make up much of the Saudi work force, especially for menial or low-paying jobs. First used by U.S. army engineers working in the kingdom, the phrase originally meant anyone not from the United States or Saudi Arabia, including Europeans. The meaning changed later, possibly by confusion between "third country" and "third world."

Thunayan, Al   A distant branch of the Al Saud.

tribe   A social unit made up of several clans. *See* clan.

Tuwayq Mountains   A long, narrow ridgeline that runs across the Central Plateau, south of the Najd.

Umayyads   An early Arab dynasty that took over soon after the initial conquests of the seventh century, ruling from Damascus, Syria, until being overthrown by the Abbasids in 750.

upstream   The producer's end of the oil-refining process.

Wahhabism   The strict, puritanical version of Islam dominant in Saudi Arabia, founded in the eighteenth century by Muhammad ibn Abdel Wahhab. Wahhab allied himself to the Al Saud, and this alliance between the rulers and the clerics remains the foundation of the Saudi state. *See* Muwahiddin.

wukala   These "deputies" greet arriving pilgrims at the Jeddah airport and usher them through customs. They also help them leave Jeddah on their flights home.

xenophobia   Fear or hatred of foreigners and things foreign.

Yamamah, al   Lucrative arms deal between Britain and Saudi Arabia that led to bribery and corruption charges in Britain.

Zamzam   The sacred well near the Great Mosque in Mecca, where God is thought to have struck water from the ground to save Hagar and Ishmael from dying of thirst. Ishmael is believed to have been the father of the Arabs.

zamzamia   Assistants to the mutawaffin. *See* mutawaffin.

Index

I

X-Y-Z

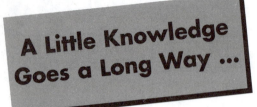

A Little Knowledge Goes a Long Way ...

Check Out These
Best-Selling
COMPLETE IDIOT'S GUIDES

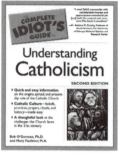

Understanding Catholicism
SECOND EDITION

1-59257-085-2
$18.95

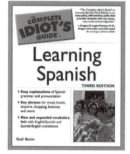

Learning Spanish
THIRD EDITION

0-02-864451-4
$18.95

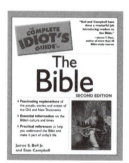

The Bible
SECOND EDITION

0-02-864382-8
$18.95

Feng Shui
SECOND EDITION

0-02-864339-9
$18.95

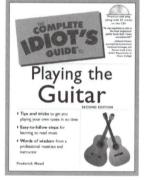

Playing the Guitar
SECOND EDITION

0-02-864244-9
$21.95 w/CD-ROM

Personal Finance in Your 20s & 30s
SECOND EDITION

0-02-864374-7
$19.95

Creating a Web Page
FIFTH EDITION

0-02-864316-X
$24.95 w/CD-ROM

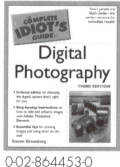

Digital Photography
THIRD EDITION

0-02-864453-0
$19.95

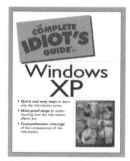

Windows XP

0-02-864232-5
$19.95

More than *400 titles* in *26 different categories*
Available at booksellers everywhere

ALPHA